ASSASSINATING SHAKESPEARE

Thomas Goltz

ASSASSINATING SHAKESPEARE

The True Confessions of a Bard in the Bush

SAQI
London   San Francisco

ISBN 10: 0-86356-718-5
ISBN 13: 978-0-86356-718-6

This edition published 2006 by Saqi Books

A full CIP record for this book is available from the British Library
A full CIP record for this book is available from the Library of Congress

Manufactured in Lebanon

SAQI

26 Westbourne Grove, London W2 5RH
825 Page Street, Suite 203, Berkeley, California 94710
www.saqibooks.com

To my parents,
Deborah and Neill,
from #2

' ... would there were no age between sixteen and three-and-twenty, or that youth would sleep out the rest: for there is nothing in the between but getting wenches with child, wronging the ancientry, stealing and fighting.'

William Shakespeare, *The Winter's Tale*, Act III, Scene III

'Es fehlt Weisheit.' ('It lacks wisdom.')

Bertolt Brecht on his first play, *Baal*

Contents

Acknowledgements

The book you hold in your hands is more than half my lifetime in the making, and I am fifty-one years old at the time it is going to press. Accordingly, there is half a lifetime or more of people to thank for their aid and assistance at the time of gestation (Africa, mainly, between 1977–78), many of whose names I cannot possibly recall, and whom I have had no contact with since. One exception to this lost telephone book is Jiri Bores, who let me camp in his Berlin flat at the end of the journey, and where I left a colony of lice. Sorry, Jiri! Bet you didn't think you'd see your name in lights 28 years later!

The first people to see any form of a manuscript (circa 1979–81) were my NYU professors of Arabic and German, David King and Volkmar Sander. Whether by mistake or design, I started using discarded sheets of the first manuscript as scratch paper for their courses, and both took an interest in what I had been scribbling on the underside of my homework ... After a very long hiatus of interest on my part (and that of the world at large), and on the demands of my wife Dr Hicran Oge, I started fiddling with the manuscript again, sometime in the late '80s, whereupon my literary agent Diana Finch dared shop it around the New York publishing scene. It went nowhere, but received some of the most peculiar rejection letters ever written.

And so the project languished once again until the late '90s, when I received crucial (and completely coincidental) encouragement from Margie Kidder to try and move the beast into print before I got killed in a war zone, or something. At exactly this time, a long-lost friend from Fargo, Judy Gunderson Muncy, fortuitously (specifically, via my book on Azerbaijan ...) resurfaced in my literary life and asked if I had anything else she could read. I sent her the Shakespeare, and she sent me back an edit. I took that edit and gave it to another of my expert readers, Natalie Sudman – and she, too, demanded to know why I had been so lax in trying to find a publisher. Maybe because I was scared?

Then in late 2004, my friend and fellow writer, Hugh Pope, called from Istanbul to suggest I make contact with a publishing house he knew of in London. I almost laughed at the idea, but the next time I was in the UK I picked up the phone to Mitch Albert at Saqi Books – and the rest, as they say, is history.

Thanks to everyone involved in this long and drawn-out process.

I have dedicated the book to my folks, Deborah and Neill Goltz, but I am thinking of you all as the albatross starts to take wings to fly.

Thomas Goltz
Livingston, Montana
March 2006

Stratford in Front of the New Stanley

ENTER Stage Right, The Bard, A Younge American Youthe Of Naive Aspecte. He Carryeth A Shoulder Bagge Filled With Sundry Stuffe, Including A DOZEN WOODEN PUPPET FIGURINES And Severale WOODEN MASQUES.

ENTER Stage Left, The CROWDE, Which Consisteth of Divers Folke of the Streete Varietee, The Majority Of Whom Are Blackamoors. They Banter and Joke Until The Bard Calleth for Silence, Upon Which Time The Bard Slippeth A Masque Over His Countenance Whilst Placing A Seconde Masque Upon The Pavement, Thus Creating A Body. Alarums sound; A Long Trumpet Flourisheth (it is actually a bus), And The Bard Continues, Now Bellowing Over the Trafficke:

> Friends, Romans, countrymen – lend me your ears!
> I come to bury Caesar, not to praise him
> The evil that men do live after them
> The good is oft interred with their bones ...

It is Mark Antony eulogizing Caesar, in a soliloquy that many might recognize from an annual Shakespeare In The Park production. I had to memorize parts of that speech in English class with Mr Jacobsen, at Shanley High School, Fargo, North Dakota. Mr Jacobsen. He was mainly a basketball coach and didn't know too much about Shakespeare or scansion, but he had a good sense of humor, and gave you extra credit on the vocabulary test if you gave the answer 'a couple of doctors' as the definition of 'paradox'. I wonder what he would have thought of this guy bellowing iambic pentameter over the growling traffic? Extra credit for public exhibitionism? Why not?

> The noble Brutus hath informed you
> That Caesar was ambitious

But I am not in Fargo. Being a trained observer I have noticed, for example, that the weather is sticky hot, not bone-numbing cold. Also, most of the audience gathered to hear the Bard are black and not white – and the only black man I knew in North Dakota was Michael Collins, Christian Brother principal of Shanley High School.

In fact, I have determined that the venue is the pavement outside the New Stanley Hotel in Nairobi, Kenya, a place once frequented by the literary likes of Ernest Hemingway and Alan Moorehead. I rather doubt, however, if these grand old men of Africa-related literature would have felt comfortable here and now. In the main, the crowd gathered on the pavement in front of the bookish *bwanas'* old haunt consists of shoeshine boys, ladies of the night caught out during the cruel light of day and a few Japanese and German tourists, peeking over the rim of the crowd, with idiotic grins plastered on their faces. A couple of pickpockets and petty thieves are also on hand, working the outside of the crowd. One of them is even now sneaking a stealthy hand towards the collection bowl, primed with the Bard's own cash to encourage the assembled to toss in a coin or two. The Bard sees this, and steps on the young thief's fingers without breaking scansion, resulting in a collective cackle from the crowd:

> You all did love him once, not without cause –
> What cause withholds you then to mourn for him?

Oh, Judgment! Thou art fled to brutish beasts
And men have lost their reason! Bear with me,
For my heart is in the coffin there with Caesar
And I must pause 'til it come back to me ...

The Bard is now taking a bow. A horn honks and a collective cough seems to ripple through the audience. The three or four tourists who stopped to listen are walking down the street with smirks on their faces, having made no movement towards donating any money. A cigarette butt flies by the Bard's nose, followed by a paper cup.

'Thank you very much,' says the Bard. 'Are there now any requests?'

A murmur passes through the throng, and a large well-dressed African man steps forward. He is wearing a three-piece suit, with the button of the ruling political party pinned to the jacket lapel, and he is smiling far too sweetly to bode any relief.

'Yes, *bwana*,' says the man, using the form of address employed by colonial black servants towards their colonial white masters. 'My request is that you stop.'

Another howl of delight rises from those gathered along the street, and the crowd presses in closer to eavesdrop on the conversation.

'Why?' asks the Bard, pathetically.

'*Why?*' the interloper asks rhetorically, in an even louder voice. 'Brothers!' he thunders. 'The *bwana* asks us why he should stop! Brothers! He should stop not because he is bad, which he is, but mainly because we all had to memorize that same speech in school at the knee of colonial school mistresses and masters! And what does that speech have to do with Africa? Shakespeare is English and we are not!'

The feckless crowd roars its approval, and the Bard seems to cringe behind his Masai mask.

'*Bwana* Brutus,' the man continues. 'You are like the missionaries who came and gave us the Bible and took our land in exchange! You are a missionary of Shakespeare, come to take away our African culture! Go back to your own country and leave *Africa for the Africans and Kenya for the Kenyans!...*'

I want to help the Bard, but I cannot. He has gotten himself in this mess and will have to get himself out, by himself. For a year and a half, he has been a self-styled Johnny Appleseed of Shakespeare in Africa, surviving by his wits and *élan*. But now he is too tired, physically and emotionally, to even consider countering the attack being made on him. In fact, he is about to snap. It is time to duck, collect his props, pack his bags and go – and the sooner the better.

The crowd has grown bored and starts to disperse, with the exception of the jowly man in the three-piece suit who stands triumphantly over the Bard, arms akimbo. Then a young street kid drops a shilling into the Bard's collection bowl.

Clink, goes the coin, and the Bard looks up.

'Please, *bwana,* you play Macbethi?' the young urchin asks tentatively.

'Not now,' mutters the Bard, trying to shut out the world.

'I see you do Macbethi last year, *mzuri sana* [very good],' says the lad, and smiles.

The young patron is dressed in what would generously be described as rags. His feet are without shoes, and his trousers are too large, filled with holes and held up with a belt made of string. He produces another brass shilling and drops it on top of the first donation, resulting in another meek jingle of appreciation.

'Ha!' It is the fat politician in the three-piece suit again, his Rolex watch weighing heavy on the street kid's scrawny shoulders. 'Not only does this *bwana* mean to rob us of our national culture, but he also means to steal the hard-earned savings of this young citizen! Don't let them eat bread! Let them eat Shakespeare! Hahaha!'

'You eat Shakespeare,' says the street urchin, writhing away from the fat man's embrace. 'You too fat, anyway!'

'You make good Falstaff,' adds an anonymous voice, and a snicker runs through the throng, followed by a chanting chorus. 'Falstaff, Falstaff, you play Falstaff!'

They are not referring to the Bard. Dysentery from Cape Town to Cairo has long robbed him of any claim to play that role. They are now mocking the interloper, who is indeed corpulent.

'What do you know about Shakespeare,' sneers the suit-man, turning on the remnants of the crowd. 'Half of you cannot even read English!'

'Julius Nyerere write *Julius Caesar* in Swahili,' someone says, invoking the Tanzanian leader whose brand of African socialism had always made the post-colonial Kenyan elite nervous.

'Macbethi!' someone else demands, and another coin is tossed at the collection bowl. It hits the fat man in the three-piece suit on the head. A howl of laughter erupts from the crowd, which is taking its pleasure at the expense of the politician, not the Bard.

'Macbeth, Macbeth, Macbeth!' chants the crowd, and a small shower of coins rains down on the Bard and his tormentor, with those that bounce off both into the street hotly pursued by the younger thieves and urchins, who then sling their windfall profits back at the stage. 'Macbeth! Macbeth! Macbeth!'

'Yes, please, do perform that scene you do from *Macbeth*,' says a well-dressed African woman who has now come forward, pressing a paper note into the Bard's hand. 'It is certainly apropos today, given the state of affairs in Congo.'

'Down with dictators!' crows the crowd, demanding action.

'I shall call the police!' bellows the fat man in a last-ditch effort to stop the show. But it is too late. There are already several policemen in the audience, waiting for the curtain to rise, and the Bard is now digging in his performance bag for the *panga* blade that serves as the knife used to dispatch the doomed King Duncan.

> Is this a dagger I see before me?
> The handle towards my hand?

If the changed mood of the crowd is not enough, the appearance of the *panga* in the hands of the masked man does the trick, and the interloper leaps from the stage with a yelp while the restored audience roars its approval and initiates yet another shower of coin.

> Come, let me clutch thee –
> I have thee not and yet I see thee still ...

Now the crowd is silent, attentive. Only the grinding gears of a bus out on Kenyatta Avenue break the silence of the streetside stage. The Bard has received a reprieve, a second wind, a second life, as he follows the upheld dagger around the stage, feet miming disturbed steps down cold castle stones.

> Art thou not, fatal vision, as sensible
> To feeling as to sight? Or art thou but
> A dagger of the mind, a false conception
> Proceeding from the heat-oppressed brain ...

His meter is intact, caesuras, too. The Bard might be leaving Africa the next day, but he will have his farewell performance. His voice, which had felt weak and gravelly before, is now responding like he had trained it in Greco-Roman amphitheaters and not African streets. The crowd has grown silent and attentive, tying the classical texts into concrete, local experience. They have all seen coups and counter-coups and unexplained assassinations. They might not understand every word, but every nuance is as familiar as last year's leader.

> While I threat, he lives
> Words to the heat of deeds too cold breath gives!
> I go and it is done; the bell invites me.
> Hear it not Duncan, for it is a knell
> That summons thee to Heaven – or to Hell!

A flourish, then a bow. Hoots and hollers. But the Bard knows it is applause. It washes over him like a magic balm, ointment for the cuts and nicks and gashes incurred by his fragile ego over eighteen months on the road in deepest, darkest Africa.

'Thank you, thank you,' says the Bard, now speaking in something closer to American English with a Midwestern twang than the round, quasi-Elizabethan accent of Caesar or Macbeth.

'For any of you who would like to help me get out of Africa the way I came in, please! Put money in my purse!'

With another flourish and bow, the Bard reaches towards the crowd with his collection plate in one hand, while removing the mask with the other.

I am stunned. Through the haze of twenty years I recognize this man. He is younger and thinner and certainly has more hair on his head, but – he is me.

Only now, after having spent the subsequent twenty-nine years of my adult life as a much-wandered adventurer in the non-Western world, do I have the nerve to put the details of this difficult journey down on paper. Herewith, then, my secret history as a one-man wandering Shakespeare show in Africa, my life as a Bard in the Bush.

ONE

A Once and Future Bard

At the risk of offending long-deceased ancestors, I might blame it all on my great-great-grandfather, Ignatius Donnelly. No, I am not referring to his involvement with the Grange Party and his Jesse Ventura-like jabs at the late nineteenth-century Minnesota political establishment. It was Shakespeare that he yoked around the collective family neck, thanks to his obsession with proving that Sir Francis Bacon had been the real author of not only Shakespeare's but also the Greene and Marlowe plays.

> In the winter of 1878–79 I said to myself: I will re-read the Shakespeare Plays, not, as heretofore, for the delight which they would give me, but with my eyes directed singly to discover whether there is or is not in them any indication of a cipher.

Ignatius wrote this in *The Great Cryptogram: Francis Bacon's Cipher in the So-called Shakespeare Plays*, a 998-page work published in 1888 that destroyed his reputation as the 'Sage of Ninninger [Minnesota]'.

The first thing that struck Ignatius as odd about the plays was the multiple and totally unnecessary recurrence of the word 'bacon' in *The Merry Wives of Windsor*. Soon, he discovered a veritable double helix of embedded codes and mathematical formulae that ultimately revealed Bacon's darkest secrets and commentary on the Elizabethan Age.

If a certain passage did not fit the number grid, Ignatius felt confident enough in his discovery to reverse the flow of words:

> ... as the Cipher flows out of the first column of page 74, its mode of progression is different from the Cipher referred to in the last chapter, for that grew out of the first column of page 75, which is broken into two parts by the stage direction 'Enter Morton', and hence the root-numbers were modified at one time by subtracting the upper half, and at another time by subtracting the lower half; that is to say, by counting *up* from 'Enter Morton', or counting *down* ...

Roll the clock forward twenty years from the scene in front of the New Stanley. I am sitting around the Murray Hotel Bar in Livingston, Montana, waiting for my pal Margot Kidder (Margot is Lois Lane of *Superman* fame to most of you, and the poster girl for manic depression after her flip-out in Los Angeles, when she decided that exactly thirty-eight CIA operatives were out to get her) to have a goodbye drink before she takes off to Fiji to shoot a new movie.

'What's it about, doll?' I asked.

'The script is really weird,' Margie replied. 'There is this New Age cult leader who discovers that the key to the return to universal peace and happiness is found in a cipher that proves that Francis Bacon wrote the Shakespeare plays ...'

The scenario rings bells.

'I think you better tell the director that the family takes a proprietary interest in maintaining the good name and reputation of our illustrious forefather.'

'What the hell are you talking about?'

'Come over to the house tonight and I will show you the book.'

The Divine Miss K comes round and I show her not only *The Great Cryptogram*, but also another work by Ignatius that resulted in a cult following among New Age enthusiasts: *Atlantis – or the Antediluvian Age*.

'Seems like the writer ripped off both books,' says Margie, perusing both, which together probably weigh ten pounds.

'What do you mean?'

'Well, the point of breaking the code used by Bacon to write the Shakespeare plays is to get back to the Antediluvian Age, that is, Atlantis.'

I am tempted to show her another book by Ignatius titled *Caesar's Column*, a pre-Orwellian account of working-class revolution and the collapse of American society. The survivors escape the bloodbath and general chaos via long-distance balloons, to Uganda.

At the time I graduated from high school in Fargo, I had already adopted some form of Great-Great-Granddad Iggy's obsession with the Bard. I wrote sonnets to girlfriends and packed along both *The Collected Works of William Shakespeare* and the *Great Cryptogram* when I left my parents' house and my seven siblings to move into a crash-pad commune. I also lugged the hefty tomes along when I transplanted myself to my grandmother's townhouse in St Paul. They came with me to Chicago when I went to study theater at the Goodman School of Drama (my audition piece was young Henry V's 'Once more into the breach' speech), and followed me to New York City, where one of my first was an experimental version of Macbeth in which I played both Banquo and a witch. It was a flop. I also had some other choice roles which no doubt caused extreme jealousy among the hundred thousand wannabe actors in the city always so awash in broken dreams: a bit part in a movie about escaping balloons and a supporting role in an off-off-off-Broadway musical that had something to do with King Kong.

Then my girlfriend left me, and the boss of the painting crew I worked for had a heart attack and almost died. Accordingly, I did the only reasonable thing in such circumstances. I packed up *The Collected Works* (*The Great Cryptogram* was too large and fragile to take) and moved to Berlin.

It was the summer of 1976, and I was twenty-one years of age.

I was soon ensconced in a *Wohnungsgemeinschaft*, or communal apartment, working as a house painter by day and attending theatrical performances every night. Bertolt Brecht's old theater, the Berliner Ensemble, was one obvious draw, but the niftiest production of all was a tremendous experimental show directed by Peter Stein at the Schaubüehne. It was titled *Shakespeare's Memory*, and it was a three-day Robert Wilsonesque romp through Elizabethan times, replete with simultaneous multi-stage performances of relevant bits of the Bard, wandering Indians brought in from the 'New World', public executions, jousts and battles and diverse Magna Carta-like speeches from the contemporary British parliament, all selected or thoroughly imbued with left-wing German social consciousness. My favorite moment was when a clown actor playing Launce from *The Two Gentlemen of Verona* had a dialogue with himself, changing characters by flipping into a handstand, a second head attached to his rump.

It was all very edifying, and I began thinking about going back to university, studying German literature and writing a dissertation on the 'Theoretical Difference of Dynamic Between East and West German Dramaturgy and the Practical Aspects of Politics as Theater In the Post-Marxist Age', when another commune member decided my reluctance to share my cigarettes with the rest of the members on demand set me apart as a New World bourgeois of the worst order; I was evicted.

What to do? At exactly that moment, I received a letter from my younger brother Eddy extolling the beauties and rigors of Africa. *Africa?* It seems he had taken a semester's leave from studying music at Oberlin College in Ohio in order to do work in the department of musicology at a university in Nairobi. Sadly, those plans had been put on hold for the very good reason that the seasons are reversed below the Equator, and he would have to wait until the new school year opened in March, as opposed to September. It was all rather confusing, but the main point was that he was now playing guitar in a local band, and conducting an investigation into the roots of the Swahili music culture of the Indian Ocean coast, especially on a certain island off Kenya called Lamu, which just happened to be a piece of heaven on earth. The various words and references meant nothing to me, but as a recently cast-out actor, unemployed house painter and aspiring German philologist, I weighed my options, parked a suitcase of clothes in the workshop of an East German puppetmaster refugee and, with about $200 in cash, a change of clothes and a thick winter coat on my back, began hitchhiking south. To fend off roadside boredom, I brought along *The Collected Works*, marking scansion aberrations in the various plays to pass time.

Sitting in the middle of nowhere determining that a certain line from, say, *Hamlet* should be read with a trochee/dactyl combination as opposed to straight iambic pentameter. If this sounds like a warped version of my great-great-grandfather Ignatius's obsession, dear reader, let it be, let it be. If he could have had no idea that one of his offspring would wander off to perform Shakespeare on the Dark Continent, neither did his offspring at the time.

I traveled fast. I traveled so quickly that the first 2,000 miles were nothing but a blur seen through the dirty windows of trains, buses, cars and trucks I hopped or stopped along the way. I pushed through Austria before hitting Italy, tried and failed to find an old girlfriend in Belgrade and took the train to northern Greece, almost all in one and the same day. An empty tour bus brought me across the border into Turkey; I remember something about dancing girls in the Topkapi bus station outside Istanbul, getting shaved in the bus station in Ankara and having to change money in a crowd of threatening-looking folks in Antakya before crossing the border into Syria, across which I hop-scotched in two days.

I had no inkling or even inclination to anticipate the future marriage of my personal and professional interests in the Arab and Turkic worlds and languages, ranging from Algeria to Azerbaijan. No, I was on my way to Africa, and places like Aleppo, Amman and Aqaba were merely in the way, pit-stops along the burning road south towards

Saudi Arabia, which I cruised through in a series of overheating trucks and air-conditioned cars, sleeping on elevated straw platforms by the side of the road and drinking gallons of half-sugar tea in my mad rush to North Yemen.

I have been assured that the only way for a non-Muslim foreigner to acquire a Saudi visa is to be thoroughly stitched into a multinational corporation doing business there, and that foreign residents are essentially restricted to complexes in order to minimize contact between local and infidel. But the only restrictions I encountered were those pertaining to non-Muslim entry to the holy cities of Mecca and Medina, around which I was obliged to take the detour road to Jeddah and the Red Sea. And I was hitchhiking.

Finally, after descending a grand and green escarpment at the southern end of Saudi, I neared Yemen. After waiting for hours at the point where the gravel road disintegrated into a desert track, a Palestinian truck driver stopped and called me aboard. We brought a case of his cargo – Jaffa oranges from Israel, packed in crates labeled 'Product of Lebanon' – into the cab with us, and plunged into the sea of sand.

For two days of blistering desert heat and two nights of bone-chilling desert cold we plowed on through the land of the Queen of Sheba, moving from one oasis village to the next. It was hard to believe that this was once known as Arabia Felix, the land of myrrh and frankincense. The ubiquitous goats were quickly taking care of whatever saplings had survived the ravaging of firewood-and-charcoal collectors, who lived in the mud-and-wattle huts dotting the shifting sands by the roadside. At every stop we were greeted by screaming children and graybeards teary-eyed in anticipation of breaking into a crate of the precious cargo. Even the camels sensed they had a dessert of orange rinds coming, and would stick their ungainly heads over the bramble and bush fences that surrounded the individual compounds in the settlements.

At the end of the sand road lay al-Mukha (Mocha), a sleepy little Red Sea port town that gave its name to the coffee originating in the highlands of Ethiopia before being shipped to Arabia and then Europe. It was also the export point for another stimulant moving in the other direction, from Yemen to Ethiopia and the Horn of Africa as a whole: *qat*, an amphetamine-like weed that had the triple effect of killing hunger, reducing the libido and inflating one's self-esteem. As such, it seemed like a perfect drug for a Third World country with a growing population problem, or for wandering hippies with no dough (and no women, for that matter). I started an acquaintance with *qat* that would finally result in the sort of withdrawal symptoms one usually associates with junkies on meth.

The reason for coming to al-Mukha, however, was not to sit up and chew *qat* with the guys, but to find boat transport to Africa – meaning that I had to make arrangements to get aboard a lateen-sailed, high-backed pirate ship called a *dhow* when it pulled anchor, and hope it was going in the right direction – the French colony of Djibouti, a sort of city-state-brothel for French Legionnaires carved out of the best Red Sea shoreline. Daily I went to the harbormaster to badger him about boats sailing to Djibouti. Daily I was told either '*Insh'allah*' ('God willing'); '*Bokara*' ('Maybe tomorrow') or '*Ma'lesh*' ('So what?'). Reading *The Collected Works* helped pass time.

At first I was alone. But within a few days of my arrival, there came some other foreigners – two French rustics in a converted armored personnel carrier that they were driving to West Africa in the hope of selling it there for a tidy profit; then a pair of Parisian newlyweds, followed by two rude Australian brothers; then a couple of queasy Canadians. We all slept out near the docks, crab fishing by night and wandering the dock area by day, lest one of the *dhows* leave for Djibouti without us. In addition to the crabs we caught, our diet consisted of damaged cargo – especially the huge sticky sacks of Iraqi dates that had a tendency to split. We ate ourselves sick more than once. Perhaps the tummy trouble had less to do with too many dates, though, than the fact that the tea we drank was made from seawater. It was all rather tedious.

But there was no quick egress from al-Mukha. Most of the *dhows* at anchor were captained by Somalis whose people had been plying the waters of the Red Sea and the Indian Ocean for centuries. Their boats would arrive overloaded with dates, preserves, coffee, spices and other sundries, be unloaded by the tried and true method of slave labor (the coolies were black, worked constantly and slept on the docks, having no other apparent reason for existence than to haul huge loads on their naked backs) before again raising anchor to sail seemingly to any other port but Djibouti. Then one day, God, in His infinite wisdom, willed a boat to be ready. More to the point, the port authority refused to let one Somali captain set sail until he agreed to take us across the waters. We suspected he was just plain sick of dealing with us.

The French APC was hoisted by crane to the *dhow* deck; all the windows were shattered in the process. Then, rather than simply board the craft as it wallowed near the crane, we were obliged to follow it out to a new anchorage at sea, and aboard a dug-out canoe at that. We reached the hull, at which point someone threw down a rope ladder and we hoisted ourselves aboard. Once on deck, I wondered if it wouldn't be best to climb right back down and check out other transport options. Our craft, like its sisters at anchor, was a crowded tub that rose impossibly high in the stern and seemed ready to capsize at any moment. The outhouse, sort of a box set on runners extended over the starboard side, actually touched the waves when the vessel tipped to that side, rendering every bowel movement an encounter with eternity; and these were only the reassuring parts. The crewmen furiously loaded bales and boxes ever higher aboard the fo'castle, stripped to their waists and singing in rhythm as a wicked-looking man in a long, white gown and turban stood watch. From my perspective, towards the back of the boat, I swear I saw whiplashes on their backs. None appeared to have much to lose if caught slitting the throat of a hippie foreigner for a dollar or two. The whole scene conjured up visions of real-life pirate ships and high-seas banditry, of galley slaves and *hashish* in the hold. I thought it prudent to start chewing as much *qat* as I could in order to stay awake for the duration of the journey, lest I end up as the captain's forced male concubine before being jettisoned to the sharks.

Meanwhile, the slaves or crew or whichever had ceased loading the cargo and began heaving anchor and hoisting sail, singing as they tugged and hauled. Then the scowling captain, his face a leathered wreck, lifted his hands to the searing blue sky, breathed a blessing and turned the prow of his *dhow* out to sea. Soon all the flailing arms along the docks of al-Mukha diminished into dwarves, and then to less, and then to memory as we dove through trough after trough of perfectly directed, absolutely beryl-blue and froth-tipped waves, ever downwind, towards Djibouti. I was moved to utter a recently memorized bit of the Bard, from *The Tempest*:

Heigh, my hearts! Cheerily, cheerily, my hearts!
Take in the topsail; tend to the master's whistle –
Blow, till thou burst thy wind, if room enough!

The Somali captain and crewmen looked at me strangely but carried on with their given tasks, including the ritual casting of a baited fishing line from the outhouse outrigger.

We had barracuda for dinner that night.

TWO

Haile Selassie's Revenge

The skinny little conductor wearing a beach towel for trousers, a worn suit jacket and sandals made out of old tire treads cried out the Somali equivalent of 'All Aboard!', and the weekly train between Djibouti and Dira Dawa, Ethiopia pulled out of the station.

Actually, the call was only a warning, because the train was so overloaded with human, animal and material cargo that one could have purchased a ticket five minutes after the first blast of engine steam, sauntered to the platform and climbed aboard any wagon without fear of being left behind.

There was still the problem of finding a berth, especially aboard the third-class carriages. Knots of men who looked exactly like the tiny conductor, along with burly matrons cinching the ends of their black veils in their teeth, stuffed huge bundles and live animals through the windows, crushing anyone seated there for a bit of air and elbow room. Meanwhile, legions of roaming vendors meandered through the crowd, hawking cigarettes, candies, flashlights, radios, watches and fried lumps of dough, picking pockets when not cheating on change. Last came the customs people, climbing over rack and infant with an open sack into which everyone was obliged to toss a piece of contraband. Thus all were satisfied, the officials having obtained proof of having done their duty as evinced by their sack of confiscated sundries while the smugglers (nearly everyone on the train) were able to bring in their goods with only a minimal loss.

Finally, mercifully, the train pulled out of the station. It chugged along at five or ten miles an hour, for hour after sweaty hour, towards and then across the frontier until morning found us in the dump called Dira Dawa, in an Ethiopia in the midst of a civil war.

Now, I was vaguely aware that there had been a revolution in Ethiopia in 1974, but not that it was still going on. In fact, it was a four- or five-ring circus of ethnic and political violence. Tigreans were in revolt in the north, as were the Galla in the south. Eritreans were fighting for independence in the provinces along the Red Sea, while Somali guerrillas were infiltrating through the Ogaden Desert to the east. At the center, student groups which had originally sparked the revolution were now 'enemies of the people' and hunted down like animals by peasants and farmers armed by the state. Finally, there were the Rastafarians, who had made the mistake of declaring the late Ethiopian emperor and 'Lion of Africa', Haile Selassie, to be the Messiah according to their peculiar theology, and then accepting Selassie's invitation to his deifiers to leave the West Indies and settle in his kingdom on the Horn of Africa. The Rastafarians enjoyed special status until Selassie was putsched from power, when open season was declared on anyone sporting dreadlocks and who listened to that great 'counter-revolutionary', Bob Marley.

At the Dira Dawa bus depot, situated more or less in a sewer in the middle of town, I purchased a ticket aboard the first bus leaving for anywhere. As chance would have it, my destination was the 'forbidden city' of Harrar, the last major Ethiopian town on the Ogaden plateau – a disputed scrub desert that eventually becomes Somalia somewhere very thoroughly in the middle of nowhere, over which Ethiopia and Somalia were fighting a border war.

If Dira Dawa was a dirty dump, Harrar was a horrible hole, a city consisting of streets that served as open sewers, redolent with human and animal waste. The ancient walls only exaggerated the sense of claustrophobia and filth, and one might argue that the town acquired its reputation not because of the ferocity of nineteenth-century native slave dealers but because of the ferocity of contemporary flies, crawling in and out of the eyes, ears and noses of the children who followed me around. It was difficult not to make an association between the flies, the filth and the astounding number of lepers crowding the streets.

The main tourist attraction in town was a dilapidated mansion in the Italian-African style where the young poet Rimbaud resided when employed as a gun-runner. The house itself seemed to come straight out of a novel by Poe – which, in fact, is what the brochure given to me by the current residents of the house said: 'The Rimbaud House In The Forbidden City Of Harrar Looks Just Like A Haunted House In A Novel By Edgar Allen Poe'. The brochure also informed me that it was in Harrar that Richard Burton – the explorer, it took me a while to realize, and not Liz Taylor's twice-husband, the actor, despite the fact that I was reading *Antony and Cleopatra* at the time – had his face slit open by a Somali spear, while on his way to Central Africa in search of the source of the Nile.

After observing sunset from the town's ancient walls, I followed a crowd down to the east gate of the city where a man was amusing the masses by feeding a pack of hyenas. Move over, fire-eaters and acrobats! Keeping the crowd at a good distance, he coaxed his carnivorous pals out of a nearby ravine, barking commands. The beasts put on their show, standing, sitting and howling in a weird chorus before their trainer fed them their meal of raw meat. In a country with famine just around the corner, feeding scavengers slabs of steak seemed a little odd, but I guess everyone must set their own priorities.

My own priorities were twofold: to get some chow and find a bed for the night, and both for as cheaply as possible. I found an inexpensive-looking restaurant down a side street where I wolfed down an order of raw, spicy beef on *injera*, a sponge-like bread. Next, I set out to find one of the two hotels I had seen near the old city gates. The manager at the first said it would cost me $10 a night, so I set off to find the second, which cost $15. By the time I got back to the first, it was locked up. Returning to the second, I discovered to my dismay that it, too, had closed its doors for the night.

It was looking like another evening *al fresco*, and soon I cursed my fate. The logical places to camp – along the sides of buildings – all seemed to be occupied by small knots of lepers, huddled together beneath communal blankets against the evening chill. I moved on from the Old City gates down a ceremonial avenue into 'new' Harrar, eventually finding myself in a small park across from a large, solid-looking building – the first I had come across that was not surrounded by lepers. It also sported two ceremonial cannons, one on either side of the door, which seemed to offer protection from any malevolent persons who might consider disrupting my rest. Then, as I started clearing the twigs and branches for my bedroll, I felt a strange rumble in my belly. The raw beef on *injera*. *Gurgle gurgle*, went my intestines, and my mouth began to take on the taste we Goltz kids used to refer to as the 'smelly burps'. It was no use holding off until morning to find a toilet. As the street was deserted, I thought the best option was to add a little night soil to the boulevard, and dropped my drawers.

That is when a light went on in the building across the way. Funny, I said to myself, that someone should be at their office at this hour of the night. Then a thin sliver of light flashed as the door creaked open again, and a hunched figure darted into the enveloping darkness. Thieves, I thought, and chuckled. A second later, the door creaked open again, and another figure dashed out, carrying something long and heavy in his hands. A dull alarm began buzzing in my brain when a third man leapt out and rolled behind the stairs.

Twin cannons outside a well-kept building on the main avenue into town? Guys with guns taking cover? Rebel gunfire in the hills? With a jolt of adrenaline, I suddenly knew where I was: camped in front of the regional military HQ of the Ethiopian Ogaden Desert Command. The men who were rolling out of the building carrying the heavy-looking objects were soldiers carrying guns who thought I was trying to kill them. Before that, of course, they would try and kill me. Time was only left for prayer, or better, a last attempt to reverse my incredible stupidity.

'*AMERICAN!!*' I wailed at the top of my lungs as a searchlight blasted over me, revealing five more men bolting out the door. Their bayonets shimmered as they charged, my trousers dropping as I shot my hands up in the air, desperately trying to surrender.

The only reason I am still alive today, I am sure, is that the soldiers had no bullets for their vintage rifles. Although the prospect of being disemboweled by a bayonet is not very pleasant, the form of the attack did allow the soldiers time to notice their target: in place of the expected guerrilla planting a bomb, there was only me, a bumbling clown with his pride dangerously overexposed, and fresh shit up and down his legs.

It was still questionable whether I would survive the night. Hustled off with muzzles trained at my chest, I was carted around from one military authority to the next. My escort would shout a password, jump out of the vehicle and run in to speak to his commander while my guards, their fingers greasy and slick from gripping their weapons' triggers, spoke in low tones to one another and jerked their heads in my direction. It wasn't clear if they were talking about the best place to aim for, or simply that one was best advised to stay upwind of the stinking prisoner.

We arrived at a low, flat building with bars on the windows, at the edge of town. It was flanked by a long, ugly wall, riddled with bullet holes in a horizontal line about the height of a man's chest. I was told to get out of the truck; I got out. My guard jerked his head tower the wall. My head swam, and I moved forward to meet my maker. Idiotically, Claudio's scene with the Duke in *Measure for Measure* came to mind:

For thou doest fear the soft and tender fork
Of a poor worm ...

I was half way to the wall when someone called, and I turned to see a figure framed in the doorway of the building, a very handsome Ethiopian man dressed neatly in a khaki uniform with sufficiently braided epaulets to designate fairly high rank. He also bore an uncanny resemblance to Brother Michael, my high school principal (and only black man) back in Fargo, North Dakota.

'Sit down,' began the officer, leading me into a spartan interrogation chamber consisting of a desk with two telephones on it, a shortwave receiver-transmitter, a two-year-old calendar in Italian on one wall and the obligatory picture of Colonel Mengistu, leader of the *Dergue*, or Committee (of the Ethiopian Revolution) on another.

'Why were you trying to blow up the regional headquarters of the Ogaden command?'

No, it was certainly not Brother Michael, but an Ethiopian army officer in the middle of a counter-revolution who thought I was out to kill him and his friends with well-placed bombs. If I had anything left in my bowels, it now flushed down my leg.

My plea for mercy was interrupted by a commotion at the door. Two new enemies of the people had arrived, their eyes downcast, their arms pinned behind them by soldiers.

'We have quite a problem here,' the officer confided after listening to his men brief him on the crimes committed by the pair. 'The one chap was pissing in the street and the other is an adulterer, or rapist. It's not clear which. Now the problem is how to make punishment fit the crime. Should the urinator be obliged to clean the streets or drink his own urine? How do we revolutionaries impress on him the need for raising our national consciousness, which has been urinated on for centuries? Perhaps you may regard this as trivial, but look: Who is the greater offender to society, the urinator or the fornicator? The latter only sought to gratify his immediate sexual needs, whereas the former pissed on society as a whole ... A dilemma, what? To be just, that is the main thing ...'

Beads of sweat appeared on the officer's forehead as he pondered his decision, upon which the very nature and quality of the Ethiopian revolution seemed to rest. The two individuals who stood before the law cast their eyes towards the floor awaiting the verdict. The officer rose to his feet and all the eyes in the room were drawn towards him. Slowly, softly, he announced his judgment, and the blathering thanks of one captive mixed with the wailing of the other as his pants were lowered to his knees. The officer had taken off his belt, and using perhaps ten inches as a thick whip, delivered a quick five lashes to the man's groin. The offender collapsed to his knees in agony; whether he was the urinator or the fornicator was not clear, nor did I bother to ask.

My own trial, I knew, was next. Once more, I began to blubber and babble, assuring the officer again that I had no intention whatsoever of blowing up anything, and that far from disliking him or his men or their revolution, I had learned a profound respect for the changes wrought over the past few years, and that clearly, you cannot make an omelet without breaking a few eggs ... As Marx said and Lenin enjoined and Brecht suggested ...

'Oh, shut up!' said the officer, threading the belt through the loops of his trousers. The room filled with a pregnant silence, augmented by the sound of the howling dogs and rifles barking in the distance. 'Next time, take a room.'

I walked out as dawn began to break, alive because I was clearly too stupid to be a spy.

After an excruciating journey in the back of a truck (or trucks – I was obliged to dismount every two hours thanks to 'Haile Selassie's Revenge', or Ethiopian tummy trouble), the thatched roofs of roadside villages began to give way to more permanent structures and the sparse vehicle traffic on the roads started picking up. Then, with a suddenness that surprised me, we were on a monumental avenue driving towards the center of Addis Ababa, the capital of the People's Republic of Democratic Ethiopia, then in the throes of civil war and a dying revolution.

I was indifferent to the politics of the place. Feverish, radically dehydrated from my illness, weakened because I had eaten nothing for days and utterly exhausted because I had not really slept since al-Mukha, I had one objective only: find a bed, and at any price. Well, not any price. Mine was a low-class hotel near the market. It was not pretty, nor was it clean. But it was cheap and, moreover, it had a bed. And the bed was for me. Yes, there were parasites, and the sheets had not been cleaned for several weeks, but it was a mattress on a frame, sagging under its own weight, skewered by its own springs, scarred by inch-long cigarette burns and stained with the dreams of a hundred itinerant men lost in the remembrance of their favorite toothless, long-breasted whore. The bed was set perfectly and logically in a damp, squalid room, its four paint-peeling and chipped walls dropping dirt and bug-dung half an inch deep on all. Yes, it was a mess, but it was mine. I stripped the filthy sheets, stuffed my dirty laundry in a T-shirt for a pillow, and collapsed into one of the most profound sleeps I have ever known, waking twenty hours later – the mattress soaked in sweat and the room smelling of my unwashed feet.

My fever had broken, and I was starving. So I sallied forth from my hostel to find some food, any food. The fruits and vegetables in the market nearby looked very tempting, but caution got the better of me. Soup, said my stomach. Soup. But this was easier dreamt of than done. I stumbled across one street and then another, looking for a salubrious café. As I stood on a corner, deciding to go left or right or cross the street, I felt something pass over my face as another body bumped into mine.

Mugged.

Whirling around to face my assailant, I braced myself as best I could for the second blow, but it never came. A blurred shape was distancing itself from me, merging with the hues and tones of evening into the shadows of a side street. Perhaps it had only been a bump, an accident. But there was something very wrong with the world. It was out of focus. I put my hand to my face, and wiped a trace of blood off the bridge of my nose. A sick feeling welled up in my stomach. My windows on the world, my glasses, were gone: someone had stolen them right off my face.

I do not want to exaggerate the condition of my eyes – they are not good, but neither am I legally blind. I remember the first time I got glasses: my Little League baseball batting average improved so dramatically that I was moved from ninth to sixth or fifth in the batting order. I could actually see the hurled ball, and not merely a whitish blur moving towards me from the mound. My fielding got better, too. Most shocking was the realization that you could actually identify people on the other side of the street, and did not have to rely on shouted greetings to identify friend from foe. Now, suddenly, I had been reduced once again to my previous, myopic state, and did not like it at all. If not as blind as Gloucester in *King Lear*, neither did I have a Poor Tom to lead me to safety.

Night falls quickly on the Ethiopian highland, and there was – I now knew from my travails in Harrar – a dusk-to-dawn curfew in force, and for good reason. I had not gone far when I began to hear the clatter of small arms fire down alleyways and the explosion of a distant bomb. An armored personnel carrier roared around a corner and I dove for cover behind a heap of garbage, scaring the rats out into the street to seek a new hiding place. As I made my way deeper and deeper into the rabbit warren of winding alleyways, it became increasingly clear that I was completely lost. Still I pressed on, hugging the sides of buildings and dashing across the open spaces that represented streets. Suddenly, a hand reached out from the darkness of an alleyway and pulled me to the ground while another hand quickly wrapped around my mouth to stifle my cry.

'*Friends!*'

It was one of my captors, hissing in my ear. My heart beat somewhere in my throat, but over its pounding I could hear the sound of the booted feet of a squad of soldiers as they stumbled down the street, the noise soon swallowed by the renewed rattle and pop of gunfire on the other side of town. Slowly, my captor released the grip on my mouth, and allowed me to look around. I was in the company of six intense young men who seemed to be cast from the same mold: graceful, aquiline noses and thin, taut lips, all sporting perfect Afros such that one might have asked them about their hairdresser, had it not been for the impassioned look in their eyes and the guns in their hands. They were urban guerrillas, remnants of the student groups who had toppled Haile Selassie but who were now being exterminated by the military junta they had brought to power.

Silently, we moved on, three of the student warriors in front of me and three in the rear, making our way through the labyrinth of alleyways and side streets, plastering ourselves against doorways or behind heaps of garbage whenever soldiers stomped by, flashlights poking the darkness for life to put to death. After an hour – or was it only two or three or fifteen minutes? – we turned a corner, and tears began welling in my eyes: my hotel, dark but for one naked bulb dangling above the door, casting an eerie glow down the deserted street. The man who appeared to be the leader of the group – a tall, finely chiseled fellow with tired, martyr's eyes and a firm grip despite the feminine delicacy of his hands – pointed to my destination, smiled a tight, hopeless smile and led his little band back into the shadows of the side streets along which we had come.

How did he know where I belonged? Was my savior a receptionist in my fleabag hotel by day and revolutionary by night? I do not know, but would still like to thank him whoever he is and wherever he might be, even if he is one of the hundreds of Ethiopian or Eritrean taxicab drivers in the Twin Cities who cannot find the way from the airport to the Guthrie Theater ...

In the morning, I made a perfunctory search of the flea market in the hopes of finding my glasses on sale, but had no luck. In Africa, they say, you can steal and sell one shoe, so the idea that the thief intended to hawk my prescription specs to some other myopic guy was not so strange. It was only sad that the glasses in question happened to have been mine, and that I was effectively blind.

The road south to Kenya was tarmac all the way, but traffic was so light that beautiful wildflowers and strange weeds sprouted in the cracks and potholes of the highway. Perhaps the landscape was verdant and beautiful; maybe it was austere and boring. I don't know because I could see nothing but a fuzzy, hazy mass of colors, starting with the blue sky and ending with the gray-black tarmac of the road in front of my nose.

I walked a great deal. I walked more than a great deal. I walked in and out of a score or more of lethargic villages, whose residents would collect along the side of the road to watch me pass. I would shout the most histrionic bits of Shakespeare to them that I could remember, howling a little *Lear*, perhaps, or a fragmented passage from *Coriolanus*:

All the contagion of the south, light on you,
You shames of Rome, you souls of geese
That bear the shapes of men!

I ended up walking twenty miles (or so it seemed to me) before I spotted a slow-moving, overloaded sedan moving in my direction. I stepped out in the road to stop it, and to my amazement, discovered the driver to be a white man. Next to him sat a white woman holding a white child, while the back seat was packed with five or six black people.

'Hi,' I said, as naturally as if the vehicle had stopped for me on Interstate 94 between Fargo and Jamestown, and not on a deserted road at dusk in southern Ethiopia.

'We have no room for you,' said the driver, with a singsong Norse lilt to his English.

'I'll ride on top.'

'We are overloaded already. I'll come back.'

'You won't!' I shouted. 'Don't lie to me!'

'I am not lying!'

'Goddamn it, don't leave me!'

The car moved down the road and I ran alongside it, screaming into the window. Then I was running behind it as it moved up a hill, and then it was gone once it started rolling down the far side.

'Goddamn you!!' I wailed.

The sun set; night fell – and on I trudged. It was pointless to stop, and almost as pointless to go on. Then, as the moon began to rise and the first blink of the great, almost equatorial panoply of stars began to emerge, I heard the sound of an approaching motor from the south, and saw distant headlights. I crossed the road and stood in front of the approaching vehicle, waving my arms. With keen embarrassment, I recognized it as the now-unloaded car that had spurned me hours before.

'Sorry about shouting at you,' I said. 'I have been out here walking all day and –'

'Get in,' said the Norseman curtly.

I did.

'What in God's name you are doing here?' he demanded. 'You must be out of your mind and I must be for returning! The entire countryside is rife with *shifta*.'

'What's a *shifta*?'

'You truly are clueless, aren't you, young man.' breathed my driver. '*Shifta* are bandits, guerrillas. They steal and rob and kill and generally disregard the word of God.'

'Oh,' I said, now nervously reaching for a cigarette.

'We do not allow smoking or drinking at our mission or in any of our vehicles.'

'You are a missionary?'

'I am here teaching the word of God. Are you are Christian?'

'Depends on what you mean and how you define the nature of Jesus,' I began, ready to start using all the modern, relativist Catholic qualifiers to theological questions drummed into our little heads by the Christian Brothers at Shanley High.

'Good God!' whispered the Norseman. 'We sacrifice years working in the name of Lord Jesus for the Christian West, and it is people like you who show up!'

We drove in silence until we got to the Norwegian Episcopalian Mission, at which point the missionary who had saved me from the *shifta* pointedly reminded me that there was no smoking on the premises, and that but for the love of Jesus he would rather that I not bunk down in the mission at all. In the morning, I was dropped by the highway to find my own way to the nearby town of Mega.

Mega wasn't much. A big camel market town in better times, it was slowly but surely being starved out by the *shifta*. There was neither food for the beasts nor for the residents, save for camel chops for breakfast and camel chops for supper. I ate camel and smelled camel and thought camel for two days in Mega, wondering if I would ever get out, when word went round that a supply truck was going to run the *shifta*-gauntlet to Moyala, a town on the Kenyan frontier. Producing a dollar bill and a winning smile, I was able to join a motley crowd of goats, chickens and human beings atop the load, and waved goodbye along with the rest as we pulled out of town, heading south.

For two hours we plowed into the parched landscape, a single, defenseless merchant ship in a sea of pirates, every grunt and groan of the gearbox screaming our approach to anyone who cared to know we were coming. But as time drew on without event, the mood atop the truck lightened: the silence of the first hour was replaced at first with circumspect mumbles, then by more elaborate conversations punctuated by the cackle of the ladies and the knee-slapping of the men.

The driver had just changed gears, and at first I thought the reverberating bang was just engine backfire. Then came the first splinters of superstructure wood and the sharp whine of hot steel ricocheting off the metal frame, followed by the delayed clickety-clack of automatic rifle fire. *Shifta* were raking the truck with hot lead.

Pandemonium broke loose as human and animal fought tooth and hoof to dig deeper beneath the cargo. My immediate rival was a nasty-smelling goat who nearly had the better of me when it suddenly squealed, shivered and appeared to urinate on me. I was about to punch the beast in the nose when I realized that it had selflessly collected a stray bullet meant for me and was dead. Red Badge of Courage for Billy. Then, as swiftly as it had descended on us, the rain of bullets ceased – and the sudden silence rent by the wailing of the wounded. No one had been killed.

We arrived in Moyala to be greeted as heroes, the first supply truck to have braved the road in weeks. A month before, a Land

Rover had attempted to run the gauntlet south and been ambushed. The occupants – Norwegian missionaries – had all been killed and mutilated. A week later, a military convoy had engaged the rebels in battle, and lost.

I hoisted my pack off the truck and descended into the crowd of relatives, onlookers, doctors and nurses who gathered to help the wounded or collect their merchandise.

'Hey, what happened?'

A white man was standing next to me, newly arrived from Kenya and heading north.

'We got hit by the *shifta*,' I replied, amazed at how cool I was.

'Shit ... I've been waiting here three days, and there's no traffic.'

'Yeah,' I acknowledged, 'I had a bit of a wait coming this way.'

'How long have you been in the country?' the stranger queried.

I had to think about it for a minute, because the answer didn't seem to tally.

'Eight days,' I finally confessed, and walked across the border into Kenya.

Stanley Misses Livingston

Given the singular dearth of traffic on the Ethiopian side of the frontier, it was hardly surprising that a similar situation prevailed south of the border, two feet inside Kenya.

I was not alone, however. I was kept constant company by clouds of vicious flies. They swarmed around me, alighting and nibbling away at any piece of exposed flesh. My only recourse was to wrap myself into a mummy bundle with my blanket bedroll, keeping a slit open to breathe and peer myopically down the road, anxiously awaiting the musical whine of a distant Land Rover or the poetic backfire of an ill-tuned truck. Studying Shakespeare was not even a recreational option, although I rolled over various pieces of previously memorized material in order to fend off total boredom and madness.

When night fell, I gave up my futile roadside vigil and camped on the steps of the Kenyan customs house. The customs guys snickered and predicted that I would be waiting a week or more for transport. They were kind enough, however, to offer me a repast of barbecued corn and a glass of water.

The next morning, I again wrapped myself in my blanket, planted myself on the road and waited. After a number of false starts (the sound of a generator in the nearby town sent me scurrying, throwing off my blankets and exposing myself again to the vicious flies), I finally heard it: the dulcet tones of a diesel engine with compression problems. A vehicle soon came into view, and I threw off my flynet. But as it neared, the driver raised one fist and smashed the other palm into it. I took the gesture as the driver's way of telling me that I had no business in his country or anywhere near his daughter or, possibly, that he fancied me. Disregarding the obscene implications, I stepped out into the middle of the road and gave the driver a choice of running me over, pitching his vehicle into the ditch or, I hoped, stepping on the brakes.

Happily, he chose the last option, and as soon as he stopped I launched my kit into the back and clambered aboard, where the perfectly innocuous meaning of the hand language immediately became apparent. The driver had simply tried to warn me that his vehicle was already full, and that it certainly was: the back was packed shoulder to shoulder with a small clan of African tribespeople in traditional regalia. Both the men and women had their hair stained red and ochre and festooned with intricately beaded headbands, while the earlobes of the ladies were weighted down to their necks with a variety of gaudy charms, including bottlecaps and the tops of tin cans. The men also carried cruel-looking spears, whose use seemed confined to swishing away clouds of flies. The Stone Age weaponry seemed tame after having been blasted with automatic rifle fire on the other side of the frontier.

The tribespeople bouncing along with me in the back of the truck were quite friendly, too. They laughed openly and offered me questionably clean water from their gourds as well as tiny crunchy-munchies for snacks. I assumed these were bits of dried lizard, slugs or whatever passed for delicacies in the Northern Frontier District, and thought it impolite to refuse.

'You Masai?' I asked one of the men, trying to prove my ethnographic awareness and cultural acumen.

'Rendille, Rendille!' came the response.

'You Turkana?' I tried again, remembering something about Richard Leakey's work around the lake by the same name, which had to be somewhere around here.

'Rendille, Rendille!' my interlocutor repeated insistently.

'You Rendille?' I finally asked.

'Ayii!' crowed two dozen cackling voices, as the men did a tribal stomp in the back of the truck while the women trilled, shaking their breasts.

Apparently I had hit a chord.

'They are savages!' came a new voice. 'They circumcise their women and kill any girl who becomes with child before she is married and eat slugs and worship cattle the way any civilized man worships his car!'

Thus I met Johnson, the only other passenger on the manifest wearing pants and a shirt. He was also so incredibly black that his skin looked almost blue. Later, I would learn that this was one of the distinguishing characteristics between the jet-black Bantu and other agricultural tribes and the much lighter-skinned pastoral groups such as the Masai, Turkana and Rendille (one theory even posited that the latter are lighter in skin color because they descend from one of Caesar's lost legions). But in the meantime I had Johnson, who would become my traveling companion for the next few days.

Perhaps I should be grateful, because Johnson did teach me quite a bit about the basics of political and economic life in Kenya, albeit always with his own, uniquely Luo slant. That was the tribe to which Johnson belonged, who were subjected to any number of indignities and inequalities by the governing Kikuyu tribe. The biggest indignity seemed to be the fact that Johnson was bouncing along with the Rendille in the back of a truck in the Northern Frontier District. The reason for this, as Johnson related, was that some utterly corrupt and totally duplicitous administrator in the Ministry of Education, who owed his sinecure to his membership of that perfidious and greedy and traitorous clan known as the Kikuyu, had decided that the only way to prevent the rapid and well-deserved rise of one Mister Johnson in the ministry was to banish him to a one room school in Rendilleland. That had been two years earlier, and for Johnson it had been two years of hell. He had prayed every night for deliverance and now, at long last, the prayers had been answered. Mister Johnson was on his way home.

'To Nairobi?' I asked.

'No, no!' said Mister Johnson, a look of horror on his face. 'As I told you before, I am a Luo, as was the martyred Tom Mbuo of whom you may or may not have heard but who dwells in the hearts of all Bantu people in Kenya due to his martyrdom at the evil hands of the unwashed and uncut Kikuyu who loathe us due to the fact that we dwell in a veritable Eden on the shores of the Great Lake Victoria, where true Africa resides and where man first descended from the ape, should one choose to believe Darwin and not the Holy Scriptures! You must come to Kisumu and smoke *bange* and drink *pombe* and enjoy a Luo girl, for we are civilized and not to be confused with the other, unwashed and uncut and generally unspeakable people of Kenya!'

Mister Johnson was about to launch into a more detailed critique of the political system of Kenya when the driver kicked his machine into gear, slamming Johnson and me to the floor. Our sudden start sent a wall of dust over the assembled tribespeople, and we roared off into the depths of the Northern Frontier District.

The reader cannot possibly be more disappointed than the writer about the latter's inability to describe the great natural wonderland of northern Kenya, that rough-and-tumble region between Lake Turkana and the Sudanese frontier in the west and the Somali border and the Indian Ocean in the east. A vast land of sweeping plains, mirages and dormant volcanoes, the area has long been a favorite setting for adventure novels about great white hunters and the movies subsequently made from such fictions, not to mention all manner of anthropological and animal studies conducted by real-life academics drawn to the strange compelling beauty of the region.

I could see none of it, save for a few blurred shapes in the distance moving like Macduff's men from Birnam Wood to Dunsinane. Johnson pointed excitedly to what assured me to were herds of giraffe, gazelle and zebra. They might have been cattle, dust devils or rocks for all I could tell; my advice to all other nearsighted travelers is to carry an extra pair of glasses, always.

Time, too, became obscure. My only gauge was the relative whiteness of Mister Johnson's shirt, with the passage of time calculated in increasing shades of gray. That worked for a while, but at a certain point in the journey his white shirt had turned black from sweat and grime and road dust. I vaguely recall turning off the main road – a rutted, spine-shaking affair – and onto completely uncharted tracks, stopping at an encampment outside a mission house to pick up another load of country folk; re-boarding under the full moon; stopping at another nameless place to eat roast camel while an awe-inspiring dawn broke to the east; then plunging ever deeper into the austere terrain of towering buttes and twisted mountains and mirage-filled horizons that make up the Chalbi Desert.

Finally, after what felt like weeks but was probably only two days, we arrived at the town of Marsabit, a small administrative map-dot that sits at the lower flank of an ancient volcano, atop which – they say – is a perfect crater lake, with misty forests on the slopes of the mountain populated by herds of elephant and greater kudu. Travelers kill to get there, but without glasses it was a useless trip for me. It was also the end of the truck drive, and the end of the road for Mister Johnson: the road forked around the Great Rift Valley, and he took one road while I took the other. As a matter of course I promised I would track him down in Kisumu to enjoy a little *pombe* and *bange* and a Luo girl with him some future day. Alas, I never did.

Another Norwegian missionary; the back of another truck. Progress was slow. Then, somewhere under the snow-covered crest of Mount Kenya, a Land Rover pulled over.

'Hi,' I began. 'I'm trying to get to Nairobi, and was wondering if –'

'Eee, Gad and Ho!' crowed the driver, or something to that effect. 'You are so filthy I thought you were a silly black beggar! Good God! But you're *white*!'

As the driver inspected me, I inspected him. He was huge, though whatever muscle he once had had long turned to fat. And white he was

– skin the color of porcelain and with a white beard and white hair and even white eyebrows, the exception to his general whiteness being his nose and the one elbow cocked out the car window, which were deep red. It almost goes without saying that he was wearing a white, short-sleeved safari suit, although his calf-length socks were blue, as I recall. As a generic type, he was a 'white farmer,' one of the holdout colonialists who had not bolted back to England (or Rhodesia or South Africa) when Kenya became independent in 1960. I thought of him as Falstaff on the Equator.

Apparently, the true color of my skin beneath the accumulated grime of the road necessitated some adjustments in the seating arrangements inside the Land Rover. Instantly, Falstaff's companion (or servant) was consigned to the back of the vehicle along with the baggage, while I was directed to the now-empty front passenger seat.

'Have a beer, boy!' crowed Falstaff, handing me a cold bottle of Tusker, the local brew which boasted an elephant motif on the label. I slurped the suds down in seconds. 'Thirsty, what? Been on the road a bit, eh? Well, have another cup of sack ...'

Then we hit the road, cruising through a variety of landscapes – the remaining desert, then the first green cultivated fields and finally into jungle. After the third bottle of beer, coupled with my poor vision, I began having trouble distinguishing between the diverse climatic zones, general hue of vegetation and ethnographic makeup of the towns and villages we wheeled through.

'Well, young man,' inquired Falstaff after we both belched and bolted down another half-pint of 'sack'. 'What the hell are you doing in the back country? Anthropological research, perchance? A little wildlife photography?'

I tried to explain that I was, well, not exactly sure what I was doing in Africa, aside from looking for my younger brother Eddy in a general sort of way, although the search had become considerably more problematic due to certain experiences in Ethiopia such as the loss of my glasses to an urban nose-thief.

'Stole your glasses off your nose, now did they, the cheeky bastards!'

muttered Falstaff, shaking his shaggy white head. 'Reminds me of the time my boy stole one of my shoes ... Had him flogged for that, I did. Did it myself, in fact ... And he learned. That's why I keep him with me today, although I still can't trust him as far as I can throw him.'

I do not remember much more, and certainly nothing of what other travel writers relate about the stunning beauty of the Great Rift Valley. I was stone cold asleep, the multiple beers resulting in an adrenaline letdown of profound proportions. I drifted into dreams about high-school sex and hockey heroics mixed with bits and pieces of shattered Shakespeare, only returning from the ether into this abode of tears with a jolt some two or three or four hours later.

HONK!!

I was staring at the grille of a Mercedes 220 sedan, its motor revving inches from my nose and its driver determined to move the machine through the last obstacle blocking a congested intersection: us.

'Blighters!' growled the fat white man at the wheel. 'In the old days, a wog would never have the nerve to try that move, much less drive a Merc!'

Reality came flooding back . The driver was Falstaff from Marsabit, the *bwana* with his 'boy'. They were in Kenya, Africa, and so was I.

'Well, Yank!' said Falstaff, pulling over to the curb. 'This is it, Nairobi – and the Thorn Tree Bar!'

'Thanks,' I said, as I got out.

'Good luck finding your brother,' he continued, extending me a meaty chop of a hand. I took it, and it held me like a vice.

'This is for your glasses,' said Falstaff, stuffing a wad of money into my breast pocket. 'Just remember me, and turn the favor to someone else when you can.'

Upon emerging from the optician's shop, it was as if I had opened my eyes to the world for the first time. And what a world it was, growing increasingly wonderful with each step: Kikuyu girls dressed in outrageously patterned dresses, and wearing tumbleweed, train-trestle, beehive hairdos that rose a foot or two above their scalps, strutting next to Masai Moran, hair plaited and ochred and perforated earlobes flapping in the breeze. Here beefy, black businessmen wearing Brooks Brothers' best in the midday heat waddled between business and bar, while Sikh bridegrooms in pink turbans, beards braided up under their headdresses, shouted matrimonial luck to one another across the thoroughfares. Then there were the tourists: overweight Americans in garish jumpsuits, knots of Japanese people with cameras on automatic shutter, Germans, French, Italians and Spaniards, tumbling out of or into caravans of white- and black-striped safari buses affiliated with one or more of the dozens of game camps in the country.

Shoeshine boys shined, turning natural brown leather blue; beggars begged, their tailor-made maladies paying better interest than a bank; hawkers flogged fake elephant-hair bracelets and camel-bone ivories, and pickpockets plied their craft. It was all fine and active and great and nifty, especially because I could see it all unfolding like a brand new movie before me.

What I wanted to see more than anything else, of course, was something familiar – namely, the ugly mug of my little brother Eddy. I planned out the theatrical elements of the moment Stanley met Livingston: 'Hi, stranger – what are you doing in a place like this?' No, not quite right. 'Fancy meeting you here.' *Naw.* It wasn't every day you ran into your younger brother some 5,000 miles from North Dakota. 'Doctor Livingston, I presume?' That would probably be best, though it was a horrible cliché. 'Doctor Livingston, I presume?' Yeah, that would be the one I went with.

The natural place to make a stakeout and surprise him was the local American Express office, where little Eddy maintained a *post restante* account, and where I had instructed concerned individuals to mail me as well.

'Hello!' I announced myself to the clerk. 'Got any mail for me?' The man behind the counter found my name and hauled out a huge package.

Sitting outside the AmEx office, I started to read and savor each and every epistle. There was a Christmas card from my Aunt Eleanor, with the same $20 cheque she had sent for the past ten years; a brittle postcard from my ex-girlfriend Kim, asking what I had done with the cat; and a calling card from a bank representing a student loan-lending institution I owed a couple hundred bucks to, threatening to destroy my credit into the seventh generation unless I immediately paid up. On the opposite side of the ledger was a letter I made sure no one saw, lest I die of shame: a money order for a thousand bucks from my parents, who were worried about me.

Then, towards the bottom of the stack, I picked out an aerogram postmarked Berlin. The handwriting was familiar, and I wondered whom it might be from. Cracking it open, I began to read the contents.

'Dear Eddy,' read the first paragraph, and I realized I was reading my brother's mail. Who did he know in Berlin? Feeling a little sneaky and curious, I read on.

'I have decided to travel to Kenya in order to –'

With a sudden, sick and sinking sense, I realized the handwriting was my own, written on a letter posted over a month earlier. Eddy did not even know I was in Africa. Livingston, the object of my insane journey, was gone. Beating off despair, I walked around the block in the thin hope that maybe, just maybe, my brother would bump into me, or me him. Perhaps he had been out of town and was on his way back to pick up his mail, even today? But Eddy was nowhere to be seen and after several hours I decided it was time to go proactive, and started buttonholing likely-looking people in the street to ask if, by chance, they had seen or heard of such-and-such a person meeting such-and-such a description. It sounds pretty ridiculous, but there were a few tantalizing traces. A gorgeous Indian girl fond of hanging around the Thorn Tree Bar admitted to having had a liaison with my sibling, but didn't want to know anything more about him. A more curious clue came when a couple of local lads stopped *me* on the street, saying quite simply that I must be Eddy's brother.

'Yes!' I exclaimed. 'How did you know?'

The pair replied that there was a striking family resemblance. This was strange indeed, in that I was born a blond and Eddy dark-haired, that I have blue eyes and he green and that I am some five inches taller.

'Well, where is he?' I asked.

To this the pair had no reply. They had played in a band with him some months before, but he had disappeared – maybe to the resort areas dotting the Kenyan coast, or possibly to Tanzania and beyond. But if I found him, they requested that I remind him of the money Eddy owed them for the last gig …

The coast, of course! Little Eddy was no doubt down there, wowing them with his music.

The dice were cast and my course was now clear. I cashed the check, cleverly hiding the moola in a secret compartment in my bags, and after crashing in a Nairobi flophouse, started down the road towards the Indian Ocean and the coastal city of Mombasa.

I figured I would give myself about a week for a last look around, and if I failed finding Eddy there I would book a tramp steamer to take me to the Seychelles or the island of Diego Garcia, where I would catch a merchant ship back to Europe or the US.

But the gods of Africa had something quite different in store.

FOUR

A Con Man Among the Makondi

The wail of the *muezzin* calling the faithful to midday prayers drifted in through the mosquito net like a siren, and it took me a moment to realize that I was sweating because of the heat and humidity and not because I was in the middle of a four-alarm blaze. It was filthy hot and sticky as a Turkish bath, and I had no idea where I was.

Dabbing the sweat off my brow with a damp bedsheet, I put on my new glasses and surveyed my environment: another filthy room filled with sagging beds inhabited by rank strangers, two of whom were naked and busy screwing on an adjacent bed, indifferent to the five other, snoring bodies in the room.

It was a fine and proper introduction to the capital city of the Kenyan coast. Mombasa was sultry, and the scent of sex and cloves was nearly cloying in the muggy air, each molecule of which seemed to be imbued with licentiousness born of indolence and ease.

I was not in Mombasa looking for sex, but for Eddy. I began asking the diverse travelers in my fleabag hotel about my brother, but received no concrete identifications. Perhaps, I figured, he was working at one of the large hotels dotting the coast, or more likely in a bar, and I would just have to wait until evening to start searching.

With the afternoon to kill, I ventured forth into the labyrinth of the old town, and immediately got lost as the streets shrank from colonial thoroughfares to cobblestone lanes where two donkeys would find it difficult to pass. Mud-and-wattle, whitewashed houses, many sporting elaborately carved wooden doors and latticework balconies, lined the alleys. Due to the slow settling of the foundations of the houses into the sandy ground, or perhaps by design, several balconies actually touched each other as they leaned over the street, allowing the pious Muslim ladies to peer out at life on the street without participating in it, as well as keep an eye on their less pious daughters.

There was good reason for maternal concern. For no sooner did night fall and the cooler breezes of the evening wash over the town than did Mombasa give herself over wholly and without reservation to the skin trade. The instant I was back on the main street looking for bars where Eddy might be working, I was literally assaulted by knots of prostitutes, cat-calling from dimly lit doorways leading into a dozen red-lit bars, and aggressively grabbing at any and all arms and other peripherals strolling by. It was mad, mad. There were tall whores, short whores, fat whores and skinny whores, blue-black women from up-country, freckle-faced, red-haired black girls who could pass as white. Miscegenated creations abounded, reflecting the centuries Mombasa had served as a port of call: There were girls descended from Arabs, from Japanese, from Finns and from Argentines – a genetic pool that recast itself anew every fifteen years, which seemed to be the average age of the streetwalkers crowding every corner.

Looking for Eddy, I checked out hotel lobbies and was pawed and clawed; nightclubs where the gender ratio was perhaps four times in favor of women; sailor bars with rooms in the back for quickies; and assorted speakeasies best described as 'sexeasies'. Then I was assaulted by a sensuous fantasy that would give a priest pause – lewdness and wantonness personified, overflowing flesh stuffed into a far-too-tight red satin dress.

'I love you *too* much!' she cooed, opening negotiations. 'Give me 100 *shillingi* and I make you *too* happy.' (This use of 'too' instead of 'very' was the convention, and could lead to confusion – such as when someone related how a destination was 'too far'.)

'And you are *too* beautiful,' I said, and offered her twenty.

'You have *too* much money,' she replied derisively. 'Seventy-five *shillingi.*'

'Fifty.'

'Seventy.'

'Sixty.'

'Show me.'

The problem was that I was low on dough. Cleverly, like a maniacal gambler who knows his vices, I had stashed most of my cash in the hotel room and was stalking Eddy (and thus, really, women) with scarcely a dime to my name. But I could stand it no more and, in a raw sex craze, I sprinted back to my hotel room to get the requisite fee.

It is remarkable how a little physical exercise will dampen one's libido. I got back to the empty room with my lungs panting but with ever less pounding in my privates. Even more remarkable is how a sudden shock can rob one of one's sexual appetite: I shook my pillowcase until feathers began to fly, but nothing else came out. A dull pain forced its way from my stomach to my throat. My ticket out of Africa, or at least the cash to buy it with, was gone.

My mind raced through the various possibilities that would explain away the missing money. The pillowcases had been changed by the staff, perhaps? But no – the sweaty sheets were the same I had slept on. Nor was my wad tucked beneath my mattress, or any of the others in the room. I was frantic, checking a third time by pulling the various bedframes from the walls and heaving mattresses on the floor, when the female half of the couple screwing next to my bed that morning walked into the room with yet another man – this time a tall Frenchman with bad teeth, who I recognized from my hotel in Nairobi..

'Hi,' she said, as she began to disrobe, oblivious to the state of the room. 'Having a good time in Mombasa?'

'I've been robbed,' I said.

'The town is filled with thieves,' she said.

'You should not leave your mon-ees in zee room like zat,' said the

Frenchman with a peculiar, nonchalant sneer. 'Now leave us to make love.'

They were too casual. Too friendly. Too sure. *It was them.*

The nympho was down to her panties already and the Frenchman was pulling his dirty T-shirt over his head when something snapped, and I launched myself on the pair.

'*You* took it, *you*!' I shouted. 'Thief! Thief!'

She was screaming and scratching and he crying and bloodied, and the hotel staff was suddenly all over me, pulling me off the poor sod and escorting me down the hall, down the steps and out the door onto the street. My shabby bundle of clothes and pack arrived with a thud, separately, on the pavement next to me, as the cacophony of shouts and curses and cries in French, German and Swahili was suddenly muted by the hotel door swinging shut.

Booted, abused and broke. The situation looked bad.

In retrospect, perhaps, I should be grateful to the thief, whoever he or she really was; no one had yet heard of the 'slimming disease' that would cut a deadly swath through the Mombasa streetwalkers in the coming years: AIDS has a very high incidence among the port prostitutes, and I could well have been spared HIV infection that abortive evening of planned sin.

My digs that night were several large pieces of cardboard. My laundry served as bedding and my *Collected Works* as a hard pillow to keep my head off the ground; aside from my glasses – now tucked down my underwear – it was the only thing left to steal.

It was a long and lousy night's sleep. The noise of the bars mixed with the grunts of trucks and taxis and the mosquitoes from the malarial harbor would not let me be. I tossed and turned in my cardboard bed and pulled my surrogate sheets this way and that, but to no avail: I woke feeling grimy and bad with welts on all exposed parts of my body. Through blurry eyes, I discovered that I had camped beneath two, huge cement elephant tusks slung over the entrance to Mombasa. This was essentially touristic ground zero, an area of small shops and portable curio stands, and the owners and workers were just starting to trickle in for another day of gouging foreign fools.

Logic would have seen me walk off to the American consulate and throw myself on the mercy of officialdom. Fate, however, had other tricks in store.

'Whence and why hast thou descended upon me?' asked one of the men setting out wooden totems and other kitsch of the tourist trade.

'Well, I got robbed last night –'

'Invidious world! To the hearth comes the stranger, and it is open and warm.'

This was Joseph, master carver of ebony trinkets, and I have difficulty remembering him saying anything that should not be given brackets. Mission school rhetoric class and street Marxism commingled and ran mad in his speech. 'Procrastination is a thief of time' was one of his favorite lines.

Joseph led me to his workshop, where his assistants were already hard at work, hacking and hewing blocks of ebony, teak and other African hardwoods into strange, spiraling statues of the 'African Mother' as well as the whole range of wooden elephants, lions, giraffes, zebras and forks, knives and spoons. The wooden trinkets were mass-produced with factory precision: the apprentice carvers would rough in the sundry figures with three-inch axe blades before the block was passed on to the older boys with their one- and two-inch axes for further detailing (the blades were interchangeable in what were allegedly rhinoceros-skin heads). Eventually, the piece would reach Joseph. Whittling away with a razor-sharp knife forged from an old screwdriver, he would then put the final touches on before the piece was given over to filers, sanders and painters: applewood was much easier to work with than ebony, and most tourists did not know the difference between the two with the aid of a little shoe polish or stain. Besides, it was Joseph's sales pitch about the ancient craft of carving that was half the attraction to clients.

'You see this monumental statue,' Joseph would intone in his strange, pedantic English. 'The Mother is Africa, and her children revolve about her supple body like the stars around the moon, albeit one edifice looks preferentially in the opposite direction of the other offspring, symbolic of the primal need for individual differentiation within the context of traditional society, where man first emerged, and whose values are rapidly evaporating. Procrastination is a thief of time.'

'Hey, Joe,' I said after some time. 'Mind if I try my hand at this whittlin' business?'

'Pride cometh before the fall,' he replied, passing me an axe.

I began chipping away at discarded lumps of wood to the great amusement of the other carvers, and soon developed a motif of my own: pipes, with the bowls fashioned into quasi-human faces or animal heads, the hollow stem being either the neck or, in the case of an elephant, the trunk.

'You sell these to *mzungu*,' said one young carver. '*Too* much *pesa*.'

'Much money' was a pretty relative idea, especially coming from some kid to whom Joseph was probably paying a buck a day to carve ten times my output, but what the heck – I was broke, and any income was welcome. 'Our sacred tradition can only be applied by the sweat of the African brow,' said Joseph, meaning 'no'.

'Well, I'll just make my own stuff and say your grandfather made it, and that I bought it from him out in the bush.'

'That, my good man, is an insidious lie!' Joseph shot back. 'Our ancestors never carved! You sully their memorability!'

This was a horrible *faux pas* and the master carver knew it the moment the words slipped out of his mouth. The ancient craft of Makondi carving in East Africa had been set up by an Italian in the 1940s, who realized that the abundance there of good wood and idle hands were a perfect marriage. Joseph, I had discretely found out, had been carving for only about two months before my arrival. Prior to that, he had driven trucks.

'In the final disposition, veracity shall reign supreme!' Joseph shouted after me as I walked off. It was a bad way to part with a man to whom I would eventually owe so much, but sometimes that's just the way it goes.

Sisal plantations and coconut palms swayed in the breeze as I traveled north along the tourist coast, and the numerous roadside stands were crowded with delicious and sticky mounds of fresh oranges, mangos, cashew nuts, bananas and kiwifruit, hawked by bandana-draped African women to groups of safari-suited German tourists. I had plenty of time to study, because I was hitchhiking – and failing miserably. None of the zebra-painted touristic dune buggies would stop, and eventually I was obliged to flag down a *matatu*, or group taxi made from a pickup truck, the back so full of standing passengers that the vehicle swayed dangerously with each shift of weight. The greater danger was that I planned on riding for free, a notion I was obliged to dispose of after watching the driver chase down and beat up one unhappy character who tried to run away without paying his fare. When it was time for me to disembark I produced some change for the driver to pick at. But he laughed and refused, and produced a bottle of his home-brewed, fermented coconut hooch for me to sample instead. Perhaps he felt that I really deserved a free ride: I had provided much entertainment by swimming the shark-infested mouth of Kilifi Creek while waiting for the ferry, and that was worth something (especially as I was only informed of the sea-beasts after I had made it to the far side).

My destination was Watamu Beach, an exquisite stretch of fine sand dotted by palm and coconut trees with fine fishing and diving for those willing to brave the dangers of the deep. In addition to the Great White sharks said to prowl the edge of the reef, unconfirmed rumor had it that the local species of grouper grew, like flies, until death, eventually becoming eating machines of incredible size. Divers were advised not to prowl into offshore sea caves, lest an opening represent nothing so much as the mouth of one of the monsters which had inadvertently claimed the cave as home when a minnow, but was now grown so huge that it was unable to get back out.

But my plan of action was a different sort of diving.

Watamu was Neckermann turf. The motto of this ubiquitous German tourism agency, synonymous with mass, packaged holidays for sun-loving Krauts, is *Neckermann macht's möglich* ('Making it all possible'), which in this case meant creating a little Düsseldorf in the tropics. Without exception, everyone in Watamu, from the whores to the busboys to the kitsch vendors in the 'native village' down the road, spoke German. This state of affairs was encouraged by a local school built to educate the offspring of tourists and locals in the *Kultur* of the Fatherland, the better to serve future generations.

Acting like a guest, I managed to breach the security gate and, after a quick dip in the ocean to take off the smell of wood resin, sweat and shellac, I sauntered up to the bar with two of my best pipes – one an elephant head with the trunk as the smoking stem, and the other a human head set upright with a two-inch bowl. I ordered a beer and waited. Within minutes I got my first nibble.

'Ver did you get zeez?' inquired a plump vacationer from Stuttgart at my elbow, removing his hand from around the waist of his lithe Somali escort and slowly inching it towards the larger, humanoid pipe. I only had to set the hook and reel him in.

'I was up on the border, you know, with the Turkana, and we were sitting around the camp-fire smoking *bange* and camel dung when the Rendille hit us. It was bad.'

'Really?' the man's eyes opened wide with admiration and adventure envy. 'I vood gif mein auto to see ze *real* Afrika! I haf been here for von veek, but haf not left zee hotel.'

'Its rough out there, it's bad,' I continued. 'If I hadn't run away, they would have shrunk my head. Cannibals. They say they don't exist but I'm telling you they do.'

'It must haf been terreebell ...'

The man had his mitts on the pipe now, turning it over again and again. Then he noticed the red splashes in the carved eye sockets.

'Is zis blut?'

'Yes, but holy blood, taken from the vagina of a twelve-year-old virgin on her wedding night. Wards off the evil eye. Without it the pipe is useless.'

'Tell me, my frint, how did you get it?'

'The chief invited me to the circumcision of his first son, and the boy placed his foreskin in the bowl, but he died of a hemorrhage and they said it was because the gods were angry because there was a white man present. So I stole the pipe and ran away.'

'But you just tolt me zat ...'

'It's a cursed pipe; I can't live with it anymore. Take it away from me, now.'

'But I couldn't do zat after all you haf been tru ...'

'Give me 200 shillings and it's yours.'

'Vat? Two hundret shillink for a stinky olt *pfeife? Nein!* I gif you von hundret.'

'One-fifty.'

'Vell, I hope it is vurs it,' he coughed, peeling off three crisp fifty-shilling notes.

I could hardly believe my luck. One hundred and fifty shillingo-smackers on the first cast! My customer was still talking, plugging me for more details of my escape, or was it the circumcision ceremony, or the significance of the left eyebrow being larger than the right, but I wasn't even listening anymore. I was tallying future profits, and setting up an itinerary for the morrow, thinking of Autolycus in *The Winter's Tale:*

Every lane's end, every shop, church, session, hanging yields a careful man work ...

FIVE

Romeo and Juliet on an Indian Ocean Island

I fled ever northward, hawking my pipes and selling my lies at every tourist trap and beach resort along the way, keeping an eye peeled and an ear perked for Eddy at all times. The end of the line was Lamu, the island Eddy had so extolled, separated from the Kenyan mainland by a saltwater swamp teaming with mangroves. Could he still be there? Climbing aboard a rickety barge, I soon found myself among a throng of chattering men wearing flowing white robes and skullcaps, and ululating women enveloped in black. The reason for all the excitement became obvious when we pulled up at Lamu's wharf. No sooner had the dockhands secured the barge to the quay than a swarm of equally festive folks came pouring over the seawall to drag everyone towards the town square, where a great public wedding was in progress.

The town was alive with the wail of the fife, the thud of the drum and the wild cries of the veiled women. From a balcony overlooking the square, the bride and groom – a handsome-looking couple, the virgin bride looking radiant in a white dress – surveyed the crowd swaying beneath them, throwing flowers down to knots of eager children. Then a blast of a bagpipe shattered the air, and a group of about thirty men trooped into the midst of the crowd, swaying to the rhythm of the beating drums and wailing pipes while forming a circle. A pair moved into the center, squared off and brandished long, wooden staffs like broadswords. They smiled through set teeth and began to tap their poles, keeping time with the beat of the drums. Suddenly, one of the men stepped back and let loose a bone crushing blow at the other; the second man stepped lightly out of the way and then launched his own attack, which the first parried. The crowd roared in approval – and on and on it went until the entire team of duelists had done their thing, namely, cover up whatever noises were emitting from the bridal chamber.

The ceremony ended when the groom's mother emerged on the balcony waving a bloody napkin, retrieved from the maiden's bed. The crowd, as they say, went wild.

Finding a real virgin on Lamu was apparently going to be much easier than locating Eddy. Guitar-playing hippies were a dime a dozen on the island, but none of the string-strummers there fit his description. In fact, very few of the foreigners on the island seemed to care about much of anything aside from their next bowl of *bange* or dope. Time seemed to flow to a beautiful and liquid halt on Lamu, and resulted in a curious lethargy. The absence of all motorized traffic lent a special quiet to the winding, narrow lanes of the town which, in turn, inspired pedestrians to limit their talk. The only bar on the island was inside the only hotel, a place called Pentley's. The loudest noise to be heard from the patio was the rhythmic pounding of the surf during high tide and the creaking of *dhow* masts in the harbor. One soon moved into a groove. The primary concern on any given day was whether to stroll through the swaying palms shading the miles of perfect, white sand dunes between the town and the ocean or saunter the long way around along the beach. By night, when the cool breezes blew, a decision would have to be made to wander over to the hotel for a drink or simply to stay home with a cube of *bange* and dream dreams.

My own piece of paradise was a cell-like room in an old house up a cobblestone lane off the one main street in town. Built in the Arab style around a courtyard, the house was entered from a massive wooden portico inlaid with mother-of-pearl in a rigorous, geometric design. The only other tenant was Franz, a sweet-natured homosexual from

Amsterdam, whose proclivity for the bottom was amply rewarded by the lads of Lamu, who formed a virtual line outside the Dutchman's door.

My own amorous intentions were focused across the street: Brony, a strangely wistful and beautiful Australian lass who inspired my dreams at night and haunted my waking hours by day. In the mornings, I would rise early and wait at my window to catch a glimpse of her in her window, or try to time my exit from my lodging to coincide with hers. I would let her pass and then follow her through the narrow lanes to a tea stand on the waterfront where, at the distance of a table or two, I would watch her flick her golden hair and smile through her perfect teeth before meandering across the sand dunes to the beach. I was in love, or lust, and of the worst, bumbling, unrequited variety, and even started composing sonnets as I sat glancing towards her in the hope that one day, perhaps, she might inquire about the contents of my daily scribbling.

I found solace in the Bard. In addition to his opus of sonnets, I paged through *Love's Labours Lost*, *As You Like It* and, inevitably, *Romeo and Juliet*, where I found a secret sonnet within the play at the moment when the two star-crossed lovers first meet:

Romeo: If I profane with this unworthiest hand
         This holy shrine, the gentle sin is this:
         My lips two blushing pilgrims ready stand
         To smooth that rough touch with a tender kiss

Juliet: Good pilgrim, you do wrong your hand to much
          Which mannerly devotion shows in this
          For saints have hands that pilgrims' hands do touch
          And palm to palm is holy palmer's kiss

Romeo: Have not saints lips, and holy palmers too?

Juliet: Ay, pilgrim, lips that they must use in prayer

Romeo: O! Then, dear saint, let lips do what hands do:
         They pray, grant thou, lest faith turn to despair

Juliet: Saints do not move, thou grant for prayers' sake

Romeo: Then move not, while my prayer's effect I take.

I memorized the scene, using two of my new humanoid pipes as rude puppets to play it, hoping that someday I would have the chance to show my ardor, amazing Brony with the skit and elevating myself head and shoulders above her myriad other suitors.

Alas! The evening I had planned to perform for her at Pentley's, I fell into a sewage trough; knee-deep in the town's shit and urine, I was obliged to postpone ...

Alack! The next afternoon, I followed my fair damsel from the café through the town and over the dunes to the far side of the island, in the hopes of finally summoning the nerve to inform her of my passion. There I found her not alone as planned, but frolicking naked in the surf with another: she browned by the sun, he blackened; her golden hair bleached yellow; his dark curls straightened by the salt water – both bodies glistened, perfect in all their proportions, a picture of joy and happiness, Othello and Desdemona with me, Iago, spying on their bliss.

Jealous and lonely in my own despair and isolation, I left Lamu the next day.

I doubled back along the coast, looking for Eddy in Malindi, Watamu and, finally, Mombasa again – to no avail. My Livingston was nowhere to be found. I was about to give up and see about sea passage out of Mombasa aboard a tramp freighter bound for Diego Garcia when I ran across a new rumored sighting of my brother, or someone who looked like him, at a hippie hangout on the Tanzanian frontier called the Twiga Lodge, also known as 'The Castle'.

The name was apt, because the Castle looked like an impregnable fortress, replete with turrets topping windowless walls and a massive door to serve as a drawbridge to the beach. The reason for the defensive architecture was pretty simple. The beach was a no-go zone after dark. Word had it that a week before an English girl, smooching with her beau beneath the full moon, had been attacked by *panga*-wielding thieves, or *mwezis*, the crashing surf extinguishing the sound of their pleas for help. The boyfriend was beaten senseless, and the girl lost the fingers of her right hand when some brute got tired of trying to pull a ring off a digit and simply cut them all off. True? Even if apocryphal, the story was believed ...

The lord of the Castle was a fellow known as Colorado Ken, an ivory-smuggling, white supremacist who rented the estate from an anonymous Indian owner. Travelers, in turn, rented out space in the Castle's dozen rooms or, when those were filled, on the tiled floors of the lobby and hallways. The palm-lined cove with its perfect white-sand beach stretching from the front door down to the surf was open to all, but in exchange males were obliged to act as muscle and females as fodder for Colorado Ken's private pleasures. It was his disagreement with following these rules and regulations, it would appear, that had forced Eddy's exit and thus put the final kabosh on our Stanley-and-Livingston meeting.

'Yeah,' snarled Ken when I brought up the subject of Eddy and provided a description. 'There was a short, brown-haired guy with a guitar who come down here and stayed for a while. Tried to screw Sally. Thought he did, so I threw him out.'

It sounded like Eddy – always trying to use his guitar to horn in on someone else's girl. He had done that sort of thing to me, well, too many times to recall and feel fraternal affection at the same time. The rest of the ID seemed to fit as well. 'Five-foot-five, with green eyes?' I asked.

'Like a swamp.'

'Stares at you ...'

'... like a lizard.'

'That's Livingston.'

'Thought you said your brother's name was Eddy.'

'It's a long story,' I said. My quest, it seemed, was over.

Once ensconced in the Castle, however, it was difficult to check back out. The snorkeling, diving and sunbathing were so pleasant that the idea of leaving Paradise seemed absurd by day, and when evening finally fell it was simply too dangerous to depart. Colorado Ken darkly suspected his night watchmen of collusion in the bump-and-run on the beach, and strongly advised his guests to travel in groups of at least ten after dark. Funnily, everyone just stayed inside, safe behind the crenellated walls.

While the others busied themselves with playing backgammon and writing postcards, I engaged myself with carving up chunks of wood into a new selection of pipes to hawk. I was getting quite proficient, and had gone so far as to acquire my own axes, knives and files. The other guests at Colorado Ken's were largely indifferent to my whittling skills. But the local staff were intrigued. 'Are you devil doctor?' the cook asked, implying a voodoo-like function to my pipes.

'No,' I replied.

'Then what good this thing, anyway?' he asked, twirling a pipe in his fingers.

'You can smoke *bange* in it,' I said. 'Or you can make them tell stories.' I picked up two of the pipes, draped a napkin around the stem of one and a sweat-soaked handkerchief around the other. Then, flapping my fingers like doll arms, I began improvising a puppet show. It concerned the story of a man and his girlfriend and how they wanted to marry, but the man had no money. So the girlfriend took to prostitution; the man became a thief and was killed by the police, but then came alive again and saved his girl and they were married and lived happily ever after. The show was dumb and the plot stupid but the assembled crew of Castle laborers laughed and clapped and, before I knew it, a few of the sunbathers wandered over from the bar to gawk. 'What else do you do?' a pretty young English girl asked.

'I knew a guy in Amsterdam who put on pornographic puppet shows,' someone said.

'Well,' I mused. 'I guess I could do a little Shakespeare.'

'*Shakespeare?*' A silence settled over the residents of the Castle, and all eyes turned towards me. It was inane, I knew, but the looks of incredulity spurred me on. Flipping a towel over my head to create a sort of backdrop to play against, I launched into the seduction sonnet from *Romeo and Juliet* I had memorized for Brony in Lamu, ending the mini-show with the male puppet giving the female puppet a big, slurpy smooch.

Then someone threw a brass shilling, and someone else chortled and threw another. 'Hey, Bard,' said Colorado Ken, handing me a ten-shilling note. 'Take this.'

Slowly but surely, interest waned and everyone went back to playing darts, backgammon or cards – or disappeared into their rooms to perform their own private acts. But I could not sleep. An insane idea had lodged in my brain: A Shakespearean puppet show? It was weird, wild ... but why not? I hauled out my *Collected Works,* and started going over all the lines I had previously underscored.

SIX

A Bard Is Born

'*Shakespeare?*' the burly, surly, half-breed manager of the Sunshine Club asked. 'We sell women and beer here, not British culture.'

'I'm American,' I added, as if it made any difference. 'Please?'

'Well, I guess I could give you the ten o'clock spot during the band break and before the Masai maiden strip show,' he said at last. 'But no politics, OK?'

A gig, at last! Indeed, I couldn't think of a better venue than the Sunshine: the lights were dim, the customers drunk and anonymity reigned supreme.

I arrived early, at eight, just to get the feel of the place. Already, the Sunshine was filling up with 'professional' ladies, and every eye in the bar turned to coolly appraise me. Nimbly leaping over a beefy thigh, I claimed a place at the bar, where I continued to cram lines as a succession of whores came over to grope me: 'Darling I love you *too* much!'

'Darling, I told you I am *too* busy!'

Hours passed with no call, and I was about to give up and go when the band stopped playing and I noticed the manager whispering something in the lead singer's ear. The latter nodded, reached for the microphone and then announced: '*Ladies and Gentlemen ...*' A decibel or two dropped as the sailors and whores paused for a moment to gawk at the stage. The man said nothing more, and walked off the platform. It was my cue. I hit the stage with dirty feet in open sandals, wearing black stretch slacks cinched with a red bolt of some cheap material, into which I had stuffed a wooden dagger and an assortment of brightly colored cloths. A large and rather pungent towel served as a sort of cape to flourish, while a sheet of white muslin cloth tucked under a black beret soaked up sweat and acted as a curtain when I pulled it over my face.

'Sirs and honored Madams, for your pleasure this eventide, Bits from the Bard!' said I, flipping the muslin cloth while whistling a would-be Renaissance tune. My couplets were heavily distorted through the PA, as I launched into Romeo's seduction pitch:

> If I profane with my unworthiest hand ... anD ... aND ... AND
> This holy shrine, the gentle sin is this ... isS ... iSS ... SSS
> My lips, two blushing pilgrims stand ... anD ... aND ...AND
> To smooth that rough touch with a tender kiss ... isS ... iSS ... ISS

At first, the swell of noise coming from the back of the room seemed to be encouragement. *They like it*, I thought, continuing in a falsetto voice for Juliet:

> Good pilgrim, you do wrong to much ... ucH ... uCH ... UCH
> For mannerly devotion shows in this ... isS ... iSS ... ISS –

Suddenly, my amplified voice went dead. In the void that followed, a wave of noise rolled towards the stage. But, in place of the expected praise, came jeers. 'Bring back the band!' shouted a sailor.
'Fuck 'er, Romeo!' came another critique.

It was going downhill fast. But I had to persevere, convince them, carry on and finish at least the one scene, amplification or no. I started shouting – but to no avail. The heckling grew until I could scarcely hear myself. Still I carried on, projecting, shouting, *screaming* Shakespeare to my audience of b-girls and their sailor suitors. *FOR!*

SAINTS! HAVE! HANDS! THAT! PILGRIMS'! HANDS! MUST!
TOUCH!

Then, with a clump and bang, the PA system came back on, magnifying my voice twentyfold in mid-sentence. But before I could get another caesura in edgewise, a hand reached in front of my face to remove the microphone.

Testing, testing, one, two, three, testing ...

It was the band, and I wasn't halfway through my piece, much less my entire prepared act. Then, with a rude shove from behind, I was propelled from the stage to land in a heap on the dance floor. Howls erupted as I picked myself up, dazed, bruised and confused.

'Hey!' I cried, trying to claw my way back to the stage. 'I'm not done yet!'

The band, however, was playing, and couples were moving out on to the floor. My grand debut was over – and it had been a disaster. The sensible thing to do would have been to get as far away from the Sunshine Club as possible. But my pipe-puppet Romeo had fallen from my grip. With the obsession of the insane, I determined that I would find it, and began looking under tables, between people's legs – asking everyone to help me search for the missing pawn.

'Give it back!' I accused a fat whore with wild, trellis hair.

'Romeo, Romeo wherefore art thou, Romeo?' she cackled. 'Hahaha!'

It was bad and getting worse, my ignominy only feeding my indignation until finally, blissfully, the manager called on his bouncers to drag me out of the club and deposit me on the street. The howls of laughter were only silenced when the door slammed shut behind me – or almost. A group of taxi drivers calmly observed my humiliation, and then began to chortle.

I stumbled away, weeping. I had been reduced to public groveling in front of bawds and whores, and I had been utterly rejected, utterly. I had bottomed out, crashed. There was nowhere to go but up.

The first place to try and dive, however, was down as deep as I could go. Junkies might beg to differ, but I maintain that there has never been better pseudo-solace from the self-perceived evils of this wild and wicked world than the comfort of the bottle, and I that is what I sought that night, big time. I was into my sixth level of incoherence when I felt a hand on my shoulder.

'I thought I was the only crazy one around here,' a slightly accented voice whispered.

I whirled – or lurched – around and stared at a familiar-looking woman with henna-red hair. It was the nympho half of the pair I believed had stolen my money so long ago (actually only a couple of weeks), come back to haunt me again. 'You!' I snarled. 'You are responsible for all this!'

'Be calm, be calm,' cooed the witch. 'I saw you at the Sunshine Club tonight.'

The reminder of my shame hit hard.

'Just leave me alone!' I wailed. 'What do you want from me?!'

'You are actually quite good,' said the Siren, speaking with what I gathered was an Austrian lilt. 'But you just chose the wrong venue. Sailors' bars are designed for sailors. They go there to get laid, not for Shakespeare.'

'Oh,' I said, confirming or admitting a profound truth.

'Tell me, where do people go to listen to Shakespeare?' she asked.

'They go to the theater,' I replied.

'If people who want to listen to Shakespeare go to the theater, why don't you?'

I was dumbfounded by this insight, and wanted more – but as soon as she had drawn a small map detailing the location of the Mombasa Theater and Arts Club, a horn honked outside the bar.

'Sorry,' she said, brushing her lips against my cheek while nodding subtly towards an idling Mercedes Benz. 'Gotta go.'

'What's your name?' I managed to ask before she made the door.

'Elizabeth,' she said, and then was gone.

After hiding out in a flophouse hotel, afraid to show my face in Mombasa during the long, cruel light of the next day, I emerged in the early evening and slunk over to the Mombasa Arts and Theatre Club to pitch my show to the manager. 'I say, Shakespeare *wallah*, what!' he replied with a grin.

'Shakespeare *whata*?'

'You know, the chaps who busked around West Africa with such success, although I believe they were financed by the British Council or some such. Who finances you?'

'I was actually sort of thinking of passing the hat.'

The manager bought me a double scotch and told me to hang around until after the evening movie had finished (Burton–Taylor's *Shrew*). Finally the doors to the clubroom opened and out spilled a crowd of just plain regular folks: Englishmen with their wives, Indians dressed in safari suits with their families, middle-class Africans chatting softly at the bar and even the oddball American Peace Corps volunteer.

'Well, Bard, the floor is yours,' said the manager, snapping me out of my shock at the wonderfully mundane. Then he raised his voice above the general din of clinking beer glasses and the cough and cackle of club conversation.

'Ladies and Gentlemen!' he said. 'Tonight we have a special guest, who claims he is a wandering actor, a peripatetic player of Shakespeare! Let me introduce to you, tonight only, the one and only ... Bard in the Bush!'

Heads turned, and a murmur passed through the crowd. I lifted two puppets and screwed my courage to the sticking place, like Macbeth knifing Duncan. Actually, the curtain rose on the Desdemona snuff scene from *Othello*.

Put out the light, and then put out the light.
If I quench thee, though flaming minister,
I can again thy former light restore
Should I repent me; but once put out thy light,

Thou cunning'st pattern of excelling nature,
I know not where is that Promethean heat
That can thy light relume ...

The deed done and Desdemona dead, I finished the scene with a flourish, took a deep bow ... and was met by silence. Disaster had struck again, I was sure. But then, from the bar, came the first murmurs of praise circulating around the room. It spread like a blissful contagion and as I emerged from my bow and threw back the facecloth, everyone was applauding and smiling.

'Thank you, thank you,' I said, unsure of what to do next.

'I say, a little *Romeo and Juliet*?' asked someone.

Why not, I thought.

'My next scene is a piece from that well-known play of the two star-crossed lovers. But what is not well known is that their first meeting is actually cast as a secret sonnet ...'

I chipped in the Porter's monologue from *Macbeth* which I somehow remembered from the off-off-off Broadway production years earlier, finishing my limited repertoire with a badly hashed version of Launce from *The Two Gentlemen of Verona*; for an encore, I reprised Desdemona's death scene. My audience did not seem to care. The manager came back from passing around my beret, which was filled with cash notes and coins to the tune of some 250 shillings, a sum representing about 100 bucks, if memory serves. Others plied me with drinks and suggested new scenes. The night's revelry went on, and I emerged from the club deliciously drunk, my head spinning with new ideas and my pockets brimming with honest loot.

Back to the flophouse that night? No way. I hailed a cab and went straight to the train station, where I got myself a ticket aboard the Lunatic Express. It was still cattle class, and I ended up sleeping on a piece of floor somewhere behind a stove, but what the heck; I was going to Nairobi, the Big Town, bringing my show on the road. Finding li'l Livingston Eddy could wait for a while – I had a new career.

SEVEN

Mzungu on the Make

It was opening night of the National Theatre of Kenya's production of *Jesus Christ Superstar*, the cast made up of local luminaries playing the key roles, with a thick padding of Peace Corps volunteers in the chorus. All of culture-conscious Nairobi was there, applauding wildly despite the occasional discordant guitar chord or singer out of sync.

Jesus Christ! Jesus Christ! Who are you, what have you sacrificed ...

When the doors swung open for intermission, the audience emerged for a little fresh air, only to be greeted by a strange apparition standing at the bottom of the steps.

'Twas I, in deep disguise.

'Ladies and Gentlemen!' I announced from behind a Masai mask I had altered to fit my face. 'For your intermission entertainment and edification this evening, I would be so bold as to present you with Shakespeare, Scenes from Diverse Plays! I will begin with *Othello,* a tragic tale of race relations and miscegenation ...'

I reached into my belt and seized a brace of puppets, one stained black with shoe polish to make the Moor, the other the natural grain of wood, but with long strands of cowhair glued to the scalp: the doomed Desdemona.

It is the cause! It is the cause, my soul
Let me not name it you, you chaste stars.
It is the cause ...

I switched back and forth between a fake baritone and a squeaky
falsetto until finally, the Othello puppet stuffed the head of the
cowhaired puppet into the folds of the cloth, and Desdemona was
no more ... The intermission gong sounded early, but the audience
was still outside and with me as I launched into Launce from *The
Two Gentlemen of Verona*, using my kit as a surrogate dog Crab.
I had been hard at work for the previous week, and ready for the
grand debut:

> Nay, 'twill be this very hour ere I have done weeping: all the kind
> of the Launces have this very fault. I have received my proportion
> like the prodigious son, and am going with Sir Proteus to the
> Imperial's court. I think Crab, my dog, be the sourest-natured
> animal that lives. My mother weeping, my father wailing, my
> sister crying, our maid howling, our cat wringing her hands, and
> all our house in a great perplexity, yet did not this cruel-hearted
> cur shed one tear ...

Applause and laughter, the filling of my collection plate – and then
again the flickering of the lobby-lights by an irate management.
'No! No!' cried the cheering audience. 'We want more!'
Finally, the guards were sent to drag me away. Pockets filled with
loot, it was time for a beer at Brunner's, to wander over to the New
Florida Disco to check out the new batch of Ugandan talent or
simply to stumble back to my domicile. It was called the Hotel al-
Manzura, and it is a wonder I am not still there today.

There are, of course, the Great Hotels of the World, those uniquely
elegant, obscure or historical hostels-cum-watering holes owned,
managed or frequented by the exceedingly wealthy, notorious or

renowned. There is Zelda Fitzgerald frolicking in the fountain of the New York Plaza, T. E. Lawrence doing his thing with some Arab boy in Baron's of Aleppo, Somerset Maugham sipping his sling at Raffles in Singapore, Eric Ambler contemplating a dark tale at the long bar of the Park in Istanbul ...

The Hotel al-Manzura was none of these. There was no bar lined with pink gin fizzes and red noses, only a raunchy kitchen with greasy slop for food and tea boiled in milk to drink. There were no easy chairs in the lobby from which to watch the world walk by, because there was no lobby and the world without consisted of a trash-lined street. Nor were there balconies, balustrades or even curtains on the windows of the rooms. The rooms themselves were small, had cement walls and floors and were crammed with beds – usually four to a room, but often six. The ceiling fans, showers and toilets never worked, and folks were obliged to go to bed in the stultifying air, dirty and farting. But it was cheap. If the haze of twenty years does not mislead, a room – that is, a dirty mattress tossed atop a steel-frame bed with sagging springs – cost about a buck a day. The result was that the al-Manzura attracted a certain clientele, and it was this group of sometimes-unsavory guests that gave it rank in the category of memorable hostels of the world.

Belgian ivory smugglers snored next to Dutch sociologists, both only recently back from a month with the Masai. Canadian drug dealers shot dice with Ethiopian refugees, while Greek globetrotters traded tales with the odd traveling Turk. While there were always plenty of wannabe Hemingways who passed through its open doors, easily identifiable by the stacks of books next to their beds, it was the modern-day mercenaries, adventurers and just plain con men and women who gave the al-Manzura its particular flavor. The al-Manzura attracted them all; it attracted me.

A typical evening centered on boiled milk tea, harsh Rooster cigarettes (bought individually from the counter) and perhaps an oversized joint of *bange*. Tale-swapping was also enhanced by the institution of *mihra*, the local version of Yemeni *qat*. No sooner did the green saliva begin to drip from the mouths of consumers than self-aggrandizing talk began to pass around the room, usually focusing on fantastic yarns of paradise found, or deeds of derring-do too outrageous to be true. If you hadn't seen your best friend rot away with jungle fever or get crunched by a herd of stampeding wildebeest, or hadn't utterly lost control due to the effects of some impossibly potent dope, you simply had not traveled.

Sadly, no one could afford to trust anyone else. Guests slept behind locked doors with their wallets under their pillows, and woke to find all their money gone and their wallets still there. Travelers' cheques, strangely enough, were regarded as fair game due to the simple fact that they were replaceable. But having someone else take your cheques was not the only game in town: if someone ran through the halls of the hotel crying, 'Thief! Thief! Someone stole my travelers' cheques!', it was just as likely that the victim had fallen on him- or herself, registering the tragedy in order to get an official statement from the hotel to present to the AmEx folks, who would then replace the loss. The 'stolen' cheques would remain in the victim's wallet to flash as a cash wad when crossing hippie-phobic borders, or used to dump on unsuspecting store or hotel clerks in different towns or countries: no one in Africa believed for a moment that American or European computer systems could pinpoint a hot cheque before months, or even years, had passed, and such canceled cheques were regarded as a viable currency. In India, it was rumored, travelers' cheques drawn in another's name were purchased for half the stated value with no questions asked. The joke was that somewhere in the world, Burma perhaps – or, more cruelly, 'somewhere in Africa' – there was a country that used the bad notes as legal tender.

Despite the general lack of trust, I did become acquainted with travelers at the al-Manzura whom I would meet again and again. There was California Jimmy, always looking for an 'expatriate' job with such perks as company car, apartment and paid home leave. There was Franz, the gentle Dutchman I had met in Lamu, who seemed even more of a greenhorn than me – until I met him again in Cape Town a year later, and found myself talking to changed man: he had just been released from some hideous Zambian jail, and had in mind to join the Seloux Scouts squad in Rhodesia to take revenge upon all black people with the aid of a gun. There was Michael, a Jewish South African with his girlfriend Pam, a gal from New Zealand with one wandering eye; they had traveled overland by motorcycle from Bangkok, dealing LSD all the way. (I would later see them in Namibia, running from the law.) There was Gino, the Italian-Brit intent on making his next run between Nairobi and England with a dozen opium gum-filled rubbers strung down his stomach from a string tied to his teeth; he roomed with Günther, a chubby German baker from Stuttgart who doubled as a holiday photographer and was constructing his own custom-made bush bike to go shoot the last of the elephants. Then there was Marco, a former French Legionnaire traveling with his Swedish-Lapp wife Lena, trying to smuggle gold out of the country, and who wanted to hire me as his 'mule'.

To all these people I was known as 'Bard' due to my obsession with memorizing Shakespeare. Admittedly, it was pretty hard to see the connection between *A Midsummer Night's Dream* and the al-Manzura, but I was determined to find one.

'That's a pretty fat book you got there,' someone would ask as they plunked themselves down next to me in the first-floor restaurant. 'What is it? The Bible?'

'Oh, no,' I would answer. 'Just a little Shakespeare.'

'*Hamlet* and all that, right?'

'Well, this is a little passage from *Richard III*.'

'Say what?'

The easiest way to explain was to demonstrate, usually to the embarrassment of those sitting near me as I spontaneously launched into histrionic, half-memorized scenes.

A horse, a horse! My kingdom for a horse!
I think there be six Richmonds in the field
Five I have slain today instead of him
A horse, a horse! My kingdom for a horse!

Eventually the show would break up with Ali, the proprietor, turning up the volume on his tape deck to a pitch I couldn't compete with. A merry gang of travelers would hit the fantastic fruit and vegetable market to pick up an avocado lunch followed by a visit to the local zoo to see the baby elephants, a look-see at the museum, a flyby at the central park to catch a new Zairian band playing at the Gazebo, an afternoon snack of cheap beans in a tin shack down by the river or at an all-you-can-eat Indian-style vegetarian restaurant, followed by an early evening *kung fu* flick at the cinema down the street before stumbling home for another night of chewing *qat* and telling lies.

Ah, the al-Manzura! If I ever become rich and famous, the management should put up one of those plaques designating the place where the poet or statesman rested his head. The problem is that I changed rooms so often they would have to plaster an entire floor. 'Bard stayed here – and here, and here, and here ...' Not likely, alas.

Still, I might have become the most conspicuous *mzungu* in town, playing the streets by day and the clubs by night. But I was not really making and money, which was, of course, an essential element in the exercise whether I chose to continue my pursuit of brother Eddy across Africa or simply save enough to buy an airline ticket home. For reasons of pride I had decided that I could not, would not, sink so low as to make that international call to Mom and Dad and pass the beggar's bowl in that direction – *no* ...

To address the issue of cash flow, I hit upon a stunningly simple idea: *the schools!* The English legacy fairly demanded that administrators admit a little Shakespeare to their classrooms for a fee, and I was more than happy to oblige. If the Karen Middle School was planning a performance of *A Midsummer Night's Dream* next semester, then I prepared Quince and Bottom for that season's class. If the English teacher at the Greater Nairobi Boys' Council Estate School was thinking about staging *Hamlet* the following year, then I worked up a scene or two from the tragedy of the Danish Prince ...

Drugged up on *qat* and coffee, often not sleeping for thirty hours at a time, I poured the big-ticket soliloquies into my brain: Macbeth,

Lady Macbeth, Falstaff, Henry, Mark Antony, Brutus, Prospero, Caliban, Iago ... as well as memorizing dialogues for puppet sequences that seemed appropriate, such as the 'Night Watch' from *Much Ado About Nothing*:

> Dogberry: If you meet a thief, you may suspect him, by virtue of your office, to be no true man; and, for such kind of men, the less you meddle or make with them, why, the more is for your honesty.
>
> Watchman: If we know him to be a thief, shall we not lay hands on him?
>
> Dogberry: Truly, by your office you may; but I think they that touch pitch will be defiled. The most peaceable way for you, if you do take a thief, is to let him show himself what he is and steal out of your company.

One day, the headmaster at the Banda Boarding School declared that he intended to mount *The Comedy of Errors*, and asked if I could include some material from that play in my repertoire. In fact, I had already memorized a skit from the play – the somewhat ribald dialogue between Dromio and Antipholus, a selection I referred to as 'The Fat Woman'. Within the scene Dromio, the servant, describes in detail how he has been taken for his unknown twin brother by that man's wife, the very Fat Woman.

> Dromio: ... She is spherical, like a globe: I could make out countries on her.
>
> Antipholus: In what part of her body stands Ireland?
>
> Dromio: Marry sir, in her buttocks, I found it out by the bogs.
>
> Antipholus: Where Scotland?

Dromio: I found it by the bareness, hard in the palm of her hand.

Antipholus: Where France?

Dromio: In her forehead; armed and reverted, making war against her heir.

Antipholus: Where Belgia, the Netherlands?

Dromio: O, sir! I did not look so low!

In the spirit of internationalism, I would next add a country not listed on the map at the time of Queen Elizabeth, Kenya, and then allow the scene to develop into a sort of improvisation with the audience of children guessing Kenya's position on the Fat Woman's body and the reasons why it so lay. A frequent response was 'in her hair because of the forest', or 'in her mouth because of the ocean'. Then the inevitable happened:

'Between her legs!' suggested a nine-year-old at the Banda School.

Unfazed, I continued the skit and completed the performance to a sound round of applause, packed my kit and made my way to the headmaster's office to collect my fee.

'Sit down, Mister Goltz!' he said with strained smile. 'What an ... *interesting* way of presenting Shakespeare! You must be quite popular among the expatriate schools, yes?'

I ticked off a quick list of the schools that were expecting me in the next week or two, and then asked him for any suggestions he might have to expand the tour.

'I am afraid not, Mister Goltz,' he said curtly. 'The show happens to be over.'

'I beg your pardon?'

'WE AGREED THAT THIS WAS TO BE A CHILDREN'S SHOW, MISTER GOLTZ, AND YOU'VE PROVEN TO BE A PURVEYOR OF PORNOGRAPHY!'

I was so startled I was speechless.

'RUINING OUR CHILDREN!' he bellowed.

'Sir, what are you talking about?'

'YOU KNOW PERFECTLY WELL, YOU, YOU ...' He was perspiring heavily and could not sustain his tirade at full volume, but spluttered through his spittle, foaming at the mouth. 'You *filth*! You *indecent thing*! To suggest that Kenya is *between a woman's legs*!!'

I could only groan in reply, and left the office as he began dialing the schools whose names I had been unfortunate enough to give him. When I arrived at the Karen School, I was not entirely surprised to find that my Shakespeare show had been abruptly canceled. I was washed up on the Nairobi school circuit – blacklisted, as it were.

Other aspects of the Shakespeare show were starting to sour, too, even on the street. I might have developed a dozen or so two-puppet skits, but the reality was that due to the limited range of gestures I could effect with the thumb and middle finger of either hand used as puppet 'arms', and the limited range of vocal difference possible between, say, Lady Macbeth and Desdemona, one scene appeared much the same as another unless a given audience member actually knew the lines. To make up for such limitations, I started to inject contemporary politics into various scenes: Macbeth became Idi Amin, the mad dictator of Uganda; Caliban was the 'native', whose lands had been stolen by Prospero, the colonial British or French.

When members of the audience seemed indifferent to such insights into the universal relevance of Shakespeare, I started to get angry; and when I started shouting at the staff of the New Stanley and Brunner's (who had previously allowed me to set up my show at a short but safe distance from their lunch, dinner and cocktail crowds), insisting that their clientele not only *wanted* to hear my exegesis on the state of affairs in Rwanda and Burundi, but *needed* to ... well, shall we say their patience started running a little thin and I increasingly found myself further down the street, fuming in outrage at the injustice of it all.

It was time to go, and go anywhere – but I did nothing. Days went by. A new batch of travelers arrived at the al-Manzura, talking about adventures enjoyed or survived here and there, and then they were gone again, replaced by more strangers. The only person who seemed to be going nowhere was me. One day I caught myself out on a street, literally unable to decide whether to go left or right – so I remained exactly where I was for almost two hours, torn between going over to the American Express office to check for mail as opposed to going over to the New Stanley to try and quick-mount a show and pass the hat before the guards threw me off the premises. Finally, I went left, which meant the AmEx office, and asked after mail, even though I was sure there was none: I had hardly received any post for a month. But to my surprise, the clerk handed me two letters. One was from an acquaintance who wrote of an annual theater festival held in Zambia, suggesting I go and check it out; the other was from Eddy. He had finally received news that I, too, was in Africa. Rather than having disappeared over the ocean, moreover, he was in Lesotho, the independent mountainous country in the middle of South Africa. He had arrived there via a route that included Tanzania, Malawi, Zambia, Botswana and South Africa, and was now headed for Rhodesia. Typically, he forgot to put a date on the letter.

But Eddy was in Africa. A decision was thus made for me: the quest to find Livingston had been rejoined!

I paid off my accumulated lodging debt to the al-Manzura. Abdullah the cook wept at my departure, and Ali handed me a choice batch of *qat* to keep me happy.

I was on the road again, a Bard back in the Bush.

EIGHT

Serengeti Shakespeare

The sun began to set, a foghorn sounded and a mammoth ship moved from its berth out towards the open sea. The beached fishing dinghies rose in the water as the waves licked higher on the sand, and then rest again. *Dar ... Dar-es-Salaam.* A nasty socialist city saved by its port, connected to the world beyond the vastness of the Indian Ocean by a deep, narrow channel that telescoped all shipping, right before one's eyes. Huge boats flying all the different flags of the world were constantly steaming in and out of anchorage through the defile, so close one was tempted to reach out and touch them. Nearby, dinghies and *dhows* careened onto the beach and added their barnacles to the smell of decaying seaweed, dumping the day's catch into the fish market. Sailors from around the globe mingled with Russian and Chinese diplomats, American foreign aid folks and sea-beaten Swahili-speaking boatmen, all squeezing octopus and squid for freshness, noting the discoloration in a shark's fin and nibbling on deep-fried minnows.

But I was not in the Tanzanian capital to loll around the docks. My mission was to get to Zambia in time for the theater festival I had heard about, and then push on to the enclave kingdom of Lesotho in search of Eddy. Accordingly, my first stop was the Chinese-built Tan-Zam railway station to pick up a ticket to Zambia. To my dismay, I learned

I needed not only a visa, but that the visa required me to receive a battery of shots against smallpox, diphtheria and even yellow fever. The entire inoculation cocktail took about a week, and the Zambian embassy would not even begin to process my application until all the medical hoops had been jumped through. I was stuck, and being stuck I began scouting out possible performance venues to raise a little cash while passing the time. The first of these was the street in front of the main international hotel in the middle of town.

Mwalimu Nyerere might have had translated *Julius Caesar* into Swahili, but no one on the street seemed able to recognize the original. I felt this acutely when police arrived and I was unable to effectively communicate the idea that I was not so much an agitator or rabble-rouser as an emerging cultural icon, and not a danger to the existing socialist order at all.

'*Mimi kutaka kula*,' I said. 'I merely wish to entertain.' (Actually, a literal translation would be 'I want food', but no matter.)

Then, as I was about to walk away and return to the port to watch the boats come and go, an angel appeared.

'Bard!' he cried. 'What are you doing here? Jump in!'

My fan knew me from the Mombasa Theater Club. In fact, he was an active member of a similar institution in Dar-es-Salaam, and thought it a fine idea to bring me over and introduce me. Even better, that very night was the final performance of the expatriate theater season, replete with a cast party for all involved.

A few hours later I was ensconced in the director's box as a guest of honor, viewing a production of *Annie Get Your Gun*. The leading role was played by some American Peace Corps volunteer, and Wild Bill Hickock by a *Wahindi* Indian businessman. Africans and even a Sikh in a turban played several other cowboy roles, with chorus parts played by the sons and daughters of various diplomats and United Nations personnel.

It was, alas, the sort of show that only friends and family could delight in – and aside from me, the audience consisted exclusively of friends and family. They liked the show so much that they gave it a standing ovation and demanded a reprise of the finale:

Anything you can do I can do better
I can do anything better than you ...

That was kind of how I felt when I made my grand entrance an hour later during the post-production party at the bar, with the cast and crew two sheets to the wind. My Shakespeare show opener was Launce; wild applause greeted this and every other effort I mounted, and I decided that it was just and good and rightly deserved, though disconcertingly similar to the enthusiasm evinced for the half-baked musical production I had just panned. More to the point, the management invited me back for a couple of performances the following week on the main stage of the theater itself, replete with a lighting scheme. As a wandering actor, I was moving up in the world ...

Rather than wait the week out in my Sikh temple abode (it was free, but you had to be inside the gates before nightfall), I decided to exercise an option.

ZzzzaaAnnnZzzziiiBaaaRRR!

Zanzibar, land of sordid history and romance, island of spice and slaves, the fragrance of cloves and the screams of castration combined, country of choleric deaths and harem heavens, home to Burton and Speke, Livingston and Stanley, me! The magic spice island was just out of sight across the sea, and beckoned like a clove stuck in a Christmas ham.

ZZzzaaAnnnZzzziiiBaaaRRR!!!

The problem was getting there. While there were flights between Dar-es-Salaam and the mysterious island, they were infrequent, overbooked and required special visas for foreigners, a process so arduous and time-consuming that most would-be visitors simply gave up. Then one day down at the port, pondering one of Prospero's monologues from *The Tempest*, I noticed a line forming at a small office down the quay. Closing the *Collected Works*, I ambled over and discovered people queuing up to buy deck tickets for a tramp steamer sailing that afternoon for – Zanzibar! I joined the line, kept my mouth shut and asked no questions and put down the requisite fare when it was my turn at the window.

Ticket in hand, I walked up the gangplank to the steamer along with several hundred other folks, all as neat and courteous as can be. A police officer stood at the top of the boat checking tickets and identification. When my turn came, I showed him my ticket; he started to say something, and then someone behind me shoved and I was on the deck and lost in a kicking, scratching and clawing mob, being the same people who had lined up so nicely before.

Their behavior may have been what saved me from instant eviction from the steamer. But the sudden change from public politeness and decorum to utter chaos gave me pause. The shy and retiring Zanzibari men in skullcaps who had waited in the ticket line so patiently now fought tooth and nail for a place to say their midday prayers, while the pious women covered head to toe in black, who had been so quiet and demure on *terra firma*, soon turned into territorial animals on board, stripping off their veils to stake claims near some upright object which would provide minimal wind protection for the gas stoves used to boil water for tea and corn porridge, as well as to wash the dishes. I was soon reduced to perching atop an oil drum near the starboard railing. Every time the tramp rolled or wallowed in the waves, I found myself clinging to the edge of my seat lest I be dumped in the electric blue and shimmering green shark-infested waters.

Soon, we were out of sight of land, and the chatter and commotion on deck died down to a subdued buzz. A tanker floated by on the oblate plain of water. Flying fish flew. Goats bleated. Another tanker appeared in the heat waves on the horizon. More flying fish flew. It was mind-numbing, and by early evening the monotonous pounding of the engines, the smell of diesel and the taste of salt on everything had brought me to the edge of nausea. I was starting to wonder about the wisdom of having made the trip. Then a kid came up and pointed out a pair of dolphins jumping alongside the ship. A bobbing brace of coconuts and then the trunk of a palm tree followed. *Land?* I scanned the horizon again, but it remained as empty and immense as before. But did my nostrils apprehend the raggedly sweet scent of cloves, however faintly?

Others, too, felt something, smelled something. A man in a skullcap and gown got up from his mat and walked to the bow. He was joined by another, then three more, then five. Ineluctably, I was drawn into the growing mass of humanity crowded on the prow, silently waiting, sniffing. A minute passed, then ten. I was about to return to my perch when someone said something, and a long jabber-murmur ran through the crowd, and someone reached out to point to a faint shadow in the east. In the distance, barely discernable in the haze, stood a tiny speck of gray. It grew larger and larger with each succeeding moment, and then with a piercing blast, the captain of our tramp steamer let loose a sound from the ship's horn that seemed to take on the sound of our destination, and I felt the tickle of memories experienced by the others, which I had no right to claim.

Zanzibar!

It was another two hours before we dropped anchor; the sun had long burnt down to the western horizon. One would have liked a little more light, not only to see the town but also to negotiate one's way off the steamer. The boat shifted visibly and dangerously as the crush of passengers rushed to the starboard side to disembark or just to throw bundles to waiting relatives on the quay before customs could conduct its search. Not a few suitcases ended up in the drink, bobbing like the decomposing bodies that Burton tells us used to wash up on shore during his nineteenth-century days of residence on the island.

The melee was compounded by the need to get vaccinations for cholera in the tiny sailors' mess before we debarked. Once again a mad scramble ensued, with elbows, fists and feet employed to get to the front of the line. I had resigned myself to being the last one off the boat when a hand snaked through a portal, grabbed my arm and, before I knew what was happening, dragged me through the window and had me standing dockside quicker than you can say '*sasa sana*', which means 'quickly' in Swahili.

My savior was a neatly dressed, handsome young man who, by complexion, looked more Arab than African. He also sported the most incredibly long eyelashes I have ever seen on a man, accentuated, I believe, by the liberal application of kohl.

'Thanks,' I said, reaching into my pocket to disperse a little *baksheesh* for having helped me jump the line so effectively.

'*Asante sana*,' said my savior, refusing the tip. Then he extended his hand and I reached to shake it but discovered that he was merely proffering a sheet of paper, on which two words were written in Swahili, Arabic and English: *Foreigners forbidden.*

My man clapped his hands twice in a gesture that could only mean he wanted to see my documents. The captain or some other shipboard spy had noticed me and radioed ahead to say there was an illegal on board; the local police had been waiting at the dock to intercept the interloper until the ship sailed back to the mainland, and apparently all the jails were full.

'Plea-is,' said my minder, introducing himself as 'Mister Ahmad'. 'Come.'

'Where are we going?' I asked nervously, fearing the journey was indeed to the local pokey, and having nowhere to bolt.

'*Funduq*,' he said. 'To hotel.'

We were soon walking down a broad, arrow-straight processional avenue that must have been the main street of the new town, but might have been the road to the airport. Everything was shut up tight as a drum, and the low-intensity street lamps cast a weird, cheesy glow over the rows of squat, concrete buildings, making them look dull and dirty. Zanzibar, my Zanzibar, was looking more like an Eastern European industrial town than the exotic emporium of human wares and strange spices I had imagined.

Finally, we arrived in front of a massive if formless building eight or nine stories tall, which loomed over everything else. Pinned to the façade in neon lights was the word 'Hotel', although only the letters 'O' and 'L' were lit.

'Sher-ee-ton,' said Mister Ahmad, lying or at least repeating the lie he had swallowed about the management of the cinder-block monstrosity and, in doing so, suggesting that it would cost a mint. 'All *mzungu* stay here – Russ-man, Ala-man, China-man ...'

'Mister Ahmad, I am sorry,' I said with a smile. '*Pesa* – no money.'

'Good *funduq*,' he smiled back, trying to guide me up the steps.

'No, Mister Ahmad, no.'

My escort was baffled by my reluctance. But he smiled again, took me by the hand and led me down the darkened street to another government-approved inn for friendly foreigners from the Warsaw Pact. When I rejected this guesthouse on the same basis as the first – poverty – he led me to a third, which I rejected as well.

The selection of accommodation in New Zanzibar, however, was severely limited, and Mister Ahmad's patience was growing thin. Once again, he took me by the hand and led me down an even darker lane and into the labyrinthine streets of the old town, turned a couple of corners and then ushered me through a set of iron gates. I was sure that this had to be the local jail. Then someone inside turned on a light, and we could see that we were standing in a terracotta courtyard planted with coconut and date trees and facing a stately, handsome, older stone structure. A simple wooden sign hung above the arched doorway, identifying the place as the Zanzibar Hotel.

We walked up steps and across the cool, marble floor to the reception desk, on which Mister Ahmad slammed my passport for the clerk's attention. He, in turn, silently slid a piece of paper over the counter for me to read.

'No,' I said, looking at the rates. 'Too much *pesa*.'

Mister Ahmad had been patient trying to find an appropriate abode for me. He had even been obliging enough to carry my pack. But now he stood his ground.

'No,' he said, throwing my kit on the counter. 'You – here – *funduq*!'

'Mister Ahmad!' I cried. 'I am a poor hippie traveler, and I want a cheap place, a Sikh temple or something. It is my money, not yours; I refuse to stay in this hotel!'

Although he probably only understood two words of my plea, he understood the meaning well enough. He exploded.

'*Pesa!*' he demanded, rubbing his fingers and thumb together and then slapping one hand on the other to indicate he wanted my money, now.

'I'll call the police!' I cried, forgetting that Mister Ahmad *was* the local law.

Reluctantly, furiously, helplessly, I dug into my underwear and produced the wad of Tanzanian shillings I had earned at the theater club. He looked at the crumpled bills in disgust, extracted a few of the larger ones and plunked them down on the counter. The night clerk picked them up, counted them and then produced some change with the key.

'*Lala Salaama*,' growled Mister Ahmad, and slammed the door to the hotel on his way out.

I was outraged, and stomped up to my room, refusing to tip the bellhop. I threw open the doors to my veranda and slumped into an ancient and worn if still padded wicker chair, cursing the stars and moon while my mind plotted dark thoughts. The idea! How dare they stick me in a hotel like it was a jail! I called down to reception and ordered a gin and tonic with a sprig of mint in it, and later berated the management for using too much ice. Then I drew a hot bath, soaked away the filth and sweat and grime of a week on the road and crawled into my king-sized bed between crisp clean sheets, steaming until I slept and dreaming of starkest revenge for the mortifications I had just endured.

Still seething in the morning, I was about to punch the bellboy for knocking when I realized that he would not be able to defend himself because his hands were under my breakfast tray. 'You paid for this shit so you might as well eat it,' I said to myself. I poured out a strong cup of black tea to clear my head, and then added milk and sugar to the second. There was fruit salad, too, which I had to admit was pretty tasty. Excellent, in fact. There was also a three-minute egg that was still warm in its shell and, under glass, several pieces of crisp toast accompanied by some remarkably yummy marmalade. I ate on the balcony and plotted my next move. I had best get my stuff together and check out before they charged me for a second day, I figured. But my fury and anger over having been forced to stay at the Zanzibar Hotel was abating by the minute. The veranda afforded a view not just of the unsurpassingly lovely garden courtyard, but also of the distant *dhow* harbor and the helter-skelter rooftops and ornate wooden balconies of the old town.

It was, I had to admit, rather pretty, everything considered. Perhaps I had been overly harsh on Mister Ahmad the night before. I sat down and lit another cigarette, looked at myself in the mirror and found myself reeling towards an epiphany.

Fact: my room had a view.

Fact: I was the first one to have slept in my sheets.

Fact: my underwear washed white again and my shirt and shorts were ironed.

Fact: I was paying ten dollars a day.

I totaled these and other subjective data into a formula and came up with a profound truth: I was a fraud, a fake and worse – a fool. For months I had been living as cheaply as possible, succeeding in the best world-traveler-sanctioned way of getting by on less than the poorest, unemployed native could possibly do.

How dare you do so, I said to myself. *How dare* I pretend that a ten-buck hotel bill was going to break me! *How dare* I waste hours and days standing by the side of the road hitchhiking because I refused to ride buses because tickets cost money! *How dare* I eat swill for a nickel when for a dollar I could gorge myself like a king!

The monologue went on for some time, but the sea change had already occurred: never again would I allow pretended penury to ruin my travel. If I were obliged to sleep in a ditch in the future it would be as a last resort. 'Never spend a nickel when a dollar will do', I decided, was to be my operative motto, and I have the Zanzibar Hotel to thank for that. The yellowed receipt for my five-day stay is still pinned above my desk.

Even with a changed attitude, however, there were restrictions to enjoying my newfound freedom from self-imposed penury. I was, finally, an unwanted foreigner on Zanzibar, and could not travel freely around the island. Mister Ahmad made sure I knew that when he dropped in for tea the next day with a list of rules and regulations, taking my passport in exchange. Still, a challenge is a challenge, and I was determined to make the most of my stay. The first time I attempted to leave Zanzibar town, by local bus, I was pulled off by an irate policeman and brought back to the tourism office. Mister Ahmad sighed when he saw me. I promised to be good, but managed to get around the restrictions by renting a bicycle, flying past the yawning watchmen at the city limits who only woke to check approaching motor traffic.

Still, there were no tourist maps of the island to be had, given local obsession with security. So I was never sure of the pedigree of the sights I came across, such as the ruins of an abandoned church dating to the nineteenth century or several burnt plantation houses surrounded by neglected groves of cloves. I assumed these to be the remains of the property belonging to the Arab elite slaughtered in 1964, but when I questioned a couple of soldiers guarding the place I was met with suspicion despite my claim to be a visiting engineer from the German Democratic Republic.

The sights in town were more accessible and had better labels, and I had them almost all to myself: the spice and vegetable market, several ancient mosques with exquisite paneling and carved doors, the infinitely interesting *dhow* harbor where the lateen sloops continued to set sail and, of course, the place where the great slave market had once stood. Nearby was the Tibu Tip house and national museum, which focused on the twin themes of slavery and European exploration and discovery. One exhibit read:

In 1865 the Speke/Burton expedition set off from Zanzibar on its way to voyage of exploration of the sources of the River Nile in the Great Lakes of Central Africa, and the discovery of African tribes previously unknown to the world.

'What does this mean, Burton "discover" us,' snorted a young black man reading the same exhibition literature over my shoulder. '*We* discovered *him*.'

'I guess it's all how you look at it,' I replied.

The young man spoke English; perhaps I should have engaged him in conversation, even companionship. But I did not. As each day went by, I found myself nosediving into a strange melancholy born of self-sought isolation. An Egyptian doctor resident on the island heard of me and invited me to dinner to break his own cabin fever, but I declined. Although the hotel staff and merchants in the market were civil enough, no one was really friendly – which I suppose they could have said about me, too. The texts I was working on added to the sense of loneliness and gloom. One was a monologue from *Hamlet*:

> Oh, what a rogue and peasant slave am I
> Is it not monstrous that this player here
> In a dream of passion, could force his soul
> So to his own conceit, that from his passion
> All his visage waned, tears in his eyes
> Distraction in's aspect
> And all for nothing...

On the fifth day of my open incarceration, Mister Ahmad came over to the hotel to inform me that the authorities had cleared me to leave aboard the tramp steamer the next morning, which meant that I was free to go anywhere I wanted on the island until my departure. He could even arrange a guide. I declined, because I was on the verge of some great, ineffable sadness. Perhaps other solo travelers are confronted with the Sights-Seen-Solitary-Syndrome: with no one else to refer an event to, the event itself seems to happen in a vacuum that sucks all the joy and delight from the mind of the lone beholder.

I returned to Dar not by boat but in a twin-engine shuttle airplane depositing some Eastern Bloc engineers later that day, and checked into a downmarket-if-still-decent hotel in the center of the city. The other residents seemed to all be Swedes on a 'solidarity safari through socialism', meaning they were going off to help with the coffee or tea or tobacco harvest in a collective village to express, well, whatever it was they needed to express. I checked out of the hotel and into another the next day, and then went out and had a white safari suit made for myself, both because a performer of my caliber needed some dress togs and to distinguish myself from solidarity-seeking folks wearing blue jeans and rags like the Swedes.

Then I went and did something really stupid. After delivering my lighting scheme and special-effects charts to the technical director of the theater (individual spotlights for the puppets; a bit of stage smoke for Richard III's 'A Horse, A Horse!' death scene and a red haze for Macbeth pondering Duncan's murder) I returned to town and went to a clinic to have myself inoculated for Zambia and took the entire battery of shots at one go: diphtheria, yellow fever, tuberculosis and whatever else they had lying around.

'We usually spread the cocktail over a few days, Mister Goltz,' warned the doctor.

Maybe I imagined that taking the cocktail like that would be like getting high on a mixture of pot and alcohol at once, with a couple of uppers and downers thrown in for kicks. Maybe I was not thinking at all. But within an hour or two of walking away from the clinic and delivering the report to the Zambian embassy, and a mere two or three hours before my show, I started to sweat and shake and stumble in a self-induced haze.

It is lucky I made the show at all; or maybe not. Doped to the gills, I struggled into the club about five minutes before curtain time, stripped off my street togs and slithered into my performance clothes, stuffed a list of the scenes I was to perform in the order the lighting technician expected, swallowed a water followed by a whiskey, vomited, smoked a cigarette that tasted like death and waited for the house lights to dim and the curtain to rise.

I flopped. I flopped like a dying fish giving its last, stinking gasp. I mean I really and truly fizzled, folded, failed, fried. What more can I say? I *flopped*.

Yes, polite applause greeted my every effort, but each new scene seemed to proceed worse than the previous one. The fancy lighting bore into my drug-dilated pupils, and burst like tracers at the back of my eyes and into my burning brain. The fake fevers induced by the injections made me sweat and tremble. My timing was so far off it was nearly back on; the falsetto I used for the female characters had gone baritone and was barely distinguishable from the male voices, which alternated between squeaky, high-pitched whining and breathless moans. And that was when I was trying to be chatty and coy between scenes.

I attempted to remedy things with a double shot of scotch before the second set, but half the audience was missing after the intermission and more left during the course of Part Two. My histrionic wailing for Richard III's revenge was laughable. Prospero died on his island, and Desdemona could not sell herself in the street. I did pick up some chuckles and guffaws from my standard Launce act, but that was mainly because I tripped over the bag-that-was-my-dog Crab. Finally, mercifully, the curtain fell. Needless to say there was no encore, and the dinner in my honor set to follow the main stage show was, not inexplicably, canceled. The complete disaster was mitigated by one factor: the audience of three hundred had actually paid to see me, and the house could not escape from the fact that, as per our agreement, fifty percent of the gate was mine. Money – even such a debased currency as the Tanzanian shilling – was money, and after catching a ride from my sponsors back into town, I went to a bar for a good, solid drunk and awoke in the morning in a strange room with a strange woman who, as per what she maintained had been our agreement, was asking me for some of the money I had made the night before. I didn't give her fifty percent, but I did endow her with a good chunk of change. Then I went and bought a first-class rail ticket to Zambia.

NINE

The Smell of Greasepaint, the Roar of the Expatriate Crowd

'This Shakespeare stuff,' remarked Mister Carter. 'You do it in schools, right?'

'Yes,' I answered.

'Well, I have been thinking,' said Carter. 'You could perform for me.'

'Ah ... what do you mean?'

'Does it matter?' said Carter. 'You have been staying in my house for a week, eating my food and using my phone. The way I look at it, you kind of owe me.'

Indeed, I had been staying with Carter for a week, and still did not know or could not remember his first name. Maybe he'd told me when he first invited me to stay, and by the second day as his guest I did not think it appropriate to ask, and it was getting awkward having to come up with permutations of 'Mister' as a means of address. Over breakfast: *Mister Carter*, more coffee, please ...Over lunch: *Herr Carter!* Pass the salt! ...Over dinner: *Señor Carter* ... Over our evening games of chess: Your move, *sir* ... Sometimes he looked at me strangely, but never dropped a helpful hint, like, say, 'I said to myself, Bill, I said, pick up your socks ...'

We had met at the Lusaka Theatre Arts Club, as I was on my way to being thrown out by the American manager there, Kay Koob. (I mention her name because a year after we met, she would gain fame as one of the American diplomats held for 444 days by Islamic militants in Ayatollah Khomeini's revolutionary Iran.) At the time of my arrival in Zambia, she was the director of the American Cultural Center in Lusaka, and preparing to perform the lead role in *Mary Queen of Scots* in the annual Theater and Arts Festival. Attending the festival was my reason for being in Zambia in the first place, and Ms Koob's lack of enthusiasm for my brand of theater was not the reception I had anticipated.

'Yes, we got your letter and your clips, Mister Goltz,' she said. 'But we have been awfully busy around here preparing for the annual theater festival, and really won't have any time to organize anything until after it is over and done.'

'Well, could you recommend some schools I could contact, or the American library?'

'A Shakespeare show? Sponsored by the United States Information Service? *I* am the representative of that agency here, and our purpose is to support *American* culture ...'

'But I am an American.'

'Shakespeare is not.'

This was discouraging, so I did the only reasonable thing: I launched a guerrilla performance in the lobby, and was promptly told to leave the premises – but not before a portly Brit ensconced at the bar bought me a drink and offered me a place to stay.

'They are all so stiff, Yanks,' said my sponsor. 'Got a place to kip?'

This was Master Carter, an administrator at the university and avid chess player with no one else to play against. So I checked into his house, ate his food and used his telephone, played losing chess every night and tried to remember his first name. Then came payback day, when I had to perform for Carter. The venue, he informed me, was a 'special school' on the outskirts of town.

We set off in Carter's Land Rover to a destination about twenty miles outside of Lusaka, traveling down a potholed road through the lush, green countryside of central Zambia. Finally, we approached a whitewashed building set behind a wire-mesh fence and pulled into the driveway. There was something odd about the place, but I couldn't quite put my finger on it. The courtyard was filled with old tires and other junk but seemed to have something of a playground setup. Muffled shouting, even screaming, seemed to come from the far side of the building. Then out rushed an African man dressed in the white uniform one associates with hospitals or laboratories. 'Master Carter, Master Carter!' crowed the man, first pumping Carter's beefy hand and then mine. 'We are *too* pleased to see you here! The children are ... the children are all waiting for you with the highest expectations!'

With a roar, the door leading to the tire-filled courtyard burst open, and a tidal wave of screaming, wailing and cheering children emerged, rushing as one towards the fence that separated us, beating each other out of the way to be the first to see who had arrived. They clawed at the fence, sticking fingers, tongues and noses through it to get even closer to us. I looked at them and they gawked at me, and then with a jolt I knew exactly where I was: the state insane asylum for adolescents. There were about fifty kids, ranging in age from four to twenty, drawn from every tribal and ethnic group in the country – and representing the entire gamut of social and mental dysfunction. There were those who seemed to have been retarded since birth; some had been handicapped in accidents; others would probably have been diagnosed as autistic; others appeared to have emotional problems, and didn't seem to belong in the place at all. The most heart-rending case I saw was a handsome young Indian boy who seemed perfectly normal, except that he screamed at everything. They had all been lumped together at the institution, which might have been a dump but represented a giant step forward from otherwise neglect or expulsion.

'Carter,' I said. 'This is ... insane.'

'You owe me,' said Carter.

We ambled over to the director's office and marched into a large, empty room that was to serve as my stage. I reached into my assembled props and selected the Masai mask, slowly raised it to cover my face and then reached for the carving knife, getting ready for a little *Macbeth*.

Is this a dagger I see before me?
The handle towards my hand?

I sensed a moment of silence now, as the audience members collectively sucked in their breath Then, *boom*. Before I got in another caesura, pandemonium exploded, with half the assembled kids (those with no physical handicaps to slow them) clawing at the doors to get out, wailing in terror in a dozen tribal languages while the other half hid under their shirts, sobbing or crawling after their more mobile fellows. Only the little Indian kid seemed to be enjoying himself, sitting on the floor directly in front of me, a smile on his face and a scream of joy in his throat.

'Do it without the mask,' the director suggested with as much calm as he could muster, while calling for assistants to pry kids off the doors and walls and generally restore order. 'I'll translate into dialect.'

You might say that the performance lost some pace. I would speak a line, and the director would spend the next five minutes traducing it into Bembe, Nyanja and Lozi. At first I worried about accuracy, but soon realized it didn't matter a whit. The puppets mesmerized, and I was the greatest thing since old tires were introduced to the playground. When I took my final bow, the screamer ran up and screamed; a sparkle passed through the neurologically impaired eyes of a brain-damaged girl and a young fellow who moaned and embraced chairs came up and moaned and embraced me.

'Good show,' said Carter as we drove away.

Misfits amused, it was now time to amaze the masses – in this instance, the folks involved with the annual Zambian National Theatre Network. Leaving Carter in Lusaka, I headed for the festival host-town of Chingola near Zambia's north-central frontier with Zaire.

Rides were few and far between, and by nightfall I had only reached a place called Ndola, although I was determined to press on.

'I wouldn't stay out on the road,' my last ride warned me. 'The place is rife with bandits.' The highwaymen were variously suspected of being the Katangese Gendarmes, who had infiltrated from neighboring Zaire renegade members of black South African guerrilla camps in the area, regular Zambian army draftees attempting to supplement their salaries and just plain bloodthirsty types.

'There a hotel around here?' I asked.

'Not one I would recommend.'

'A local theater?'

'Well, of course. I was going to the show tonight myself, but got stuck in Lusaka.'

'What's playing?' I queried further.

'*Enter a Free Man* by Tom Stoppard. They say it may win the prize this year.'

We got there in time for intermission, and I sat through the second act. The chief financial officer of a local copper mining concern was playing the lead role, and a Zambian teacher was playing a Cockney. After the show I was introduced to the theater club secretary, explained what I did and asked for permission to mount a show of my own in the bar. There were about thirty people sitting around the booths and tables, with another handful cluttered around the dartboard and a few more seated at the well. All looked on with keen interest as I arranged my props and then began mime-stepping my way towards the door with the help of my shell-encrusted cane and mime-dragging my bag behind me as a surrogate dog, while launching into my opener from the *Two Gentlemen*:

Nay, 'twill be this very hour ere I have done weeping: all the kind of Launces have this very fault ...

I never got in another word. An African man who had been slumped over the bar rose and lurched at me, smothering my mask with kisses while exhaling high-octane booze breath. 'I love you, I love you!' he cried, trying to jump on my back to ride me piggyback around the room. A knot of other African men near the bar wailed in laughter while the white patrons sat in stunned silence. I shook free and raised my cane, thinking a quick swipe of the razor-sharp shells across his face might not be a bad dream. Suddenly someone grabbed my arms, pinned them down, and then dragged me out of the bar.

'Don't be a fool, damn it!' hissed a voice in my ear. 'Can't you see he's armed?'

'Suck it in, old chap!' whispered another voice. 'He's with the opposition!'

'Friggin' *kaffirs*,' spat the first, offering me a cigarette. 'That's the second time this week they've pulled a stunt like that. They want a fight so they can declare the bar dangerous and off-limits and close us down for good.' (*Kaffir* was Afrikaans for the equivalent of 'nigger'.)

'Who were those guys?' I asked, catching my breath.

'The monkey on your back is a police agent – not even a member of the club, but we can't keep him out,' said the second man. 'The others were his pals – local trash.'

We smoked our cigarettes and then went back to the bar after my assailant and his pals stumbled out the door. As for the regular expatriates, the scene had taken the fun out of the evening, and most were getting ready to go home, too. My two new friends lingered, and ordered up a round of drinks, then began filling my ears with poison.

'Bloody savages,' said the elder of the pair, a transplant from Scotland. ''Twas once a beautiful country, and look what they've done to it. Destroyers, vandals, every one!'

There followed a litany of racist complaints against Zambians in particular and blacks in general – how Africans were universally shiftless, bestial and dumb, although not so dumb to be above maiming themselves to collect lifetime wages in the way of insurance payoffs. One of the men, an accountant, related in gruesome detail how several of the men working the deeper mineshafts had mutilated themselves to get on unemployment. The lecture went on for an hour and grew more slurred and scurrilous by the minute.

'You Yanks had the right idea with your Indians – wipe 'em out!' seethed another man, a farmer. 'If we had done the same, there'd be no problem at all here, no problem at all.'

'Yeah,' agreed the other. 'And now they're exporting the pestilence to Rhodesia and South Africa, the last two places on the friggin' continent with a government.'

The subject had been broached: *Rhodesia*, the breakaway state, the land of Ian Smith and the Seloux Scouts, holding back the tide of black chaos and international communism that had swept away white rule in the rest of English Africa. Was I headed there, they asked in a whisper, looking around for unwarranted ears. They had met and helped through others before, Volunteers for the Cause ...

My next stop was Kitwe, capital of Zambia's so-called 'Copper Belt' and a town with a very large expatriate population whose social center was the local theater-cricket club. Given my experience at the Lusaka club and then the bizarre and ugly business in Ndola the night before, I did not enter with great expectations. Nor did the Kitwe club appear to be a venue just waiting for a guy like me. It was Saturday afternoon, and the club was packed with members eating brunch and playing darts.

But there was a difference between the Kitwe club and the others I had seen. First, the Saturday afternoon crowd was diverse. It was not just a bunch of pot-bellied Brits bitching about the faded empire. Rather, the Saturday brunch was attended by a melting-pot mob of whites, blacks and Indians, men, women and children of all ages, who genuinely seemed to be enjoying each other's company. Underlining this communal acceptance was a big sign with European, African and Indian names posted on it, informing members who was responsible for which tasks in the fine-tuning of the Kitwe club's entry in the theater festival: *Joe Smith and Ahuru Mutabelli and Ismael Aghazade due backstage at 15:45 to set spots and paint set Act II Scene Three ...*

I sought out and found the manager, a big, strapping man named

Ken Rhodes. Originally from Leeds, England, Rhodes was a senior engineer at the Kitwe mine when not orchestrating activities at the club. He had not been back to the UK in years, and had no intention of returning any time in the future. Zambia, he said, was his home.

'A one-man-wandering Shakespeare show?' Rhodes smiled when I asked him if I could perform. 'Never 'ad one of them before! You're on in ten minutes!'

After a quick change I emerged in my mask and started with Launce. Dragging my kit behind me, I arrived at the center of the barroom, continuing my progress in mime while bemoaning my fate and cursing Crab. A very real hole had pushed into my left shoe, which I used to advantage:

This shoe is my father; no, this left shoe is my father; no, no, this left shoe is my mother, nay that cannot be so neither – but 'tis so, 'tis so, it hath the worser sole ...

I was used to at least a little chatter in the background during a bar performance. But when I hit the stage in Kitwe, there was not a chirp or whisper. Silence reigned, and I began wondering if I wasn't ruining an otherwise pleasant afternoon with an unwanted intrusion. Nearing the last lines of the scene, I prepared for the worst, abject rejection. I turned towards the door, as it were, ready to Exit, Stage Right. And then my ears apprehended a murmur passing through the bar. It swelled, and then with a shout, the patrons broke into long, sustained applause. *More*, they shouted, *more*!

My older material came rolling out as fresh as could be; newer scenes came off without a stumbled line, and the crowd laughed as if on cue. An intermission was declared, but no one got up to go. I went for another hour and then ran out of material, but then came requests for repeats and I continued for half an hour more. The hat was passed around half a dozen times, and I was dripping in sweat and rolling in loot and delighted to be alive. 'That's really great stuff,' said Rhodes at the bar after I had hosed myself down and changed. 'How'd you like to do a Green Room show next week? We can advertise it in the local paper and really bring in a crowd. And where are you staying? I've got an extra room at my place.'

Rhodes's house was a rambling ranch-style structure set back among flame bushes in riotous bloom, with avocado and guava trees in the back. Inside, it was a virtual ethnographic museum of Africana – zebra hides covering couches, a lion rug, huge, hand-carved malachite ashtrays, wall displays of pygmy bows and arrows, spears and diverse masks and religious totems drawn from the many tribes that inhabited Zambia. Fluent in several of the languages and an avid Afrophile, Rhodes knew what the totems signified and about the religions. He also knew exactly what his position in Zambian society was: a working guest. I told him about the men I had met at the Ndola Theater Club, and he nodded his head wearily.

'Yes, there are a lot of racist nuts running around,' he said. 'Most are people who were working-class in England who now think it is their God-given right to have servants and then complain about them. Nothing delights them more than when an Af screws up on the job – it confirms their own belief in innate, white superiority. But just ask them what they were doing in England before coming here.'

That evening, Rhodes took me to the final dress rehearsal of the Kitwe theater festival entry, *Sleuth*. It was a remarkable production, boasting a split-level set with a rotating lower stage and some very fine acting by the two leads. The show was all the more impressive given the fact that it had been put together in spare time, and that the two actors were smelting engineers in their working lives. I was flattered because only the cast was normally allowed to see the rehearsal, and in the bar following the performance I was consulted about the professional acting chances of the two players.

The following day, Rhodes got on the telephone and arranged a number of school and club performances up and down the Copper Belt for me, with jobs scattered from Kitwe to Kabwe and ending up back in Chingola for the festival. I played the Lusasha mine school one morning and the cricket club that night, shot down to Ndola the next day for a series of public school performances, then to Kabwe for a quick date at the local club before heading back to Ndola for the mine school and then to Kitwe for a Catholic school performance and then the slated Green Room show, preceded by an actors' workshop. I felt like I was part of the gang.

'Hey, Bard! Good to see you again!'

'Hey, are you performing here, too?'

'Listen, mate, we have a little club down in Livingston, if you could spare the time ...'

At the end of the week I arrived in Chingola for the festival. The population of the town (or, to be specific, the expatriate part of town) had swelled from perhaps one hundred to one thousand, with players, family, hangers-on and the culturally curious from every corner of the country descending on the town for the week-long pageant. The home theater, dedicated by the Queen when she was still a princess, was bunted out for the grand occasion, the depleted bar restocked with cases of imported booze in preparation for the event. Hotel space simply did not exist. Happily, my digs had been arranged via the Kitwe crowd at the house of Sue and Richard Farmer, a pair of white Zambians who were also the leading lights of the expatriate theater scene. We didn't see much of each other owing to their duties of staging and staggering events, but now is the time to thank them for their hospitality, even if more than two decades overdue: *Thanks!*

The most remarkable thing about the festival, perhaps, was that there was a festival at all. The combined man-hours and expenses involved in developing, staging, costuming and designing the productions must have represented something like ten percent of the GNP of the country. It was simply incredible that all the various expatriates, Zambians and embassy personnel expended so much devotion and energy on their respective projects. In addition to *Sleuth*, *Enter a Free Man* and *Mary Queen of Scots*, entries included *The Chalk Garden*, *The Sea Gull* and, if I remember correctly, *Our Town*, a very strange play to perform with English accents. Rivalry was high as each town vied for the grand prize in each category of recognition. And all this in Zambia ...

I, of course, was rooting for my pals in the Kitwe club, and was pleased when they walked away with most of the awards including best set, best direction, best supporting actor and the most prized award of all, best club. Five hundred people in the audience gave Ken Rhodes a standing ovation when he climbed onstage to collect the coveted prize. He clearly deserved it, and more, for welding a grumbling knot of expats into such a dynamic, fun-loving, freewheeling and decent group.

'Congratulations,' I told him at the awards ceremony banquet. (It seemed like an ideal opportunity for me to perform and pass the hat, but Rhodes thought it best to dissuade me, and for once I listened.)

The annual Zambia Theatre Festival was over, the prizes and awards put on shelves, and everyone gone home. It was time for me to move on. I was faced, however, with a unique dilemma: I had amassed thousands of the national currency, *kwacha*, but could do nothing with the money. At first, calculating my tips at the official exchange rate, I was delighted by all the loot I was collecting: I was making $100 a show. But then came the sobering realization that due to the extraordinary difference between the official exchange rate and the real, black-market value of the national currency, I had to divide by five – and all the pieces of paper in my hand bearing the likeness of Kenneth Kaunda, the panda-faced president, suddenly seemed like so much, well, *kwacha*. Aside from joining the legions of expatriates all trying to find someone to sell them dollars or pounds, there was only one thing to do: buy something of value in *kwacha*, and then sell that something for hard currency elsewhere.

Ivory was the natural choice, but every bracelet represented a ring of dead elephant. Even if one could stomach the purchase, there was the problem of smuggling the substance out of Zambia and into somewhere else. But there was another option, which carried none of the moral weight of dealing in dead elephant: *emeralds*.

Zambia was one of the world's largest producers of the lusty green gems, and maintained a state monopoly on mining and sales. But an estimated fifty percent of the raw emeralds taken from nearby mines were smuggled out of the country for eventual sale to Israel and India, where the stones were cut and polished. Fortunes were to be made by the fortunate buyers: Rhodes told me of being approached by beggars wandering around the better neighborhoods, trying to hawk uncut stones from their pockets. Some buyers got lucky and turned a $20 investment into a $10,000 necklace. Others discovered that they had invested a month's wages in pieces of green glass.

It was a risky and illegal business to get involved in, but I was properly motivated. Unless I managed to convert my *kwacha*, I might as well have thrown the wad away.

Accordingly, I went down to the obvious place where transactions might occur: the vegetable and curios market in the middle of Kitwe. I wasn't poking around for five minutes before whispers tickled my ears: *'Shhh! Brother!* Bwana*! Look here! Lion's claws, leopard skin, ivory and more!'*

I made my commercial interests known to one of the merchants in discrete terms. Yes, he whispered, he did have emeralds, but not there: it was far too dangerous. The police made spot checks and the other stalls had eyes and ears. We had to meet secretly, he said. The taxi stand near the entrance to the market was a good, anonymous place. At a certain hour, I would see him there, get in a communal taxi and ride to a certain station. He would take the taxi behind me. We would meet by coincidence; I would ask him for directions, and then we would take separate routes to his house, meeting out back by the chicken coop.

Filled with trepidation and pockets brimming with loot, I followed the plan. My concern grew with every minute: at every taxi stop better-dressed folks got out and rattier looking folks joined the ride. Finally, all my companions in the car were dressed in rags and eyeing my relative finery. At the agreed-upon station, I got out of the car and waited, trying to act as inconspicuous as possible – no mean feat for a lone white man in an all-black African slum. The next taxi arrived ten minutes later, and all the passengers stared.

'Can I help you sir?' asked a pudgy lady with a kid strapped to her back. 'Not many *mzungus* come here.' Others crowded around to listen.

'I am lost,' I said, directing my words at the sole disinterested man in the group. It was the young merchant from the market, coming forward and brushing away the others.

'I will help you,' he said, and the other passengers drifted away. Then he described the path I was to take to his house: turn left at the broken bicycle, walk eighteen meters beyond the chicken coop, turn right and go straight until you see the second hole in the wire fence, and then left again at the house with the blue door and shattered window to the left of the half-built chimney ...

The neighborhood was a patchy affair of one-story cement houses with aluminum roofs, with yards delineated by bramble bushes and thorn thickets. Open sewage ditches ran alongside the dirt paths, which served as alleyways. I had to pull rank on a couple of skinny cows and scrawny donkeys blocking the road as they poked around for leftovers in mounds of trash. The acrid smell of burnt garbage and tire fires hung over everything, but eventually I arrived at the cement house with the blue door and went around to the back, sending a squadron of chickens clucking out over the bramble barrier into the neighbor's yard. I knew it was the right place when the merchant arrived by a different route, and winked at me. Then, rather than open the door, he climbed in through a window. I was beginning to wonder if this was his house or whether I had just become an accomplice in a burglary.

'Psst!' he called, peering through a crack in the door. 'Did anyone see you come?'

'Not a soul.'

I followed him into the inner sanctum he had just sprung open, and we got down to business. Groping with his hand under the single mattress in the room, he withdrew a beat-up leather purse, from which he extracted a plastic sack. Opening the wooden shutters on the room's single window to allow some light in, the merchant dumped the contents of the plastic sack on the floor.

I was sick. In place of shimmering green baubles the size of a fist, I found myself staring at a handful of dirty shards of a crushed 7-Up bottle.

'Very nice, too nice,' whispered the merchant, holding a chunk to the light. I took the stone from his hand and did the same, pretending I knew what I was doing. I did not. The light refracted through the stone, as it would through any glass. Then I noticed bits and pieces of darker material within the stone – the 'inclusions' that make every emerald distinct from the next. I sought for and found what seemed to be a crystal growth pattern in the other stones, but the truth is that what really convinced me was the fact that the objects were simply too dirty and encrusted with gunk to be glass. No, I felt this was the real thing.

'How much?'

'One thousand *kwacha*.'

'You're out of your mind.'

'You must weigh my case under the scale of your mercy.'

I pulled out my wad from my underwear and counted off the required number of bills, walking away with a pocketful of gems. If they were worth half my calculation of their value, I reckoned, I would never have to perform Shakespeare again.

TEN

Busted in Botswana

At the point where the Chobe River meets the Zambezi, pink flamingos toe their way through the shallows stalking small fish, crocodiles lurk in the mud hunting birds and hippopotamuses stomp the bottom, seeking out the crocodiles that have devoured their babes. But despite the natural violence of the place, the confluence of the two rivers appears calm, idyllic and maybe even beautiful. One would hardly guess that fifty miles downstream, the joint rivers turn into the roaring, churning, living thing that is Victoria Falls, near the place where the real Mister Stanley met the real Doctor Livingston. It is also difficult to imagine that the confluence of the two rivers is the point where four countries come in contact – Zambia to the north, Zimbabwe to the southeast, Botswana to the south and Namibia to the west – thanks to the absurd thread of land called the Caprivi Strip. Angola is only ten miles away.

Although the legal borders have remained the same, much has changed since that day in September 1977 when I stood on the Zambian bank of the river, waiting for a decrepit motorized raft to cross to Botswana. Two of the countries mentioned above have ceased to exist: Zimbabwe was then called Rhodesia, and Namibia was officially referred to as the United Nations Mandate of Southwest Africa. Both of these are mere footnotes in history today. The facing border towns of Kisangula and Kisane may have been relegated to footnote status, too: both only existed to provide a link between southern and central Africa because the main transportation bridge over the Zambezi had been severed due to the ongoing war over Rhodesia. With the collapse of white rule in Salisbury (now Harare, Zimbabwe), sanctions were lifted; the bridge linking Zimbabwe and Zambia reopened and the utility of the Kisangula–Kisane ferry came to an end.

In 1977, however, all that was quite different. The sealing of the Zambia–Rhodesia border meant that all traffic that would have traveled three miles between the Zambian city of Livingston and the Rhodesian town of Victoria Falls was obliged to take a fifty-mile detour to cross the Zambezi/Chobe confluence and then detour back another fifty miles to reconnect with the Great North Road. For the traveling white person, this was not merely a 100-kilometer inconvenience. In plain English, the closer the traveling white man got to Rhodesia, the more he was suspected of being a 'Wild Goose' – a mercenary, come to fight for white rule.

I was the only white man on the ferry, and thus suspected of nefarious intent. But even if no mercenary, I was indeed bound for Rhodesia in order to intercept Eddy. The problem was that I had no idea how to get into the country, aside from traveling the north–south length of Botswana and then swinging back up into 'Disneyland' (as travelers referred to the pariah state) via South Africa. Having no other plan than this 1,000-mile detour, I arrived at the Botswana customs shed around noon and was stamped into the country only to find myself waiting for the station to close for the evening to hitch a ride with the border guards the ten miles into Kisane. There was no other transport. Then, around 4:30 PM, the trans-Zambezi ferry returned, carrying a single truck. The black driver was in a rush.

'Just hurry up!' he pleaded with customs. 'The border closes in half an hour!'

'Excuse me sir,' I asked. 'Could you give me a lift into Kisane?'

'I am not going to Kisane,' he said, tapping his fingers impatiently. 'I live in Victoria Falls.'

'The Rhodesia border is open?' I asked.

'Why would you want to go there?' asked the customs officer, eyeing me suspiciously.

The driver, meanwhile, had been cleared and was running towards his truck. So was I.

I threw my pack in the back and clambered up after it, and off we shot, tearing down a sand road and kicking up tremendous clouds of dust, all of which seemed to settle on me.

We arrived at the whitewashed customs house on the far side of the Botswana frontier at exactly 5:00 PM. I tumbled off the flatbed, grimy from the ride, breathing a deep sigh of relief. Behind the counter stood a neatly dressed official, the first white man in that role I had seen in Africa.

'Hello!' I announced myself, putting my passport on the counter. I nearly expected him to offer me his hand and a cup of tea. He did not. Rather, he looked at the name on the passport in front of him, and then at me again, scowling.

'Yes, Mister ... Goltz,' he said, appraising me coldly. 'We close the frontier at five o'clock sharp, and it is now five after five.'

'I didn't know I was coming, that is, I had planned on coming via South Africa, but then I learned that the border here was open and thought that maybe I might –'

'Fill out these forms, Mister Goltz, while I deal with the driver here.'

He returned to the owner of the truck, who was impatiently waiting behind me, and gave his documents a cursory glance.

'Where are you coming from, Mister Mutabela?'

'Zambia, sir.'

'Purpose of your travel?'

'Delivery of South African cheese and cigarettes under false labels to Zaire.'

'Hmm, sanctions-busting at its best, what?'

'Yes, sir.'

'Well, Mister Mutabela,' smiled the white official to the black driver, stamping him into their common country. 'Best get on your way to Fort Victoria while there is still light. The terrorists have started to become active in the area again.'

'Good to be back in Rhodesia, sir.'

The driver was out the door before I could ask him to wait for me to be processed through. No matter, I figured, the customs guy would probably offer me a ride into town.

'Forms all filled!' I said cheerily, placing the customs declaration on the counter next to my passport. Under the category for 'profession' I had written 'actor'; under the category 'purpose of visit' I had penned 'entertainment'. All this was true enough. What was not completely honest was my declaring an inflated $300 as the amount of cash I was carrying in disposable assets; perhaps I should have declared the sack of probably-emeralds I had picked up in Kitwe, but decided it best not to.

The official scanned my form for a moment, and then looked at me with officially friendly eyes.

'I am sorry, Mister Goltz, but $300 will by no means suffice in Rhodesia for even a short visit.' He was courteous, all business. 'You will understand, that in our present situation, our government cannot afford to support potential wards of the state, or foot the bill for emergency evacuation for medical or other reasons, including death.'

It went without saying that there was no American embassy in Rhodesia; the closest thing to any sort of US representation in the country was a townhouse owned by Robin Moore, author of *The French Connection*. The manor was called 'The Crippled Eagle', and was a favorite hangout for American mercenaries.

'Well,' I said. 'I intend to work.'

'That's very nice, but how can I be sure that you will be able to find employment?'

'I have a unique job.'

'We all do, Mister Goltz,' he said, no doubt wondering how my claim to being 'an actor' fit into the economy of a state under international sanctions and in the middle of civil war. 'I am sorry, but you will have to provide statements and papers proving that you have employment before entering the country.'

'But do you know what I do?'

'It says here in your own handwriting what you claim to do,' said the official, the words written all over his expressionless face telling me what he really thought: that I had come to Rhodesia to kill black nationalist guerrillas for fun and profit.

'No,' I said, replying to his non-statement. 'Do you know what I *really* do?'

'I don't care what you *really* do, Mister Goltz, we all must do something! And I suspect that that *something* that you *really* do is not *something* that we in the Republic of Rhodesia find necessary to support or necessarily want at present.'

'But ...'

He was lifting a stamp from an invisible desk drawer, and inking it on a blotter. It was not the stamp he had used to announce the official entry of the black Rhodesian truck driver moments before. He was lifting the stamp and it was coming down, once on my passport and once on the declaration I had filled out. I knew what it said before I read the words: *Prohibited Immigrant.* I felt like the outcast among outcasts. Persona Non Grata, PNGed from Disneyland, as a suspected pyscho killer from the land of the Wild Geese.

There was nothing to do but return to Botswana by foot, through no-man's-land, and after dusk at that. The five-mile hike seemed to take five years. Maybe it was only two kilometers, maybe only one. It made no difference. I was strolling through a zone patrolled not only by the Rhodesian and Botswanan security forces but by the mutually inimical ZAPU and ZANU guerrilla organizations, too. Everybody was lurking around the bush hunting for everybody else. Every rustle in the bushes was a threat, every moving shadow meant doom. I was mightily relieved to see the buildings of the Botswana station at the end of my anxiety-filled trudge. My problems, however, were just beginning.

'Why did they not let you enter?' demanded the commander of

the shack-stockade that defined the Botswana part of the frontier. 'Is Rhodesia not a white man's land?' The interrogation had begun, with question after question coming at me in staccato, although often interrupted by equally expected political extrapolation and exegesis.

'You say they said you have no money.'

'Yes.'

'Then how did you get here?'

'I work everywhere I go.'

'What do you do?'

'I perform Shakespeare.'

'Really! Where do you plan to perform in our country?'

'Oh, I don't know – schools, cultural centers, expatriate theaters, that sort of thing.'

'It is forbidden.'

'Shakespeare?'

'Of course not. Working in our country on a tourist visa. It says so on the forms and on the stamp issued in your passport. Didn't you read it?'

My interrogator changed gears.

'What other countries have you visited?'

'In my life?'

To humor him, I proceeded to list all the countries I had ever set foot in, starting with the place of my nativity, Japan.

'You do not look Japanese.'

'I guess the climate didn't get to me before I left as an infant.' The attempted joke did not register.

'How do you like Botswana?'

'Fine, fine.'

How did I like Zambia? Which did I prefer, Tanzania or Kenya? East or West Germany, Europe or America? The United States or Japan?

'I don't quite understand the relevance of those questions,' I said, perhaps a little too testily. 'You asked me to list all the countries I've been to, but you have not even bothered to check my passport. What is the relevance of any of this to anything?'

The disinterested scowl on his face seemed to turn into a satisfied smile and finally into a sneer and shout. Whatever I had said was exactly what he had been looking for.

'JUST ANSWER MY QUESTIONS, NOW!' he shouted, working into full howl.

'Which ones?' I asked. 'You've asked so many!'

'IMPERTINENCE!!' he screamed, slamming his fist on his desk. 'HOW DARE YOU CHALLENGE THE AUTHORITY OF OUR SOVEREIGN STATE!!'

Faster than you could say 'flabbergasted' my arms were pinned behind my back by two previously invisible cops. It wasn't every day that the Kisane authorities managed to bag a real live suspected white mercenary, and they intended to take full pleasure from the occasion. I guess I should be grateful that I wasn't just hideously tortured and shot. Still, it was pretty sobering, and it occurred to me that I had a real problem on my hands.

I was thrown in a truck and then dragged inside a small, tight room framed by barred windows. Jail. Soon three prison officials strutted in, looking pleased that they had someone to play with. I *was* guilty. Not of being a mercenary or anything like that, of course; the most incriminating objects that could pass as weapons were the axe and carving knives in my puppet kit, the most deadly of which was just a screwdriver ground down to a blade. What worried me was hidden *under* the carving knives, files and resin dyes: my bag of emeralds. All they needed was something like smuggling to put me behind bars for a long, long time.

They were thorough, I'll give them that. They noted the name of the Tanzanian tailor who made my safari suit and the fact that I had mismatched socks. Not wanting to fall for the old 'wrap your stash in your dirty underwear' trick, they un-crumpled each and every piece of fouled laundry, disappointed at not finding an incriminating prize. A pouch of foreign coins was found, and every piece was described according to face value, year of minting and country of origin. My razor blade box was relieved of its contents to see if there weren't possibly items of contraband stashed within, and the individual blades duly noted according to estimated number of times used. As they neared the bottom of my pack and prepared to move on to the carving kit where the emeralds were stashed, I was about to despair and throw my pathetic self upon their mercy. Then a last-ditch means of procrastination occurred to me. I started demanding exactitude and precision in the labeling of my belongings. My numerous journals were not mere 'notebooks', no. They were unique 'episodic diaries' that had to be registered according to the first and last dates of entry, the color of the binder as well as existing blemishes, such as coffee stains. That burnt up a good hour, and I was just getting started.

'What are these?' asked one of the officers.

I almost sniggered. He had pulled up the first couple of my eight puppet heads.

'These artifacts,' I said, taking the pair and spinning the necks like top-bottoms between the thumb and middle finger of both hands, 'are simulated characters meant to facilitate my *alfresco* renditions of the classic cannon of the Divine Bard.'

'Speak English,' demanded the police scribe tasked with writing down the inventory. The important thing, I recognized, was not verb-noun agreement or even syntactical sense – it was to create maximal diversion from the task at hand. I had to waste time.

'Write down 'eight voodoo dolls,' the officer instructed the stenographer.

'No!' I demanded. 'They are not "voodoo" dolls! What if that is published in an official record? They'll think I was dispensing forbidden and esoteric knowledge, no!' I was adamant on this point. The objects in question were, precisely, Othello, Desdemona, Macbeth, Lady Macbeth, Romeo, Juliet and the fairy Ariel, represented in the form of puppets – they could write 'marionettes' if they wished, although this was not entirely accurate – that I used in facilitating street performances of Shakespeare plays.

The captain rolled his eyes and scowled, but instructed the stenographer to write the names of the puppets as I described them.

Misspellings abounded, which I would not tolerate. If a puppet played more than one role – both Romeo and Quince or Macbeth and Bottom, for example, I asked that it be recorded as such. My interrogators were visibly tiring by the time we finished with the puppets and moved on to the accessories – meaning the multicolored rags I used to 'define' characters.

'That would be one piece of Oregon green silk, manufactured in Dar-es-Salaam, that doubles as the death gown for Desdemona in *Othello*, Act II Scene III, and Petruchio's cape in *Taming of the Shrew*, Act I Scene II,' I began.

The captain looked at the stenographer and then back at me. We had been at the task of registering my possessions for nearly two hours. 'This bag,' he said, with a baleful eye pointed at the remainder of my performance kit, at the bottom of which was my stash of emeralds. 'This bag is one brown bag.'

'One bag, brown,' repeated the clerk, jotting down the item on his ledger.

'No!' I cried. What if someone should try and replace my bag with another, or meddle with the contents? A full assessment was needed before I was locked away ...

The leader reached down into the bag again, and gingerly brought out a carving knife, the handle sticky thanks to some stain or glue that had spilled inside. He dropped it back inside and then turned his tired, angry eyes on me.

'No!' he hissed. 'No one will steal this junk! I am tempted to burn it all right now!'

This was not what I wanted, so I thought it best to leave things where they were.

'This is the full list of your garbage!' the captain shouted, shoving the three-page itemized inventory across the table at me. 'Sign it, now!'

I tried to look cowed – and then signed off on the number and nature of my worldly goods, emeralds included. They would go into the safe, while I was heading for the tank.

I had been incarcerated before and I have been incarcerated since: North Dakota, Minnesota, Turkey, Syria, Azerbaijan and even Montana. The most frightening time was my overnight stint in Harrar, Ethiopia, when I was sure I was about to be summarily executed for spying. The nastiest was in Damascus, when I got thrown into a rat-infested dungeon with forty other men (Egyptians, mainly), many of whom had the snot beaten out of them by the guards for midnight sport. It wasn't much fun. The dumbest was a *DUI* rap in my adopted hometown of Livingston, Montana.

Within that context, my time in the Kisane prison was not so bad. While not onerous, however, it was the longest period I have ever spent behind bars: ten days. That doesn't sound like much until you have to sit there and do it. Ten days can feel awfully long, especially if you do not know what you are charged with or what is supposed to happen to you, aside from vague talk among your jailers about your maybe being a white mercenary and thus deserving to have your throat slit by one of your cellmates, who might just pick up an award for the deed ...

Happily, I got along with my cellmates just fine. One was a truck driver from Swaziland, dumped in the brig for what he maintained were trumped-up rape charges by some local prostitute who had it in for him. I forget his name but remember his face well. He was reading a book by oil lamp, the only illumination in the windowless night cell, when they pushed me in. He woke the four others in the cell and used his light so they could make room for me on the floor, over near the urine- and shitbucket, and then went back to reading his Doris Lessing novel.

'Great book,' Swazi said.

Another inmate, a guy who had been there for ten years on a murder charge, had some tobacco but no papers. So Swazi ripped out a page or two from the parts of the Lessing novel he had already read and we rolled cigarettes. The paper was heavier than the really thin stuff they use to print Bibles and other giveaway religious literature, which is the next best thing to real cigarette-rolling rice paper, but as we were in jail in northern Botswana, there was no point being overly fussy. We smoked, and the acrid smell soon filled the room to the point where we were all hacking and coughing, but that was better than having to breathe piss-laden air and gag. All my new mates seemed resigned to live out the rest of their rotten lives in the Kisane prison. They spoke to one another in Chanagula, the bastard language of the South African mines, which supposedly (because I'm not literally sure if this is so) means 'do as I do'. I was afraid I might have to start learning it myself.

We six inmates were allowed out of our cell at 5 AM and sent to the yard, a playground-sized sandy lot enclosed by an eight-foot-high wire fence. There were no guard towers, and the main security regulations were that prisoners not attempt to make contact with people wandering by outside the fence, a law that was enforced more in the breach than the rule. Folks were always wandering by and staring in. For obvious reasons, I was quite an attraction. Knots of young rascals came to take a gander and throw the odd rock, or at least rude remark.

'He say your mother perform act of child-make with dead donkey to get you,' the guard helpfully translated from the Tswana. 'The other say he want your daughter to associate with fifteen Bushmen in swamp.'

'I don't have a daughter.'

'Shall I tell him that?'

'Please do.'

The few white people who sauntered by our sandy pen had exactly the opposite reaction upon seeing me behind bars. They would cross the road or walk the other way. Most of them appeared to be Europeans, Swedes or Germans or generic Scandinavian do-gooders, no doubt working for international aid organizations, and the last thing they wanted involvement with was a Save The Suspected Wild Goose campaign. At least they could have thrown me a pack of smokes.

Cigarettes and food were indeed an issue. Legally speaking, I was not a ward of the police/prison system like the other inmates because I had not been formerly charged with anything; I was a detainee of the immigration service officer who had arrested me. This was not merely an administrative detail. As a ward of the state, it was the duty and responsibility of the police to feed the prisoners. While the fare was pretty meager – mealy meal porridge – at least they got fed. My immigration officer stumbled by a few times, but only to mock and taunt me, not to deliver my food ration. My new friend Swazi offered me some of his porridge, but I refused, announcing that as I was the immigration man's charge, he would feed me or I would not eat!

I also demanded my right to call a lawyer or at least the American embassy in the Botswana capital, Gaborone. The day guard broke into laughter, not because he was mocking me – simply because the idea was so patently absurd. Call Gaborone? How? But I was insistent. I would not eat and I would not move until I was allowed my phone call. That was fine and dandy until the 5 PM lockup was called. The guard blew a whistle, and Swazi and the four other prisoners got up off their haunches and shuffled towards our communal room/latrine. I refused to budge. Not an inch until I spoke with my ambo! Swazi and the others admonished caution, but I persisted until the night guards arrived and dragged me to a separate cell: solitary confinement. 'This is where you will stay day and night if you don't shut up!' one guard shouted. I thought it best to desist, and returned to the communal cell livid with impotent rage that soon abated into despair. I was never going to get out; my youth was ruined and I would waste away, stewing in an obscure foreign jail, forgotten by all.

Curiously, it was the cops, specifically the chief of police, who started taking the greatest interest in my case. By the third or fourth day, they were also starting to supply me with food, and expressed real exasperation with the behavior of the immigration man.

'This is not right,' said one, shaking his head in disgust and dismay.

By the fifth day, aware of the institutional neglect I was suffering, the guards unilaterally decided to allow me to remove my hack-axe and file from my sequestered bags, and use the tools on a four-foot long piece of pine. It had been relegated to the firewood heap, but I began fashioning my first-ever large sculpture, a woman, according to the midnight-remembered image of a long-lost lover. She also fit into the Shakespeare I was memorizing, the prison monologue from *Richard II:*

I have been studying how I may compare
This prison where I live on to the world
But for because the world is populous
And here lives not a creature but myself
I can do nothing. Yet, I'll hammer it out.
My brain I'll prove the female to my soul
My soul the father. And this two beget
A generation of still-begotten thoughts
Who people this my little world
With humors like the people of the world
For no thought is contented ...

On day eight or nine, I was working on the rump of my sculpture when I heard a hissing over by the perimeter fence. I looked at the guard; the brim of his cap was lowered over his eyes, so I crept towards the fence to see who had come calling.

They were two white men. Tourists? Mercenaries? One tossed me a pack of cigarettes, and the latter drew a circle on his palm, describing the act of dialing a telephone number.

'Please ...' I sighed, and then returned to my cell.

I was sitting in the pen the next morning when a car pulled up, and all the guards snapped to attention. It was the District Commissioner. Accompanying the DC was a smartly dressed yet obsequious man wearing the uniform of the immigration service. I recognized him as my nemesis, now busted by his boss. The reader will pardon my obsession, but the only thing I could think of was Angelo accompanying the returned Duke in *Measure for Measure.*

'Hail, well met!' said Angelo, throwing me a pseudo-smile.

The DC ordered the guards to let me out of the pen, and greeted me in the interrogation room like an old friend, personally stamping my passport.

'We are truly sorry for any and all inconveniences you may have experienced,' said the DC. 'But of course, you understand the extreme vigilance we must take concerning our frontiers, given the – *ahem!* – situation with our eastern neighbor.'

The DC had studied law-enforcement in the US. Had I ever been to Cleveland or Chicago? He loved both cities greatly, as he did the US as a whole. In fact, when I arrived in Gaborone, he would appreciate it if I dropped in at the American embassy. The DC had been waiting far too long for the fulfillment of the ambassador's promise to make an inspection of the Kisane region, and he wanted me relate this as his personal emissary.

'My dear friend the ambassador is welcome anytime!' announced the DC. 'Let him drop from the sky, and he will be welcome in Kisane district as if it were his home!'

I later learned that the threat of doing exactly that was what freed me: the two white men outside my jail had called the US embassy in the capital and given them some sketchy details about my case. The ambassador responded by chartering a plane to fly to Kisane. In order to avoid any diplomatic indelicacies, a decision had been taken to release me before the plane even took off.

'Thanks,' I said to the DC. 'I will convey your regards to the ambassador. I will also convey your greetings to the law-enforcement entities in Cleveland and Chicago.'

The immigration man smiled weakly, and then extended his hand like an old friend as I picked up my kit and strode towards the door, a free man, heading towards South Africa.

ELEVEN

White Man in Apartheid Land

The massive disenfranchisement of all non-whites in South Africa, known as the system of apartheid ('separateness'), was at its zenith at the time of my arrival there during the southern hemispherical spring of 1977. So was the reaction to it among blacks. Soweto (an acronym for 'South West Township'), a sprawling shantytown outside Johannesburg that had become the burning heart of black nationalism, had become a no-go zone for whites. All black schools in the country had been on strike for over a year. Hit-and-run raids on various governmental installations were growing in frequency in response to mystery deaths of black leaders, both in prison and in their homes. The country seemed to totter on the brink of a race-based bloodbath of Biblical proportions.

How time flies, and how things change ...

Thanks to Nelson Mandela, who had been sitting in his Robben Island prison incommunicado for over a decade and would remain there for over a decade more, apartheid is now in the ash-heap of history. His astoundingly forgiving style of leadership, coupled with the Truth and Reconciliation Commission of Bishop Desmond Tutu, appear to have transformed South Africa and in many ways made the international pariah state of 1978 a model for other African states to emulate.

But at the time I passed through the country, apartheid was all too real. Buses and toilets and even park benches were separated into 'white' and 'Non-white' categories, which included not only Africans with tribal associations but also East Indians, East Asians (with the exception of the few South Africans of Japanese descent, who had been declared 'honorary whites') and the mixed-race population officially known as the Coloureds. These were folks who fell in between the cracks of racial status. There were Coloureds as dark as any black African, and Coloureds as light as any white European. There were blonde-haired, blue-eyed, slant-eyed, hawk-nosed Coloureds, Muslim Coloureds and Christian Coloureds. Most spoke Afrikaans natively, but many were purposefully forgetting the language and moving to English, an amnesia born of rejection: the Coloureds were, or had been, a second-class if integral part of the larger Cape Dutch culture until the 'pure' Boers decided to relegate them to a still-lower level in the hierarchy of races that was apartheid, and associate them with black Africans. At the time of my visit to South Africa, the apartheid government was starting to think that it might be a good idea to sort of re-associate the Coloureds with whites in order to deflect international criticism of apartheid's intrinsic racist nature, as well as to shift the demographic makeup of the country. The black majority looked less large if you could further divide the Africans into tribal 'nations' such as Zulu, Xhosa and Tswana.

The Coloureds, for the most part, were having none of this genetic hairsplitting – although the neurosis engendered by apartheid continued to claim tragic victims among those who wanted to cross the line and become white.

One was my girlfriend, Shrinithea – but I am getting ahead of the story.

'Are you aware that this is a Coloured school?'

The headmistress of a Johannesburg Catholic grade school was on the telephone, warning me that I was about to traverse one of the many racial divides that crisscrossed the Republic of South Africa. It seemed that the only area exempted from color-coding were the yellow pages of the Johannesburg telephone directory, or at least the section under 'S' for 'Schools,' which I had been paging through in hopes of drumming up a few gigs.

'Is it illegal for me to perform there?'

'Not exactly illegal, but certainly not encouraged by the state.'

'Can I get arrested?'

'I don't believe so.'

'Then how about this coming Tuesday?'

'We will be thrilled to have you, Mister Goltz.'

'What's the address?'

'It would be best if we sent a car.'

My ride out to the Catholic school was instructive for what it revealed about apartheid and the parts of Johannesburg most white folks never saw. Slowly but surely, the shining marble façades and huge, tinted windows of the banks and boutiques of the pristine showcase city center gave way to an increasingly seamy urban environment as faces changed from white to brown. Soon, we were driving through potholed streets, with uncollected garbage left heaped on the curbs. Everything seemed to suffer from general neglect.

'My taxes,' smiled my driver after another axle-breaking jolt had been negotiated.

After an hour of turns and bumps and grinds, we parked in front of the Catholic school – a huge, two-story structure with gray stucco falling from the walls. In the grim, outdoor courtyard, two hundred kids in identical blue and white uniforms skipped rope or played soccer.

'Mister Goltz, I presume ...'

It was the headmistress, a freckle-faced woman with blue eyes and autumn-leaf skin, her warm and friendly face framed by her habit. Her appearance on the steps caused a small commotion as kids scrambled to finish their games and then line up to go back to class.

'Students!' roared the headmistress, and there was sudden and absolute silence in the yard. 'Today we have a special treat – all classes please repair to the theater!'

I was led into the basketball court. At one far end, a small stage been erected overlooking a sea of about five hundred chairs, now filling with giggling teenagers. I could already feel my sore throat from shouting over their whispers and squeaking metal seats. My standard opener from *The Two Gentlemen of Verona* would not set a hook with this crowd, and the puppets would not read beyond the first few rows. I needed something bigger, more dramatic – something, dare I suggest, more compellingly *relevant* to the lives of my audience.

Then I had it: the Shylock medley from *The Merchant of Venice* that I had started developing while languishing in my Botswana jail. I might have to ad-lib a bit, but I was sure it was the ticket to the hearts and minds of my audience. As the kids tittered and laughed, I pulled on a mask and black cape and selected a tall, handsome youth sitting in the first row to use as my foil – the Antonio for my Shylock.

> Senior Antonio – Many a time and oft,
> In the Rialto, you have rated me
> About my money and my usances.
> Still have I borne it with a patient shrug
> For sufferance is the badge of all our tribe ...

A silence descended as I hobbled down the stairs of the stage, pointing a crippled finger at the stand-in Antonio while sending him a withering gaze. The audience was spellbound, listening. Perhaps they were transfiguring the text into their own experience, linking Antonio's insults with the heap of subtle and not-so-subtle abuse they had been subjected to all their lives.

> Hath not a Jew eyes? Hath not a Jew hands, organs, dimensions,
> senses, affections, passions? Fed with the same food, hurt with
> the same weapons, subject to the same diseases, healed by the
> same means, warmed and cooled by the same winter and summer
> that a Christian is? If you prick us, do we not bleed? If you
> tickle us, do we not laugh? If you poison us, do we not die?
> And if you wrong us, shall we not revenge? If we are like you in

The author today with his 'temporarily tamed *tokolosh*'. The statue was carved from a chunk of train bedding in Cape Town, in 1978. Photo: William Campbell.

"Any requests?" Mr Thomas Goltz asks during a break in his performance on Greenmarket Square. The crowd asked for the dagger scene from Macbeth.

From *The Argus*, Cape Town, 1977.

THOMAS Goltz and puppets in action, and with admirers, above.

From *The Daily Nation*, Nairobi, 1977.

Still-life with Lady Macbeth (L); Hamlet (C) and Macbeth (R). The puppets doubled for other roles; the feminine one with hair was also Ariel, Juliet, etc; the beardless one, also Romeo; and so on. They were carved by the author from junkpile wood found in Kenya, in 1977. Photo: Anna Lundgren.

Still-life with statue, mask and axe. The statue, occasionally used as Ariel from *The Tempest*, was carved in a Botswana jail cell. The mask was carved in Kenya and used for the Porter in *Macbeth* and Launce from *The Two Gentlemen of Verona*. The axe was the author's primary rough-cut tool. Photo: Anna Lundgren.

The author as Prospero (L) and as Richard III (R). From the Arts section, *The Johannesburg Star*.

This brass monster sculpture cast by the author in the spring of 1978 left its legs outside Lusaka, Zambia, thanks to the mendacity of 'California Jimmy'. Photo: Anna Lundgren.

Another Ariel, this three-foot-high female figurine was carved from a chunk of pine destined for the communal fire while the author was imprisoned in Botswana. Photo: Anna Lundgren.

The celebrity and his audience, Nairobi, Kenya.

The young Bard's passport photo, taken after having imbibed a cocktail of inoculations – needed to enter Zambia – aboard the TanZam Chinese railway.

The author today, behind a mask he carved from scrap teak as a young man. Photo: Anna Lundgren.

the rest, we will resemble you in that: the villainy you teach me
I will execute, and it shall go hard, but I will better the instruction ...

I wagged my finger one last time at my student Antonio, cast a
malignant gaze over the auditorium and re-ascended the stage. Silence,
and then hands and feet and chairs and shoes and books erupted into
an arrhythmic cacophony of applause.

The show carried on for a full forty minutes after the bell rang to
call the kids back to class, and landed me multiple invitations to other
Coloured schools in the city. I never made much money at any of
them, but what the heck – I was starting to explore themes and make
connections between the words of the Bard and the contemporary
experience of real people that I had never made before. Shylock as a
member of a persecuted or disdained minority; the killing of the black
leader Steve Biko in police custody as a sort of contemporary version
of the murder of Julius Caesar, as expressed in Mark Antony's funeral
oration; Macbeth as a Scots Idi Amin. The list was long – or I was able
to start stretching it to the loose, literary length that I liked. Political
theater – *yes!* I was soon declaring that the confrontation between
Caliban and Prospero in *The Tempest* was best seen as the first anti-
colonial voice of modern literature. I figured it was my contribution
to the anti-apartheid cause:

> This island's mine, by Sycorax my mother,
> Which thou take'st from me. When thou camest first
> Thou strok'dst me, and mad'st much of me; wouldst give me
> Water with berries in't; and then I loved thee
> And show'd thee all the qualities of the isle,
> The fresh springs, brine pits, barren place and fertile;
> Cursed be I that did so!
> For I am all the subject that you have
> Which first was mine own king ...

I might have been spending a lot of time in the Coloured part of
town, but as a white man I was obliged to live in another. That was the

gleaming metropolis the white folks called 'Joeys' (Johannesburg). Looming, hollow, man-made mountains defined the broad streets and avenues, while down the side streets a cacophony of horns and beeps mixed with the cadenced chuckles of well-heeled white strangers rushing between the myriad shops and bars and restaurants and outdoor cafés. It was a world away from my previous Africa, and easy to mistake it for civilization found at long last. I spent the first five hours window-gawking at the astounding plenty available to the local consumer. There were shirt stores, socks stores, suit stores and even cheese stores – not to mention supermarkets, where you could buy real coffee. There were hardware stores and Kodak film development centers and haberdasheries featuring English wool-weaves. There were pet shops and office equipment outlets, retail and wholesale furniture joints and kitchen-supply stores, offering all the commercial and home consumer tools of the trade a devotee could ever dream of owning.

Ground Zero was Highpoint, in Hillbrow. The former was a towering commercial and apartment building complex and the tallest structure in the area referred to as the latter, with the expected result that folks like me confused the two and called both 'Highbrow', which local wags immediately corrected and declared 'Lowbrow'. The only thing not on sale or available by layaway plan seemed to be Sony multi-system TVs. The reason for this was that in 1977, television was so new to South Africa that only a select few owned one, and the idea that someone could make a living from selling different versions of the device was absurd.

There was only one television channel, and its broadcasts were censored for content, because the government knew that half the nation – or maybe the entire nation – would be watching the mystery machine every evening when it came on between six and midnight. The venues that had access to the squawk-box were limited to a few select upper-market homes, luxury hotel lobbies and a fistful of popular bars. It was truly the magic box, an electronic aphrodisiac. I was to have personal experience with the device.

To supplement the meager income I was getting from the Coloured schools (the white schools were on a different schedule for some reason, and the black schools were on strike) I decided to go back to my roots, performance-wise, and that meant the streets. The logical venue for *al fresco* shows was the open courtyard below Highpoint, which was sufficiently far away from the street to be shielded from traffic noise and had the additional advantage of being accessed via a wide staircase that could serve either as a stage for me or bleachers for an audience.

I waited until offices began to empty out for the day, and then launched the show, starting with *Macbeth*, using my carving knife to dispatch the doomed Duncan. A few people stopped, and a whispered chuckled passed among the throng as I followed the dagger around the stage, miming a walk down cold castle steps, blowing my voice into the Masai mask as a reverberating board.

> While I threat, he lives
> Words to the heat of deeds too cold breath gives!
> I go and it is done; the bell invites me.
> Hear it not Duncan, for it is a knell
> *That summons thee to heaven – or to hell!*

I froze mid-stride, paused two seconds, and then flipped off my mask to bow. The audience, my audience, had swollen to over a hundred eager black, white and brown faces, young and old, with more coming from the supermarket, putting down their groceries to watch the show. 'Bravo!' they cried in one great wave of applause. I was passing my hat when a brace of policemen approached, nightsticks in hand.

'Dew yew have permission to create a pooblic mayting?' asked one in his distinctive Afrikaans inflection.

'I was just giving a little show here, and ...'

'Ay'm surry, but yew must have a purmit, and besides, yew are stopping paypul from gaoing on their way to their trayns.'

There was little question about whom the officer was speaking: at least half of my audience was black – the maids and counter-girls and janitors who kept Joeys ticking, but who were obliged to get on their segregated buses and commuter trains to return to Soweto.

'Let's break it up here,' said the second officer (or something like that in its Afrikaans equivalent), and the portion of the crowd that was black began working its way up the stairs towards the street while the white spectators, suddenly aware that they had just participated in an illegal interracial gathering, also began to move away. But one white man stayed behind.

'Bravo, bravo!' he said, stepping forward and doubling my meager take by pressing a 10-*rand* note into my hand. 'You are a regular hurdy-gurdy man!'

My fan's name was John (or maybe Frank or Nigel), and he was a producer for a magazine program on South African TV.

'We'd like to do a show on you,' he said, flashing a card and a plastic smile. 'Why not come on back to the studio right now to do an interview?'

We jumped in his car and roared off to the South Africa Television Corporation HQ and, after the liberal application of makeup and dusting of nose, sat down in a studio to record my views on ... well, almost everything: Africa, life on the street, jail and, of course, the universality of Shakespeare in contemporary political life ... the producer flashed his smile at this, and then changed the subject back to other topics, such as how I spent my time in the Botswana jail, the difficulties I had experienced in Zambia and Tanzania and just how I had gotten started in this crazy business after having been robbed in Kenya. I felt as though I were being led somewhere I did not necessarily want to go, but hey! The camera was on, and it seemed the moment to be expansive and garrulous and profound and ... and ... and ...

A lifetime later, I now recognize I was seduced by the lens.

Ah, well ...

'Great stuff!' said the producer, wrapping up the interview. 'Now we just need a little live material.'

I suggested we tape a school show I had scheduled for the next day. It would fit right in with my remarks about how Antonio's appeal to Shylock might be compared to the government's flirtation with the Coloureds.

'Great idea!' cried the reporter. 'A Coloured school!'

When I brought the camera team to the school the following day, however, the headmaster's reaction was anything but positive.

'What? The national television people, here?' he hissed, rising angrily from behind his desk when I broached the issue of filming my show in his school. 'Just who *are* you, Mister Goltz, and what do you *really* want from us? You were recommended to us as an honest man who had something unique and edifying to offer my students, and that perhaps we might be able to offer you something in return – like some insight into this hellish country we are living in. Now, however, you want to use my students, my school, as a propaganda platform for the government! Do you know what they want? I'll *tell* you what they want. They want a film of my students' smiling faces while you perform so that they can broadcast it to the nation and to the world and declare: "Look! See how *happy* and *content* the Coloured people of South Africa are! *See* how *different* they are from the blacks!" Is *that* what you want to help them do, Mister Goltz? If so, I shall tell you my answer: *No, no and a thousand times, no!* I will not let that state-run propaganda machine anywhere near my school, thank you sir!'

The show was canceled, and the camera crew and I drove back into the city center looking for an alternative venue. The atmosphere had grown chilly, though, and I sensed they were only going through the motions out of a sense of obligation. After a couple of false starts we decided to go back to Highpoint, where they taped an uninspired Launce from the *Two Gentlemen*, followed by the Desdemona death scene from *Othello* and perhaps something else. Then the producer made some noises about having to cancel the dinner he had promised me, adding that he was not sure if the material would make it by the censor – which was a kind way of saying that he thought I stank.

I hung around Joeys for a few more weeks, picking up a some gigs – including a two-day run at The Abattoir, a newly established theater set up in a former slaughterhouse on the edge of town, in a district where somehow the zoning had escaped the usual 'Whites/Blacks Only' association laws, and was thus a place of limited interracial mingling. I figured it was the sort of joint where someone might have heard a whisper of my culture-vulture brother Eddy, but the only familiar faces I found were Michael and Pam, the South African/ New Zealand couple I had first met at the al-Manzura Hotel in Nairobi.

During the course of an extended dope party at their Hillbrow/ Highbrow pad that night, they informed me that a guitar player meeting Eddy's description had been seen in a bar in Salisbury, capital of Ian Smith's rogue state of Rhodesia. Further discussion was broken up by unexpected arrivals. First was a well-mannered Coloured guy, who seemed to be a dope courier of some sort. Next came an old schoolmate of Michael's, who was as surprised to find the Coloured guy in an all-white neighborhood after dark as the Coloured guy was to find himself under intense interrogation in what he had presumably believed to be a safe-haven amongst non-racist friends and/or dope-dealing partners. I stayed long enough to hold up the undercover cop (for that's what Michael's old friend was) for a sort of mutually agreed-upon time for the Coloured guy to escape, and then announced my intention to walk back to my hostel

'You Yanks,' blustered the schoolchum, now revealing himself to be involved in 'security'. 'I would have busted his *kaffir* ass in a second had you not been here!'

'Why?'

'General principle.'

I left Michael and Pam's abode, mounted a fat Swiss gal at the hostel that night and, in a post-coital, dope-induced fog, remembered my quest for Eddy.

With not a little trepidation I turned my search north, towards Disneyland. This time I had bucks in my pocket, and was approaching the Forbidden Land in a convoy of seemingly like-minded souls.

I was entering Rhodesia from South Africa.

TWELVE

Disneyland, or an Excursion
to War-torn Rhodesia

'Do you have a weapon, Mister Goltz?'

I had not thought a wandering Shakespearean actor needed anything but the canon of the Bard.

'No,' I said, and the Rhodesian border guard turned to the next man in line.

'Mister Jones?'

'Carbine.'

'Mister Smith?'

'Uzi.'

'Mister van der Horn?'

'AK-47.'

'Where'd you get that?'

'Off a dead terr.'

'Should report it to the government.'

'Just did.'

'Right-o.'

It was dawn, and there were perhaps forty cars waiting at Beitsbridge on the Limpopo River for the escort to Fort Victoria on the road to Salisbury, capital of the breakaway state of Rhodesia. Ours was the only vehicle without a gun barrel extending from it. 'Let's move it!' shouted a man dressed in a camouflage safari suit; an army jeep with a machine gun on a swivel roared up to lead, and we crossed into Rhodesia at war. The country was dying before our eyes, the low-level guerrilla war of the early 1970s having turned into a paroxysm of bloodletting, with scores killed every day. Everyone knew that it was just a matter of time before the twin guerrilla forces of ZAPU and ZANU rolled into Salisbury in triumph. But in the meantime, there was still plenty of killing to be done.

'We built this place,' snarled one of the pot-bellied Brits in the convoy – his beer gut was the type usually referred to as the 'Rhodesian Front'. 'When we came to live here, there was nothing but bush and if we are forced to leave, we'll leave it the same goddamn way we found it – bush. We'll send the women and children to South Africa, and then show these *kaffirs* how to wage guerrilla war. We'll burn the farms, blow the factories, kill the cattle and poison the water. We'll make the conditions we're living under now seem like a fucking picnic, a time that everyone will look back on as the Golden Age. Mark my words.'

Signs of war were everywhere as our armed caravan traveled up the road: the bush had been burnt away from both sides for a distance of 100 yards to provide a better field of fire; the few villages we passed were ringed with barbed wire, ostensibly to keep guerrillas from easy access to food and more recruits. As the sun topped the treetops to the east, we stopped at the Elephant Hills Lodge for morning tea. A sign declared that the Rhodesian Security Forces had just made it safe for tourists again. Fat chance. Smoldering huts and burnt-out cars along side the road all the way to the capital suggested that even this major artery was no longer safe. Salisbury, once known as one of the most pleasant and lively cities on the continent, was a ghost town: nearly all the able-bodied white men were in the bush, riding horses with Grey's Rangers or doing special, cross-border operations into Zambia and Mozambique as part of the Seloux Scouts or other elite 'defense' units.

Guarding their ladyfolk in the center of town stood the statue of Cecil Rhodes, scourge of the Boers, namesake of the country as well as of the scholarship founded to send promising young men to distant lands to seek knowledge and understanding of other cultures. The irony was that the only young men seeking knowledge and cross-cultural understanding in Rhodesia seemed to cluster around the International Youth Hostel, and the knowledge they sought had less to do with international understanding than about weapons systems and black-marketeering percentage points. One such Wild Goose was a six-foot-six, ex-Special Forces guy from Boston, who had just checked into the hostel after several weeks of pacifying villages in the north – a specialty he had developed in Vietnam. Another was a New Zealand psycho, kicked out of the regular Rhodesian army (but not the country) for stealing a dead guerrilla's gun.

A couple of loudmouth Aussies seemed intent on moving gold out for a third party before they were drafted – if one overstayed one's residency permit, one was immediately subject to conscription. I guessed that meant me, too, should I choose to linger longer than my one-month visa allowed. Is that what had happened to Eddy? Or had he actually 'volunteered' for service in the bush with a gun instead of a guitar? I had been trying to discretely ask about my brother among the goodfellas hanging around the hostel, and had received contradictory responses.

'Five-foot-five guitar player with green eyes like a snake?' the mercenary from Boston reflected, considering my standard description of my brother. 'Not a lot of time for hootenannies around here right now.'

'I got a .45 Mag I'll let you have for the proverbial song, mate,' replied a gun dealer from New Zealand. 'Thet'll keep both you and yer lost brother safe as peas in yer momma's pod.'

'I was asking if you had seen anyone who –'

'Oh, playing hard to git, is we? Well, for the sake of yer sister, I'll let you have it for only 200 Rhodesian dollars, and throw in two clips for free ...'

The hostel manager was hardly more helpful. Unlike the schoolmaster type one usually encountered behind the check-in desk of International Youth Hostels, the Salisbury chapter boasted a curious character with a dozen identities and an Eastern European accent behind an indecipherable smile, a man variously reported to be serving as a recruiter for the 'foreign' element in the Rhodesian army, a special agent for South African intelligence on loan from the CIA, an East German Secret Service operative, an informer for the Rhodesian police or – most likely – a Polish count on the lam with a penchant for battle-crazed boys.

'Plan on spending some time?' he asked as I checked into the hostel.

'No, just passing through.'

'This is the end of the road – you don't just pass through.'

'Well, actually, I am just looking for my brother ...'

'Oh, one of those, eh ...'

I am not sure what 'one of those' was supposed to mean, but I guess I was one, and nodded in conspiratorial agreement, which seemed appropriate.

'Try Robin's place, tomorrow.'

'Who is Robin?'

Robin, I soon learned, was none other than Robin Moore of *French Connection* fame, who maintained a house in town known as the 'Crippled Eagle', the self-styled (and surrogate) US embassy in Rhodesia. Or so Moore claimed. In fact, the house, and its pool and patio, served as an R & R outlet for American mercenaries, a place where they could eat hamburgers, drink Budweiser and catch up on sports scores.

The next day, Sunday, I got directions and wandered over to the establishment. It was packed full of men the size of professional football players – Wild Geese, to a man. Except for the servants and the dozen or so African floozies servicing the mercs, there was only one non-white in the place. Behind the bar, with his arm in a sling, was a huge, barrel-chested Navajo Indian. He had fallen during a practice jump from a helicopter and broken his arm, becoming a 'crippled eagle' himself. I thought his presence in this collection of professional killers a little odd: Here was an Indian, working to subdue the African equivalent of Crazy Horse.

Eddy, of course, was nowhere to be seen, although there were more tantalizing sightings scattered all around the country – and always just a mined road's ride away.

'Guitar player? Green eyes? Yeah, seen someone like that in the Vumba over near Umtali on the Mozambique frontier. Bad firefight there last week,' related a blond giant from North Carolina.

'There was some entertainment up in the Fort Victoria club house about a month back before that cross-border operation we mounted into Zambia, but I forget if the guy was playing piano or mandolin and I forget whether he was Canadian or Dutch or German,' said another shaven-headed, dead-eyed hired gun of the renegade state. A couple of other folks from the youth hostel had also wandered over to the Eagle, and invited me along for an afternoon outing to a natural water slide, pool and hotel complex located about forty miles from Salisbury, where someone else had suggested there had been musical jam sessions on weekends – or at least had been up until a few weeks before. It was reserved for whites, and the only blacks in the place were the waiters and busboys, scurrying for meager tips.

'Do these blokes ever wonder why it is that we always seem to have time and money when they don't?' one of the Australian smugglers asked, rhetorically.

'S'pose so,' answered another.

'You wonder when one is going to turn on you and put bloody poison in your stew. No telling with these Afs,' added a third.

'No sir, I don't trust an Af, never,' retorted the first. 'What they shoulda done, you ask me mate, was blow 'em all to blazes like you did your Indians,' said another, turning to me – the Yankee in the group. 'That's what they shoulda done, an' they'd have no problem today.' The Indian solution again, trotted out like the Red Badge of Courage.

Around 4:00 PM I suggested we go. Dusk was the favorite 'hit time' of the guerrillas, in that it gave them enough light to see what they were doing and all night to escape. The Australians, however, seemed determined to keep the hotel open yet another hour, even though the waiters were nearly begging us to go so that they, too, could make it to their huts before the evils of the night descended on the land. 'Let's ' 'ave another beer, boy!' demanded one of the Aussies, 'What, are you afraid of the terrs?'

'Yes, Master, we are *too* afraid,' urged a busboy. 'We love life!'

We, at least, had guns for the way home. The waiters had none, and of the tens of thousands dead since the 'constitutional conflict' had begun a decade earlier, all but a tiny fraction had been unarmed blacks. Finally, twilight. The sun had set, penumbral shadows enveloped the land and the Australian driver of our vehicle decided it was time to go. Smiling, he took out his pistol and whipped it on the door handle to cock it. 'Let us see what those ZAPU boys can do against Mister Smith and Wesson,' he chortled, all Clint Eastwood and false courage. It was pitch black and silent in the car when we arrived back at the Salisbury city limits.

The closest thing to a sighting of Eddy had been in the Vumba, a cool, misty highland area near the Mozambique border that produced all of Rhodesia's fine coffee. I had also been told that the regional capital, Umtali, had a theater club. I was sure the locals would be mighty appreciative of a little Shakespeare show as a relief from the war.

The idea was insane, of course. There might have been a theater club, but all the men were in the bush and the women had turned into a pretty tough bunch themselves, more interested in exchanging security information in the clubhouse bar than watching some clown packing a bunch of puppets rant and rave in the voice of Macbeth or King Lear. 'Sally had another perimeter violation last night,' said an attractive blonde packing an Uzi-style submachine gun.

'Don't say!' muttered an older woman carrying a sawed-off shotgun. 'I told her not to trust that new *kaffir* manager of hers. Next thing you know he'll be planting a new minefield in front of the daisies, he will.'

If Umtali was a cultural bust, there was still the Castle Hotel, located some thirty miles closer to Mozambique. A local planter hanging around the Umtali theater club bar offered me a ride part of the way. His snail-slow truck had been armored on the bottom because he was obliged to drive over gravel roads, the perfect bed for land mines. He also had an M-16 tucked under the front seat. 'Its main function is for my own peace of mind, just knowing it's there. If it came down to it, I'd never have time to brake this thing, grab the gun and cock it, much less get out of the vehicle to aim and shoot it at something,' he said. When we arrived at the junction of the main road and the turnoff to his estate, he invited me to stay at his more-or-less abandoned farm but then suggested I decline the invitation: it simply was not safe.

How safe it was standing by the side of the main road was another question I had not really considered until I watched the truck disappear down the side-track. Mist and fog rolled in from the valley below, showing and obfuscating the green mountains of Mozambique by turns. Once, when the fog rolled away for a moment, I discovered two African men walking up a gully in my direction. In Kenya or anywhere else I would have greeted them, and they me. But in Rhodesia, the battle lines were drawn. Strangers, especially those of different skin colors, did not mix. I clutched my walking stick like a rifle, and postured like a sentry. The two men veered slightly, not wanting to bolt, but also not wanting to come any closer within range of my 'weapon'. I continued mimicking my sentry-pose long after another bank of fog enshrouded and absorbed them, praying for the quick arrival of a vehicle.

After what seemed like hours but was probably only fifteen minutes, another car came by and brought me to my destination – the Castle Hotel. A massive, fortress-like structure built by Italian prisoners of war during World War Two, it commanded a magnificent view of the surrounding hills and valleys and was once an obligatory stop for anyone interested in the blue-ribbon trout streams of the upper mountains. But I was the only guest, and the landlady positively jumped on me at the reception and doted on me all through dinner, making jokes about eating 'terrorist' pie as she set down my meal, telling me her life history. 'Where's your husband?' I asked after dinner as an elderly black man served us coffee and brandy in front of the blazing hearth.

'The terrs got him last summer,' said the woman, as easily as if I had asked about the weather. 'Now Geoff – he's my eldest son – is off with the Seloux Scouts.'

'Where are the rest?'

'Stephen, the youngest, he took the Chicken Express to London and won't be back, and Bill, he's in Bolivia looking for a new homestead for us once this mess is over.'

'You mean there's nobody guarding the place now?'

'Guards? What could a guard or two do? If they want you, they get you. Gillian's place down the road got hit with a missile last week, but nobody touched us.' The long and lonely night grew longer and lonelier when the power was inexplicably cut. 'Here,' said the old lady, handing me a revolver and a box of shells. 'If you see anything moving, shoot. They run when you return fire. They're cowards, all of 'em.' While I guarded the entrance to the parlor, the landlady radioed to Umatli HQ to report a potential terrorist strike; but even before a patrol reached us to investigate, the power generators mysteriously clicked back on and all was well.

'Its Jonathan the cook, I'm certain,' muttered the old lady. 'He's one of them, I am sure. And we were so good to him ...'

The patrol arrived, and the staff was called in for questioning with Jonathan the cook singled out for a private inquisition. But he was no longer there.

'Beat it to the bush, eh,' said captain of the patrol. 'We'll find him tomorrow.'

In the morning I strolled around the grounds, which included a nine-hole golf course with a putting green. Sadly, there were no clubs available, though I am not sure if I really wanted to search for lost hooks and slices in the terror traps and rough.

As I stood on the acropolis, surveying the beautiful countryside, gunfire erupted not far away. Contact? I wondered. I tried to imagine which instrument of death and destruction was in use, reviewing the various lectures I had been given as regards weaponry. Was it the Rhodesian version of the Uzi, the favorite household weapon? Or was it an AK-47, the standard issue of the guerrillas which, although easy to carry over long distances, lacked the punch of the South African pseudo-M-16? I clambered down to the hotel and asked my landlady. She merely chuckled.

'Care for another slice of terrorist pie?' she said.

Back in Salisbury, I attempted to give a street show but was shut down by the authorities; the crowd would have been a perfect target for an urban bomber, the police chief explained. The only other attempt I made to stage a performance occurred at a private club frequented by Rhodesian soldiers on furlough. Unlike their international counterparts, most of the regular forces were just regular guys – accountants, teachers, doctors and farmers, as well as just a lot of confused young men grown more confused by the violence that had engulfed their country and way of life. All this meant that my audience was drunk.

The show went well, everything else being equal, and I had taken my bows and was deep in cultural conversation with some gal when I picked up very bad vibes coming from two men standing right next to me. Jealousy? Adultery? Simple bush-and-blood fatigue? They were smiling at each other, but something was terribly wrong, and I turned to my companion to push her back just as one man pulled a long hunting knife from his boot and started moving it towards the other man. Events played themselves out in slow motion. What I remember was the realization that I was the only person standing at the right angle to do anything before the knife ripped through the cotton shirt of the intended victim, and that the fist that slammed into the attacker's temple was my own, and that as the knife skidded across the floor the full force of the attacker's wrath was turned on me.

I awoke in a strange bed with two angels and a demon hovering above me.

'Hey, Bard,' said one of the *houris*. 'You just got the shit beat out of you.'

'Sorry, mate,' said the demon-man who had administered my beating, 'I just cracked. No hard feelings?'

It was all pretty confusing, but as far as I could make out I had intervened in a fight between two good friends who had lost a third in the bush the day before, and that my good deed had saved not only the intestines of one of the pair, but their friendship as well. The two *houris*, meanwhile, were a couple of lesbians who had taken me back to their abode to recover from my beating. One was a thick and swarthy bull dyke whose father was Jamaican. The other was a blonde, anorexic Brit who seemed to get skinnier before my very eyes. I cannot remember their names, and I am not sure if they ever knew mine; to them, I was simply 'Bard'.

'Bard,' the bull dyke would say. 'We're going to a party tonight, want to tag along?'

They would drag me off to some bizarre shindig or other – strange and wonderful *Cabaret*-type affairs that only happen in societies about to go under and where one quite literally lives for the day – or night, as it were. Drugs and alcohol were rife, marriage meant nothing, no expense was too high: locals had only Rhodesian dollars which, if they still held their value in the country, were worthless outside of it and there was only more booze to buy. Woody Allen's *Bananas*, appropriately, was a regular movie feature, with half the audience having memorized the lines. The theme song playing at each of these bashes that slowly devolved into poolside orgies was Joan Armatrading's 'High in the Saddle', with its chorus:

We had fun, fun, fun, fun, fun
We had fun, fun, fun, fun, fun
We had fun, while it lasted ...

And still no Eddy. With a few days left on my visa before I got drafted, I booked a flight back to Jo'burg. The plane crossed paths with Rhodesian jets and helicopters striking deep into Mozambique, killing two thousand of Robert Mugabe's ZAPU guerrillas on the very day that an 'internal settlement' was signed by Rhodesian president Ian Smith and Bishop Abel Muzorewa. It was a dead letter, the last military effort of the white administration to save itself – in vain. Within a year, ZAPU and ZANU leaders Mugabe and Joshua Nkomo were in Salisbury, soon to be renamed Harare, while Smith's rogue state of Rhodesia became a footnote in the history of Zimbabwe, a nation born in blood.

It was fun while it lasted.

THIRTEEN

Cape Town Races,
or Stanley Finally Finds Livingston

Tremendous clouds curdled over the escarpment like white, gooey frosting on the edge of a razor-sharp cake. The thick film rolled down from the heavens as if to engulf the city below, dissipating just short of the upper suburbs as the warm breezes of the Indian Ocean pushing up from the port clashed with those of the cold Atlantic.

Cape Town – the bustling, self-conscious metropolis perched at the very end of Africa, less a city than a series of towns attached to one another like a garland of roses – was mine, all mine. There was Gardens, a lovely, lovingly restored area of Dutch colonial houses set along cobblestone streets downtown; Mobray, just down from the splendid university campus, stitched to the middle reaches of the Table Mountain massif; there were Rondebosch and Stellenbosch, both former vineyards but now given over to a mixture of manor houses squeezed between orchards, grapes and pines groves. Over the next six months or so I would become acquainted with and then forget the names of a dozen other like places, with only one other lodged forever in my mind: District Six. Once the heart of the Cape Coloured culture, it was being bulldozed out of existence to make room for whites-only luxury flats, its residents forced to find domicile elsewhere.

Cape Town was also a capital, at least for six months of the year. True to the compulsion to divide everything and everybody into half-units and sub-units that was the spirit of apartheid, the government of South Africa spent half the year in Cape Town and half the year in Pretoria. When the Boers' National Party was out of town, Cape Town seemed to visibly relax, racially speaking. Then, whites, Coloureds, Asians and even blacks boarded the same buses and shopped at the same supermarkets and even sometimes went to the same theaters, parties and beaches.

Cape Town a 'liberal' city? Compared with Jo'burg (or Durban or Pretoria) it seemed scandalously so, and thus allowed one to be lulled into a sense of complacency about the real impact of apartheid on people's lives.

> Friends, Romans, countrymen, lend me your ears;
> I come to bury Caesar, not to praise him.
> The evil that men do lives after them,
> The good is oft interred with their bones;
> So let it be with Caesar ...

The words were familiar; the context was not. It was noon, and I was standing at the top of the great steps leading to the University of Cape Town, addressing a crowd of students drawn from across the country. It was a challenging performance, because for the first time during my one-man wanderings, I was among people who were essentially of my own age, education and native language.

On the train down from Jo'burg, I had memorized the funerary monologues of both Brutus and Mark Antony, and decided to politicize them. The black activist Steven Biko had been killed while in police custody a scant week before, and the 'honorable men' of the Afrikaner government had been busy defaming him posthumously, painting a portrait of Biko as an implacable revolutionary terrorist. It was my self-assigned task to set the record straight.

... They that have done this deed are honorable;
What private grieves they have, alas, I know not,
That have made them do it; there are wise and honorable
And will, no doubt, with reasons answer you.
I come not friends, to steal away your hearts,
I am no orator as Brutus is, I only speak right on,
And tell you that which you yourselves do know,
Show you sweet Caesar's wounds, poor poor dumb mouths,
And bid them speak for me ...

There was a silence on the Great Steps, and then a great roar.

'Shakespeare! Yes, go fer it!'

A pause, a passing of the cap, the collection of paper instead of coin (and not a few oblique references and invitations to various alternative forms of payment), and I was made. The liberal, white-youth audience of my peers enrolled at the University of Cape Town loved the show.

Bullseye, bingo – goal! Caesar equals Biko, and me the local Mark Antony! Fomentor of Revolution and Curse of Apartheid! Could it get much better than that?

But the South African racial authorities were resilient and cunning, and fought my one-man street campaign for truth and justice through devious and underhanded means. In fact, they resorted to the lowest, cruelest, dirtiest blow of all.

They made me famous.

I was sitting at a bar recovering from the day's rigors and rereading *Coriolanus*, to see what sort of socio-political material I might be able to cull and mold into an electrifying denunciation of South African fascist militarism from that particularly obscure Shakespearean opus. I kept an eye on the television at the far end of the room, around which a knot of regulars had gathered for the evening news. There was never any fighting over the channel clicker, because there was only one channel and no channel clicker anyway.

The bartender called over to see if I wanted another beer, and I looked up and noticed out of the corner of my eye that the news program was over and that something else was now on the telly. The screen was showing still photos of different kinds of street hustlers – gypsies with dancing bears, accordion players with monkeys, jugglers juggling knives, fire-eaters gobbling flame, guitar players working the strings while warbling and even a classical violinist playing at a subway stop. The background music was Donovan's *Hurdy Gurdy Man*. I put down my pint along with *The Collected Works* and moved closer to the television, feeling a little homesick. Street folks were, after all, my kind of people.

Then the camera starting roaming around Johannesburg, showing a pair of feet walking down a series of steps, wearing a pair of old shoes similar to mine. Next came the hands unpacking a bag filled with figurines, attaching a Masai mask over the still-anonymous performer's face. I knew what was coming but was still in shock, a state of total disbelief, even when I heard my own voice on the audio track first weeping and wailing and then talking to one shoe described as being my mother and the other shoe my father, and next bemoaning the heartlessness of my travel bag, which he or I or whoever was insisting was my dog, Crab ... There was no point trying to deny it any longer.

I was on TV.

'Crazy bastard,' I heard one of the other customers mutter.

'What the hell is he doing?' asked another.

'I don't know, but it sure is odd.' The man in the mask on the screen had finished showing off the holes in his shoes, which everyone in the bar found amusing, and was picking up some wooden objects – puppets, it seemed – and announcing his intention to perform a scene from *Othello*. One of the puppets, a black one, was soon stuffing the other, female one into a silk handkerchief. *'Put out the light – and then, put out the light!'* he moaned, murdering his puppet wife. Then he stopped and flung off his mask to take a bow. The camera panned the audience. No one clapped.

'Well,' said the performer on the tube, clearly irritated by the lack of applause, 'you all seem interested enough to waste your time staring at me. If your lives are so boring, then give me recompense for breaking up the monotony. I'll take my bows again.' He did just that, and then began passing his hat around the crowd for new donations.

Cut.

Suddenly, the same mad fellow was sitting in a television studio, rambling long and loquaciously about the universality of Shakespeare, Africa, what he thought he stood for and just about anything else that seemed to come to mind. 'Brecht once said that theater must challenge the audience,' the guy intoned. 'But I think that theater must challenge the performer as well. It is the obligation of all performance artists to meet their audience in an equal-terms venue, namely, the street ...'

Long-winded, yes. But after the weirdness with the mask and puppets and all, the performer looked decidedly sane. The contrast was phenomenal. 'What a guy! I'd like to shake his hand!' exclaimed someone at the bar.

'What balls he must have to do that! Shakespeare in Africa. Wow!'

'If I see him, I'll give him a *rand* or two!'

'Yeah, me too.'

'*Shh,* he's coming on again.'

The camera was again panning around the assembled faces of a street audience, and then back to the performer, who was doing something with a sheet pulled down over his face, a long wooden knife in one hand and a bearded puppet in the other. 'Must be from *Macbeth,*' someone opined. 'Dagger and all that.'

'Yeah, that's the one. Remember it from school.'

'Tough stuff, Shakespeare, but not bad when you think about it.'

Another chunk of studio interview, another street scene, a couple of sound-bites from the audience, and then *Hurdy Gurdy Man* again, drawing the program to an end. When I looked up from the television to the bar, everyone was staring at me.

I was mobbed in Green Market Square the next day, with people shouting '*Shakespeare!*' as they pressed money in my hand before I even unpacked my kit.

'Shook those rock spiders out of their holes, you did!' cried a Cape Town Brit.

'Never met a nicer salt-prick!' shouted a passing Boer.

(Both are ethnic slurs. A 'rock spider' is an Afrikaaner, because every time you turn over a stone one comes creeping out, i.e. they were everywhere. A 'salt-prick', by contrast, is an aspersion cast at Englishmen holding two passports, thus keeping one foot in Britain and one in South Africa, with the 'third leg' dangling in the salty brine ...)

All my pretensions to Brechtian relevance and impact on the political scene aside, clearly something about what I was doing touched the right spot in the South African soul. Just what that something was continues to elude me today: that I was a cultural outcast, like their entire ostracized society? Or was it simply that I had been in their living rooms, on their TVs?

Soon, there were dinner party invitations by the dozen, offers to stay a week or month and free drinks every night. Rank strangers came up and gave me the keys to their cars for the weekend (a gesture made only slightly less generous given the fact of gasoline rationing). Newspapers came to profile me, and people cheered as they drove by in buses during my street-side shows. There was not a school in town that would not have me, with many paying premiums to get double bookings.

One result was that I had money, real money, for the first time in a very long while. To celebrate, I rented a garage in the suburb of Rondebosch, which I converted into the first home I had had in almost a year. I used it as my base to work up monologues that required shouting; I used I to finally and safely secure my Zambian emeralds, the sale of which would change my life forever.

Sadly, not one gem merchant I approached in Cape Town showed more than a passing interest in my long-concealed treasure.

'Dealing in gems is illegal, bloke,' was the standard reply.

I did not have enough savvy about the industry to break through; my green-stone stash stayed in the garage. waiting.

Manwhile, there were other mines in the immediate vicinity to be exploited. Right around the corner from my Rondebosch estate stood Cape Town's primary cultural edifice, the Baxter Theatre and Arts Complex. I was sure my Shakespeare street show would fit right in.

The Baxter Theatre was a brand-new, gorgeous structure that was the darling of Cape Town's culture-vulture crowd. In addition to having multiple stages, it was also multiracial. All you needed was a tie and a ticket to enter the door. I arrived with neither, sure that the management was aching for guerrilla theater in the lobby between acts of Chekhov's *The Cherry Orchard* or whatever other classic was playing that night. 'It's him, the one from television ...' I could hear some fur-draped ladies whispering to themselves. 'Is he going to do that Shakespeare thing here?'

'He wouldn't dare ...' But indeed I did, beginning with the familiar Mark Antony oration.

Friends, Romans, countrymen ...

I did not get far. Within a caesura, the stage manager ordered me rather forcefully to cease and desist, because I could be heard inside the chamber stage. My response was to turn up the volume and point to the fuming stage manager as a surrogate bad-guy for Brutus.

The noble Brutus has informed you
That Caesar was ambitious ...

The audience clapped, cheered and guffawed, and showered me with coin. *Success! That will teach the house manager around here to hold his tongue*, I thought. But I was soon to learn one of the great lessons of theatrical life: never, ever make an ass out of an irate house manager. They can be sneaky and spiteful, and dump pitchers of water on your head even when you are in mid-verse. Having concluded the *Antony* oration, I was pulling out my sword to give my new fans a little *Richard III* when I noticed movement in the galley above me. It was the manager, with a bucket of water in his wrathful hands.

Splash! I ducked; some members of my intermission audience did not. In the ensuing melee, I lost my chance to pass the hat – and also my audience, members of which were either wringing out their wet clothes in the bathroom or returning to their reserved seats.

'WET CURTAIN FOR BARD OF THE BAXTER' ran the banner headline of a front-page story in the *Cape Times* the next day. I was furious as only the famous can be. The story, I informed the editors, was filled with errors, mainly concerning the identities of who got soaked. The corrections ran the next day along with a statement from me, vowing to return. I was True Theater, I declared, heir to the grand, public tradition of the Bard himself. The Baxter retorted with an ultimatum on the third day (the story now buried somewhere towards the back of the paper) that I would be pilloried if I set foot on their premises again; I replied on the fourth day, vowing to return. It was for *Art* that I struggled ...

The final showdown was a fizzle. I did indeed return, but the authorities were ready to dispose of me in the most effective manner. The house manager publicly praised me, and suggested I audition for a bit part in an amateur production he was to direct in the Baxter's chamber theater some months hence. As for performing my own uniquely powerful material inside the Baxter atrium, he deeply regretted that, sadly, fire regulations could not be bent to allow it. However worthwhile my Shakespeare show might be from an artistic viewpoint – it went without saying that it was excellent, groundbreaking, etc – there was the concern for the safety of the audience ... I was more than welcome to use the outside steps of the Baxter, he offered, and not only on weekends but even during dark nights when the theater was closed ...

The tricky twit. Not only had he publicly damned me with faint praise, but the invitation to use the foyer steps also effectively banished me to the corner grocery store, far removed from all potential admirers. 'Thanks,' I was obliged to say, shaking his hand for the cameras.

'And Bard,' he smiled, far too sweetly. 'Just remember: "All the world's a stage ..."'

Well, if not all the world, at least Cape Town's central Green Market Square. There I mounted my daily Shakespeare show, to diminishing attendance over time. 'Saturation' is a performer's worst enemy, and after some two or three months in Cape Town, my crowds grew thinner, the collection leaner, the applause softer. My fame was fading.

There was one audience member who seemed constant, however. She always hung around the audience fringe, but seemed to be the first to turn her back and go before the final curtain, as if running back to work. Then she was back the next day, silently watching as I roared through my repertoire, but always lingered an extra moment; I caught her eye and beckoned to her to have a chat as I packed my things.

'Did you like the show?' I asked, for openers.

'Oh, yiis,' she replied shyly in a lilting Afrikaans accent. *"Twas vary nayice.'*

Her jet black hair was pulled into a conservative bun, and she wore no makeup to speak of, save for a little too much rouge applied to her cheeks. She was dressed in blue jeans or slacks, and wore the sort of smock that hid any and all speculation of her figure. She looked like a schoolteacher, an office girl or maybe a nurse.

The most notable thing about her was the gap where her two front teeth were missing. I had heard that this was some sort of Cape Coloured 'beauty mark' and one with a rather explicit connotation dealing with oral sex, and was thus intrigued to find myself staring at the perverse possibility. Perhaps sensing this, my bashful fan quickly gave me to understand that she was neither Coloured nor toothless.

'Ay ahm hav Ayrab and hav Jewess,' she explained out of the blue.

In other words, she was officially 'White,' and thus fair game for an outlander white-boy like me. As for her missing front ivories, she informed me that she had taken a fall and knocked them out, but that soon she would be showing the world 'two beautiful caps of pure South African gold'.

I am not sure if I believed a word of it then. But I didn't have to: it did not matter to me, at least not yet.

'Well,' I asked, referring to my street show. 'What scene did you like best?'

'Ay layked thee one yew dew aboot virginity,' she smiled, referring to my ribald puppet duet from *All's Well That End's Well*, which focused on the dilemma of an undersexed maid when confronted by an oversexed lord. I called the sketch 'Meditations on Virginity'.

'Why is that?'

'Because Ay'm still a virgin mayself,' she said. 'But Ay shan't be for long.'

'Oh,' I said, taken aback at her sudden intimacy. 'Why is that?'

'Yew,' she said, blushing. 'Ay saw yew on teliiviision and Ay told awl may friinds that Ay will do it furst wiith hem. Yew, that iis. Ay wiish yew tew teach me how tew make love, just layk yew do with yewr puppet dolls.'

'Zounds!' I said, or something to that effect. Or maybe I was almost speechless, for once.

'You mean you saw me on television, and decided that you want to sleep with me?'

'Yiis.'

'Well, let's go back to my place right now,' I said, mocking her.

'Oh, no – yew must court me layk a gentleman, send me flowers. Now Ay must go and tell awl may friends thet Ay 'ave met yew.'

And she was gone again, leaving me holding my prop bag in one hand and trying to suppress my libido with the other. I did not even know her name.

The following noon, I searched the crowd through the slits of my performance mask, but she wasn't there. Nor did she appear the next day, and I had written the encounter off as a spoof when on the third day, a lilting voice caught my ear as the crowd moved away.

'Ay'm sorry thet Ay hev mayde yew wayt, but we had problems at the hospital with a heart paytient and Doctor Barnard wouldn't let me gao.'

'Doctor Barnard, the heart transplanter?'

'Yiis,' she sighed. 'He iis a wonderful maan, and Ay'm suo proud to work with him.'

'And while we're dropping names, what's yours?'

'Shrinithea,' she said, blushing again.

Shrinithea. Shrinny ...

This time we had tea, and Shrinithea allowed me to ride with her on the bus on her way back to work. Her car, she said, was due out of the shop that weekend, and when she got it back she would take me for a drive along the coast and treat me to a luxury seafood meal. Still unsure whether I should believe her or not, but having nothing to lose, I gave her directions to my garage abode and we set a date. The appointed day arrived, and then the appointed hour. Nothing. I waited for another hour, then two, and finally gave up and started to work on some new Shakespearean text. Four hours after the hour of our date, there was a knock on the door. I opened it to find her standing there, wearing lipstick .

'Soorry,' she said, 'Ay trayd to call – the hospital, yew knaow ...'

'Let's go,' I suggested. 'We can still watch the sun set over the sea.'

'Soorry,' she said, 'Ay 'ad another acciident with the car – may parents will be furious ...'

'Well, why don't you come inside, then.'

'Ay daon't knaow ...Yew might try and kiss me.'

'Damn right I will.'

I clasped her by the wrist and brought her into my hut, put my arms around her and bent my head to plant my lips on hers. There was no response. Zero.

'Seee?' she remarked mechanically. 'Ay don't knaow how.'

'Well, then this is lesson number one.'

Smooching is supposed to be fun, a delight in and of itself or a prelude to greater things to come, and I think most of us can remember the first adolescent brushing of lips that passed for passion, and then the first encounter with another tongue. There was none of that now. Not only would my odd admirer not let me plant a decent smacker, but neither would she get up and go. After an excruciating hour – or two or three or four – I suggested she leave so I might do the things that all saints must do to keep their sanity.

'See yew tomorrow,' she said.

'What for?'

'Lesson number tew.'

I did not think I would ever see her again, but the next day she was back. And this time, after a quick repetition of yesterday's blank reluctance, she opened her lips to mine. Although it all seemed rather tired and contrived, I responded the way men instinctively do: I put my hand upon her breast.

'Oh, that's what yew want!' she said, icicles forming in her eyes.

'Yes,' I said, forcing my hand up her blouse and inside her brassiere. I met such real resistance that at one point I felt as if I were in the early stages of date-rape, and stopped.

'Why are you here?' I demanded.

'Because Ay luv yew,' she said.

'You don't know who I am.'

'And yew do not know who Ay am.'

The next day I picked her up and carried her to my bed. It was all very clinical and sophomoric, with me doing all the kissing.

'Damn you!' I shouted at last. 'What do you want from me! You come over every day as if you were condemned to do this, and never even smile! I can beat off and get the same results! What about some sharing, a little reciprocity, a little love!'

'But I do luv yew.'

'Then goddamn show it!'

'How?'

Unable to stand it anymore, I announced that graduation was at hand.

'Nao, Ay cannot!' she shrieked.

'Why?!'

'Because ... because ...'

With tears in her eyes, she attempted to explain how all those years of being a virgin had 'wasted her', according to her doctor friends, and that she was 'all dry down there'. I gave her other pleasure options, which she performed in such a perfunctory manner as to nearly void libidinal joy.

'Tomorrow is our day,' she promised, as she disappeared again into the night.

The next day my South African hippie landlord confronted me in the garden.

'What are you doing with that Coloured girl every day?'

'What do you mean, "Coloured girl"?'

'Well, I mean that girl who comes here every day, she's Coloured, and what you are doing is against the law.'

'Coloured?'

'Look at her teeth, you fool – and by the way, I'd watch your wallet.'

Suddenly worried about my stashed bag of emeralds, I decided it was high time to confront my landlord on the issue.

'You trying to call my girl a thief?' I demanded, a little surprised at my defensiveness while casting my suspicions away from Shrinithea and onto him. 'What are you doing, snooping around my things?'

'Well, Mister Shakespeare,' said the landlord, 'I'd like you to remember that it's my garage, and you are making me liable to prosecution under the non-association act of apartheid. On that note, I'd appreciate it if you'd move.'

'I'll be out by the weekend.'

'Fine.'

That evening I waited, waited and waited some more. Shrinithea didn't show. Nor did she the next day, nor the next. I was packing my bags, convinced that it had all been an act designed to drive me into sexual lunacy while she grabbed my pot of green gold (why did I ever show her the emeralds in the first place?) when I heard a familiar knock on the door.

It was Shrinithea. She looked more than disheveled. She looked beat up, walking as though she had just dismounted from her first horse.

'What happened, babe?' I asked.

'Ay was in the hospiital, but as a payshunt,' she said.

'Why?'

Shrinithea then related how she had been out cold for the past forty-eight hours, heavily anesthetized as Christiaan Barnard and his expert staff inserted a slowly expanding tube into her vagina to solve her problem. Natural penetration, she had been told, would simply have been too dangerous.

'Ay wanted yew!' wailed Shrinithea. 'But Ay just lost may virginity to a machine!'

All thoughts of my missing millions of dollars in green emeralds were gone. I joked and laughed and felt stripped of one of man's peculiar ego pleasures. Then we uncorked a bottle of local Cabernet, undressed one another and made love like I have never made love before or almost since, waking after hours of half-conscious ecstasy, Shrinithea's eyes rolled back in their sockets, the vacant smile of one lost in pleasure for the first time stretched long and languid across her Cupid's face. Again, out of my haze, I noticed what looked like bruises on her breasts that certainly had not come from my attentions. I kissed one blue spot.

'Oww,' Shrinithea pulled back. 'Daon't touch me there – it hurts.'

'What are these marks?'

'Oh, nothing, nothing,' she said, pulling me to her again.

An hour, or two, or five later, we pulled on our clothes.

'Ay don't ever want to do it with anyone else, ever,' she whispered.

I walked her towards the bus stop, and then she turned and grabbed me. 'Let's go to Namibia tewgether – yew and me,' she said, with insistence.

'Namibia?' I asked. 'Why?'

'Because ... because there are less problems there.'

It was as close as she ever came to admitting the race business: Namibia, though still under South African control, had recently scrapped its no-sex-between-the-races legislation, and had become a haven for interracial couples under apartheid in South Africa.

'Maybe, honey,' I said. 'But I have to travel for a few weeks, maybe a month, and then we'll talk about it when I get back.'

'Yew're going away?'

'Yeah, I've got some gigs in Durban and Transkei, but I'll be back and then we'll go to Namibia. That is, if you don't have a new boyfriend, now that you're not so afraid of men anymore.'

'Yew will be the only one, forever ...' She reached up and put her arms around me. 'Ay love yew, my darling.'

'I think I love you too.'

But time can be a vicious companion, and this was one of those times when the past is better buried than restored to the light of day. The reader will have to forgive me for rolling the clock forward over time-line violations, other hard knocks and general plot development, because none of those literary devices happen to serve the particular instance. Suffice it to say that no sooner had I returned to Cape Town after a spin through other parts of South Africa than I found myself painting some pal's gallery in exchange for a room to stay in, and looking out the picture window at a sex doll walking down the street dressed in a low-cut pink blouse, skintight red jeans and bright lipstick framing two gaudy golden teeth, front dentures for her upper jaw. It was, of course, Shrinithea.

'Darling!' she cried, almost as embarrassed at seeing me doused in paint as I was smelling her doused in perfume. 'Aren't yew goying to kiiss yewr honey?'

We had a scene, the salient details of which are these: she tried to give me oral sex on a park bench, and then ran before I came. I followed her, and forced her into a car for a drive and talk. She bolted and ran, and I hunted her through the dusk and then the night until I finally ran her down at a dumpy whorehouse dive where she hid in a back room while her lady pimp tried to keep me in line.

'Thet Coloured girl has been werkin' fer us for at least a year, mister,' said the madam. 'Why yer so upset defies me.'

I waited in the filthy foyer until Shrinithea saw I was looking the other way. Then she broke and ran down the midnight street, away from me. I followed, and finally caught her in the arms of a sailor outside a bar in the area that all port cities boast.

'Shrinny!!' I cried, drunk with pain and the burden of realization that life can never be so simple as the naive believe. '*Why, why, why!*'

'Ay loved yew,' she said, as the sailor dragged her away towards the venue of a one-hour stand. 'Believe me, Ay loved yew.'

Howl, oh howl ...

I thought I would either go nuts or kill someone, maybe myself, but just roamed the night streets, weeping and wondering *why o why o why* had I been chosen to play this particular role in someone else's private tragedy, or trick. Twenty years later, late at night, sometimes I think it was all because Shrinithea just wanted to have one or two moments of joy before the miserable life she saw or sensed stretching out before her kicked in and robbed her of even those fantasies. Was I just the gullible guy who happened to be selected to provide illusion, or the leading actor on Shrinithea's private stage? Like Jaques from *As You Like It*, I rapidly fell into a state of utter misery.

> I have neither the scholar's melancholy, which is emulation; nor the musician's, which is fantastical; nor the courtier's, which is proud; nor the soldier's, which is ambitious; nor the lawyer's, which is political; nor the lady's, which is nice; nor the lover's, which is all of these; but it is a melancholy all mine own, compounded of many simples, extracted from many objects.

He was sitting on a park bench in Green Market Square, writing a letter. I snuck up behind him to read over his shoulder, and discovered the letter was addressed to me.

'Looks like I have just missed you for the last time,' the letter began.

The author detailed the times and places we had almost met – Lusaka, Llilongwe, Livingston, Lesotho and even, it would seem, the Limpopo River border point which divided South Africa from Rhodesia. He always had been where I just was, two or three days or a week before or after me. He had heard of my antics; we might even have slept with some of the same women. Did I remember that chick Nancy from New Jersey? But now, alas, the Stanley-seeks-Livingston tag team act was about to come to an end. He was flying back to the States the next day on a one-way ticket acquired on the Zambian black market which he had purchased for a fraction of the normal price, and which was bringing him from Lusaka to Cape Town and then to Rio, Jamaica and finally Miami and Minneapolis for a song. He recommended that I try and find a similar deal myself. More to the point, it was a pity – a tragedy, in fact – that we would not be able to see each other, after more than a year of roaming around the Dark Continent and on the same highways and byways. There was so much to say, but it was so difficult to put down on paper ...

'Doctor Livingston, I presume?' I said, resting a hand on my brother's shoulder.

Eddy's jaw dropped, his tongue wagged – but no words save one were forthcoming.

'You!...'

The record of the rest is best left to the eavesdroppers among the passersby, fans, fishermen, floozies and sundry others who peopled our lives over the next forty-eight hours. We did the day town and the night town, the public and the private. There was, of course, a Green Market Square performance he had to sit through, which almost sundered our fraternity forever: an attractive white woman approached me at the end of the show and announced that she, too, was a thespian of the Shakespearean persuasion, and just might consider joining her Taylor to my Burton. Then Eddy intervened, cuckolding me with his guitar, as it were.

'Ouch,' said I.

'Get used to it,' he replied.

'Have, for more than twenty years,' I retorted, as I watched them waltz out the door, arm in arm and hands on ass.

I told myself that it would also be the last time that I would ever lay eyes on him in my life.

But it was not our final parting. We arranged to meet the next day and more or less tried to pretend that nothing untoward had happened.

Then, on the morning of the day he left, we took the cable car up to the top of Table Mountain, staring at the fabulous city below, the distant Robben Island to the south and the seemingly limitless reaches of the twin Indian and Atlantic Oceans to east and west. 'Better do it before we don't,' said Eddy, employing a classic North Dakota reality line. It means: 'Now.'

'Yeah,' I replied. 'It's time to go.'

We moved towards the cable car station in the curdling clouds.

'You know, my life is different now,' said Eddy. 'Africa.'

'Yeah,' I said. We continued chatting in code as we descended from the mountain to the city, each obscure fraternal word imbued with meanings no one around us could possibly have understood.

'Hmmph.'

'Burp.'

'Fart.'

'Hmmph.'

Then we took the bus to the airport, embracing in a manner that might have had a touch of Ignatius in it but which most folks at Cape Town's international airport probably did not notice because Donnelly descendants from Dakota, even those wandering around Africa, don't go overboard with such stuff.

'See you,' said Eddy. 'Take care and don't get kilt.'

'You, too,' I replied.

Is this what Stanley felt when he finally ran down Dr Livingston on the Zambezi? A final embrace and then Eddy went west while I turned the corner, heading north.

It was, when all was said and done, so very *disappointing*.

FOURTEEN

Sand-surfing in Swakopmund

The Dakota waffled on the air cushion for a moment and then dipped to go in for a second, closer look. We were chasing a herd of gazelle.

'Hey Bard,' called the captain, who had offered me the lift from the Namibian capital city, Windhoek. 'Shall we go back and take another peek?'

Why not? Aside from the pilot's mother and father-in-law I was the only passenger aboard the old plane. It started with the take-off from Windhoek, when the pilot had invited me into the cockpit, and proceeded through the next two hours of watching how the gray-green hills of central South West Africa metamorphosed into the vast, golden expanse of the Namib Desert as the plane nosed straight west. Below, we could see herds of springbok or gazelle and ostrich, if I could believe my eyes, racing from one hidden water hole to the next, or following the traces of precious moisture beneath an apparently dry seasonal creek bed to a distant explosion of green on the otherwise uniform yellow sheet of sand.

'See that,' shouted the co-pilot over the roar of the engines, pointing to one such oasis now crowded with animals. 'It's grass, fed by underground fissures – there hasn't been any rain here for years, but all of a sudden the water will bubble up and the grass will grow and flowers will bloom, and it will all be gone inside of a week!'

Then came the sheets of desert sand dunes rising like waves on a dry ocean, higher and higher. Soon we were flying over mountain ranges of shimmering, golden sand that ended in a shroud of stark, white fog running all along the horizon, where the dry heat of the desert clashed with the cold humidity of the southern Atlantic on the coast. Over and beyond the bank of fog sparkled the deep, turquoise blue of the big ocean itself.

Pinched between the burning desert and the blue sea was Swakopmund, our destination, a foggy little chunk of faux-Germany that was as cold as Kiel until you drove five miles into the surrounding desert, when God turned the oven back up to full thermal blast.

Weird ... Everything was topsy-turvy.

Swakopmund was a foggy little town that was actually cold until you drove five miles into the surrounding desert, when God turned the oven back up to full thermal blast. In addition to illegal lobster fishing off the coldwater banks (you could not get a lobster in town; all were shipped by container to Japan or the United States on pain of high fines for poachers), there was the commercial harvesting of sea lions and seals nesting along the rocky coast as well as hunting the vast animal herds in the nearby Entosha Plains, all making for a large (and stinking) tanning industry in the town. Deep-sea diving and sand-dune skiing drew a certain type of adventure tourist, and many stayed on, attracted by the frontier spirit and sense of being at the very end of the earth. But the main pull of Swakopmund remained nearly unspoken, for it was government business, and rather sensitive: *uranium*, the stuff that fires fancy reactors that need no coal or gas, and the stuff that goes into nuclear bombs. Where was the yellow cake shipped? No one knew, or at least no one who knew was talking. There were persistent rumors that South Africa was 'assisting' Israel in this regard. There was also the persistent rumor that Pretoria was working on its own 'apartheid' bomb – although whom the government would drop it on was never adequately answered: if you bombed Soweto, you would automatically shower Jo'burg with radioactive dust. Whatever the truth about the identities and intentions of the end-users, one thing was perfectly clear in little Swakopmund: uranium was quite simply the stuff that made the town tick, and like a Geiger counter. A popular belief was that the place was so totally irradiated that it made people stay on and on and on, as if one's living tissue became addicted to the invisible nuclear bath.

Swakopmund certainly got an irrational grip on me, anyway. I planned on spending a week, but lingered on long after drifting towards a mitigated asceticism I could neither describe then or now.

I quit smoking. I stopped drinking. I became a vegetarian. I hung with would-be Buddhists, watering sandbox gardens just to watch things grow in the mineral-rich dune sand brought in from the desert. Evenings meant driving out to the sea of sand and climbing to the very highest ridges of the towering dunes and waiting for the setting sun to create a shivering and shimmering scarlet sea from horizon to horizon when the fading light hit the crushed garnet, diamond and ruby crystal motes that made up the swirling sand beneath our feet. As the burning red orb of the sun extinguished itself in the ocean to the west, a full moon rose in the east, replicating the lost, long shadows cast by the sun in mirror image. We danced and spun and tumbled down the sand dunes, ants in a sandbox, cackling at our meagerness and at the desert's might, shit-eating grins stitched from right to left over our faces, running and slipping and sliding down mile-high yellow dunes, tiny, utterly insignificant specks in the greater scheme of things, irradiated by uranium ...

Something very elemental was at play here, or else I was cracking up.

You might say that my homeward journey had begun a fortnight before, along the banks of the Orange River, about three days and 300 kilometers out of Cape Town, when a man in a van stopped to pick me up and ferry me north into the Protectorate of South West Africa, better known as Namibia.

'Say – aren't you that chappie who does Shakespeare in the streets?'

My notoriety had spread to the Namib Desert.

I jumped in the van. It was filled with hundreds of shoeboxes, all containing one style of pump, and a young black youth squatting among the mess.

'Blighters!' crowed the shoe salesman, congratulating himself for his brush with fame. 'I saw you on the telly, I did – and here you are in my van! It is you, isn't it?'

'Yeah.'

We passed over the Orange River and the South African frontier, but there was no sign or customs post to greet us – just an inexplicable sense that we had just left civilization behind. The neat and tidy Dutch farms of the Cape gave way to a Nevada-like landscape of pastel vistas painted in sand and rock and framed by distant buttes, and docile herds of grazing cattle on pasture replaced by springboks and gazelles bouncing across the endless plain.

This was the land of the disappearing Fish River, which never reached the sea; of the Skeleton Coast, where the shifting sands dragged stranded ships twenty miles inland. It was the land of salt flats the size of Belgium, populated by millions of pink flamingos. It was a place of the mysterious swamps of the Kalahari, where water rose from nowhere and then fell back, leaving a meadow of exploding color and fermenting plants and drunken elephants. It was the country with the most bizarre and delicate ecosystems on the planet, of insect-frog-and-snake food chains living in the burning sands of the world's oldest desert, the Namib – a 1,000-mile moonscape running along the Atlantic coast from South Africa to the Angolan frontier, virtually without a trace of vegetation and broken only by the fleeting shapes of ostriches dashing through the shimmering distance. It was also the land of the South West Africa People's Organization (SWAPO), a guerrilla group that had joined the alphabet soup of liberation armies up and down the continent – ANC, ANU, BANO, TANU, ZAPU and ZANU, to name but a few – determined to bring an end to white colonial regimes.

'Terrorists, baby killers, that's what they are,' growled the shoe salesman, whose name was Neal. 'Run around up in the north they do, until the Defense Force tracks 'em down and kills 'em. And my assistant is one of 'em, I swear. He goes home to Ovamboland every two months and marches around in the bush with an AK-47. Then he comes back here all smiles. Someday he'll slit my throat and run off with my goods and put all my new boots on all the feet of the bloody terrorists, the little bloody blighter.'

I peeked in the rear-view mirror for a glimpse of the terrorist: the chubby face smiled back through naive-looking eyes.

'Well, if you're so afraid of him why don't you fire him?'

'Can't,' sighed Neal. 'Then he'd come after me. It's safer to stay on good terms.'

The relationship between the itinerant shoe salesman and his suspected terrorist assistant was becoming increasingly difficult due to the simple fact that our throats were totally parched. Our engine was going through a nuclear meltdown, too, with the thermostat deep in the red. Neal pulled over to add some water to the radiator. I climbed out and nearly wilted in the full blast of the heat. The temperature must have gone up by 40 degrees since morning, and it was so hot that the tar joints of the highway had melted into fudge that clung to my shoes and made a sick, spitting sound when I picked up my feet. A road sign read: 'The Tropic of Capricorn, 235 Kilometers; The Equator, 1720 Kilometers; The Tropic of Cancer, 3541 Kilometers ...' We were a long way from anywhere but also exactly right where we really were.

Once, with the gas gauge dropping towards empty and a good hundred miles until the next hamlet identified on the map, we turned off the main highway to buy some fuel from an ostrich rancher. He fed us a single egg omelet (one ostrich egg is more than enough for three) and told us in relentless detail the story of how he had lost his right arm at Stalingrad.

'Alles, alles, für den Führer!' he bellowed, waving a shank of arm that ended above the elbow in the air for effect.

I asked Neal why he spoke German and not Afrikaans.

'Because Namibia is Little Germany in the sand,' was his reply.

Indeed, Namibia was that rarest of political entities: a leftover nugget of Kaiser Wilhelm's effor to match the British, French, Dutch, Spanish, Portugese and Belgian overseas empires of the late nineteenth century, when raising the flag over every last piece of real estate in the world (whether steaming malarial swamp, semi-dormant volcano island or sparsely inhabited desert) was regarded as appropriate behaviour for White Man's Burden-seeking Europeans. For the Germans, alas, the colonial quest started late and ended early. After Wilhelm's defeat in 1918, German colonies in Africa and Asia were quickly snapped up by the victors, who then moved to extirpate all traces of the hated Hun. The one exception was 'South West', namely Namibia, which the League of Nations turned over to the Anglophile authorities of South Africa as a 'mandate' to theoretically guide to independence. But whatever policy of de-*Deutsching* Namibia might have existed was soon thrown out when South Africa was, in effect, taken over by the Anglophobe, apartheid-loving Afrikaaners. The Afrikaaners loved the Germans, or at least wanted to use them as a foil against the perfidious Brits. The result was that the German colonialists stayed and even thrived in the forgotten sands of South West, and with every passing day it became more German than Germany itself. I noticed an inordinate number of amputees among the over-fifty crowd.

The capital of the vast non-state called 'South-West Africa' was Windhoek, a German *burg* located thousands of miles from anybody's last German Reich or Republic. The main drag was named Kaiserstrasse. It ran down to the Wienerwald Restaurant Hotel. *Schnell Imbiss* joints serving *Schnitzel-und-Pommes Frites* stayed open late into the night. The grocery stores and markets sold a dozen types of *wurst* and a score or more of different delicious cheeses found nowhere else in Africa, while the type of pastry served in the *Konditorien* scattered around downtown would delight the heart of any Munich matron. The city celebrated *Oktoberfest* in May, the seasonal equivalent in the Southern Hemisphere. Bookstores carried less an international assortment of newspapers and magazines than stacks of *Bild, Quick* and *Stern,* while the shelves themselves were crammed with German classics ranging from Schiller and Goethe to Brecht and Grass. Traffic, too, was *sehr-Deutsch*: the orderly German drivers of German cars took care to avoid the law-abiding pedestrians who always waited until the light turned green before they set foot off the curb. I was scolded for jaywalking.

But temperature and climate dictated that Windhoek would always remain an African town. The coconut palms, flame trees and brazen lilac bushes grew out of control, as did the flowerbeds in the middle of the wide, would-be imperial streets. There was just too much sun to keep growth under control. And there was also another element that was growing by leaps and bounds, and to the great chagrin of the good German burghers of Windhoek town – the African population. While city center was mainly white – Germans, Afrikaners and some English – Windhoek was ringed by squalid shantytowns, which in turn were split along tribal lines – Ovambos from the north and Herreros from the east, with a mixture of Bushmen from Botswana and the descendants of Hottentot, known as the *Bastars*, thrown in for ethnic spice. The rural tribal youths were going modern, evolving (or devolving) into urban gangs along clannish lines, and pitched battles between different groups were not uncommon.

My source for this information was a young Windhoek lawyer of German descent by the name of Anton Lubowski. We had met on the Great Steps of Cape Town University a few months earlier after one of my many performances there, and he told me that he was particularly taken with my effort to inject contemporary politics into the plays. The reason for this was that he himself was engaged politically, and was going back to his native Namibia to join the process of creating a state. I assumed from our discussions that this meant he was involved in a coalition of liberal whites, Coloureds/Bastars and conservative Namibian tribal leaders, who were working out details of a new constitution designed to ease Namibia out of the embrace of South Africa but not sever all links. Accordingly, when I dropped by his house in Windhoek I was rather taken aback when he began to badmouth neo-liberals as people only interested in keeping Namibia in political limbo. At first, I thought this meant that Anton was really a closet member of some ultra-conservative, neo-Fascist organization. Confusion reached the level of alarm, however, when he discretely confessed his real allegiance: Anton Lubowski was a card-carrying member of the baby-killing, Marxist-Leninist, mayhem-making organization called SWAPO.

'I didn't think whites could, you know, belong ...' I said.

Anton sighed, then lectured me about the number of whites who were members of that other, highly illegal terrorist organization in South Africa, namely, the African National Congress of Nelson Mandela, which was devoted to overthrowing apartheid rule in South Africa.

'The point is that one has to take a moral stand,' said Anton as his pregnant, silent and visibly nervous wife served us up some fine German chow. 'Even if SWAPO is not perfect, it does represent the voice of the majority of Namibians and is the only organization resisting absorption into South Africa. Namibia is not South Africa, and we don't want to become part of it. We are white and black and Bastar – and we all must learn to become Namibians and live together as citizens of a new nation.'

Sadly, Anton Lubowski never saw that day: a year later, on the eve of the United Nations-sponsored elections and the lowering of ·Pretoria's flag over Windhoek, he was assassinated by white right-wing radicals determined to turn back the clock ticking towards the birth of a multi-ethnic, democratic and independent Namibia.

Bis dann, Herrschaft, bis dann ...

As chance would have it, Windhoek's cultural association, or *Kulturverein*, of which Anton and his wife were also members, was sponsoring a 'Shakespeare Day' in a few weeks' time. Using his influence, Anton managed to get me included in the event – which soon became 'Shakespeare Week', replete with readings, lectures, and a Center Stage Show featuring yours truly.

Having time to kill before my debut and encouraged by Anton to get out and explore his country, I decided to mosey on up to amboland to see what I could see of SWAPO.

In retrospect, I guess I should be grateful that I got back alive.

The road north out of Windhoek towards the Angolan frontier traversed land so oblate that rivers ran both ways, depending on which end last saw rain. The towns I passed through scarcely deserved the name, save for the fact that they were there, had a store, maybe a bar, and a jail. Given the dearth of hotels, I usually found myself asking for incarceration every night, simply to find an enclosed place to sleep.

There was also a singular absence of traffic, and as a result I simply took every ride I got to the end of the line, no matter where it was going. It was by this method that I managed to slip into Ovamboland. I had been repeatedly told that the vast, semi-desert place was a no-go area, where one needed special permits to even walk down the streets of the occasional town, let alone amble along the mine-laced roads; that said, permits were almost impossible to obtain for the very good reason that the South African security forces did not really want anybody witnessing what they were doing: trying to eradicate SWAPO using the tried-and-true method of 'pacifying' villages behind barbed wire and killing anyone who moved around at night. Thus I was rather surprised when I woke up in the back seat of a car driven by two South African businessmen inside the security zone.

'Well, here you are!' said the driver, pulling to a stop in front of a market area.

'Where are we?' I mumbled, sitting up in the back seat.

'Rehoboth,' said the man in the passenger seat.

'But isn't that inside the no-go zone?' I asked.

'That's right,' said the driver, with whom I had been having a rather spirited discussion about apartheid and the future of Namibia before dozing off. 'Have a good time with your friends in SWAPO!'

With a cackle they were off, and I found myself on the fringe of the local market, the only non-African for miles. Hundreds of dark and sullen eyes turned towards me.

I felt very white.

I flagged down a pickup and got in the cab. The problem was that it was moving in the general direction of the Angolan frontier. The driver, a black priest, apparently assumed I was a South African Special Forces man on my way back to my unit, because when he discovered my true mission – that I had none – he exploded with the sort of moral indignation that only morally indignant priests can have.

'Are you insane?' he shouted. 'Have you no respect for life? If not your own, mine? Are you aware that you have put me in jeopardy by associating with you? Get out!'

Thus I found myself walking alone and unarmed in the middle of guerrilla-filled Ovamboland, a place where white men were not supposed to be unless they were hunting terrorists or being hunted themselves. A boy rode by on a donkey, staring at me, not waving. In the middle distance, two men appeared, walking across a field in my direction. Clutching my walking stick like a weapon I posed like a sentry, muzzle in profile – the same stupid trick I had pulled in Rhodesia, which did not seem so cute now. That I had made an enormous blunder was perfectly clear to me. I had no business being in the security zone, period.

I had turned around and begun the long walk back to the relative safety of Rehoboth, when I heard the musical whine of a truck, headed my way. Standing in the middle of the road, I began to wave as the vehicle approached. It was a pea-green, camouflaged armored personnel carrier belonging to the South African army. The APC ground to a halt, and out of the back leapt about a dozen African boys no older than fifteen. They trained their automatic weapons at me. Then the door to the cab opened, and three white men dismounted. I felt a wave of relief.

'Hi, guys,' I said. 'I'm on my way to –'

'This is a restricted area,' said one of the South Africans. 'Let's see your papers.'

'Maybe he's a Cuban,' suggested another. 'Let's waste him, now.'

'But I know him!' said the third. 'This is Mister Shakespeare from the telly!'

My admirer turned out to be an English literature student in

Jo'burg doing his service on the frontier, and it was soon old home week there on the road.

'You were great on television,' said my fan. 'I really liked that bit with the dog.'

'Thanks ...'

'And your Hamlet, man. I once played Polonius in school.'

We could have carried on chatting about the Bard for hours – but the other two South African officers thought it a best to get back to camp.

'Hey, let's go,' said one.

'What about me?' I asked lamely.

The three looked at each other and then back at me.

'We can't very well fucking leave him here,' said my fan.

'But its against the regs,' said another.

'Look,' said the second South African, scowling. 'I'll get you up to D-Base. After that you are on your own.'

Those who have never had the pleasure of riding in an Armoured Personnel Carrier or APC don't know what fun they're missing. Metal hooks and braces stick out from every flat surface, presumably to hang ammunition and helmets on, but likely just to remind soldiers that they are worth less than dirt in the eyes of their superiors: it is impossible not to whack your head while bouncing along a bad road. Then again, an APC is not designed for style or comfort. It is designed to protect those inside it from flying pieces of steel like bullets or shrapnel, and, to a lesser extent, from direct explosions applied to its thick metal surface.

In later years I would spend quite a bit of time inside or on top of the Soviet-style APC known as a BTR, as well as the US military equivalent, the Humvee, famously now favored by wealthy sportsmen who believe that pseudo-military transportation enhances their masculinity. But this was my first ride ever aboard an APC, so I studied it with care and asked a lot of questions. The most noticeable thing was that the bottom of the chassis was shaped like a V. Enquiring why this was so, I was informed that the unique V-shape, while making the vehicle top-heavy and thus problematic in terms of performing sharp turns, was specifically designed to allow the vehicle to negotiate mined roads like the one we were on. The theory, based on experience, was that if the vehicle hit a mine the explosion would blow off a wheel, but the blast would ricochet up the side, possibly overturning the vehicle but leaving the passengers alive even if they ended up hanging from the ceiling. At exactly the moment this was being explained, there was a thud and a crash and the APC lurched to its side.

'*Contact!*' howled one of the white officers. '*Move, move, move!*'

Pandemonium broke out as the Home Guards whacked their fists into their release buckles and then piled helter-skelter out of the ass-end of the vehicle, blazing away with their M-16s at the unseen foe. *Wham-whama-wham-whama-wham-wham-wham!*

'Hold your fire!' screamed one of the officers. Then there was silence while the dust settled and the Home Guard lads formed a defensive ring.

'Shit,' said another white officer.

The ambush appeared to be nothing more than one of the heavy fenders having cracked its weld and fallen off. The 'explosion' we had assumed to have been the blast of a mine was nothing more than the clatter and bang of shoddy workmanship, and everyone was looking at each other sheepishly for having wasted so much ammunition in response to what was nothing more than the equivalent of a flat tire.

The fender was lugged into the back of the APC, and off we roared, arriving at the D-Base perimeter at sunset. There was a huge hole in the road in front of the guard post.

'Shit,' said an officer. 'That wasn't here yesterday.'

'Yeah,' said the sentry. 'The terrorists mined it and we blew it when we went off to help Company B last night. Regular friggin' ambush.'

'Anybody buy it?'

'That new kid from Durban, but we got 'em back good. Twelve terrs and a Fidel.'

(Translation: the South Africans had mounted an illegal revenge raid into neighboring Angola and killed twelve SWAPO guerrillas, including a Cuban advisor.)

'So who's this guy?' another sentry asked, waving his gun at me. 'Captive?'

'Na – he's just a tourist,' said one of my escorts, and a nasty guffaw passed around me.

'No hotels up here, mate,' chuckled one soldier.

'And no late-night bus service anywhere but to heaven.'

'Yeah,' said one of the men from the APC. 'Where do you plan on staying?'

'Well, I'm not sure it's really a good idea to hang out with you guys, I mean, what if you get attacked tonight?' I lamely replied.

They all laughed battle-hardened laughs at that one, and I felt stupid and small.

'That's good, mate,' said the camouflaged sentry. 'That's rich. Pitch your tent by the side of the road and have your own balls for dinner. SWAPO specialty.'

The group of soldiers began walking around the mine blast into their camp.

'HEY!' I shouted after the men, 'Don't leave me here!'

The response was a malicious cackle.

'So, you decided to stay at our house tonight, eh?'

The commander was less than delighted at my unexpected arrival, but short of condemning me to death by refusing me a safe place to camp, there wasn't much to do but wait until morning to get rid of me. Meanwhile, he had some organizing to do: it was 'last light', the time when guerrillas like best to attack because they can see what they're doing in the falling dusk and still have the whole night to escape into. The South African soldiers and the contingent of Home Guards filed off to their posts on the camp periphery, and I was left alone in the mess with the camp's mascot to wait through the night. We were both baboons, but I was clearly a step or two lower in intellectual development: I had chosen to come here; my mate was chained to a tree. Then it began to rain, and it rained until dawn, when the mud-caked soldiers straggled back to the mess for coffee and stale biscuits, soaked and weary to the bone but delighted to be alive.

'Having fun yet?' One of the grimy lads asked me.

That next day was spent worrying about mines. The problem was that they came in all shapes and sizes, and were hidden under bogus tire treads, leaves, small branches and piles of dung. There were even crank mines, so that not the first, second or third wheel to drive over them would trigger the explosion, but the fourth or fifth, long after all trace of planting had been effaced. Soldiers often drove cows down the roads in front of them; if a beast stepped on a mine, at least they'd enjoy a meal. Progress was slow.

My own progress was completely dependent on transport provided by the security forces. They did not assist me because they liked me so much as that the only way to get rid of me was to bring me further and further down the road and bunk me down in the next camp before bundling me off with the next transport going further on. One night I stayed at a generator complex built on the side of a fabulously beautiful lake reservoir; the station had been hit by a rocket attack the night before, with one un-exploded missile still embedded in the concrete ceiling over my bunk. It was all very frightening but there wasn't much to do except hang out with the boys and try and keep from flipping out.

'You're utterly and absolutely nuts to be here,' said the English literature student, who did not want to talk about Hamlet anymore. 'I've got one friggin' week left and I don't know if I can take it.'

I can't say that I made lifelong friends among the soldiers, but as the days went on they grew to trust me and in so doing talked about a range of different issues, maybe just out of a sense of loneliness and the relief I afforded because I was a civilian. They were lawyers and doctors and teachers and farmers and factory workers, brought into the army in a staggered conscription system that put them six months in and then six months out, and many confessed to being totally confused about fighting and killing for a country that was not their own. Why were they there? For apartheid? To save South Africa from Communism? To ensure democratic elections in Namibia? For De Beers diamonds?

'This is our bloody Vietnam,' I was told more than once.

The ride with the rangers ended at the Ruacana Falls power plant, located on the Angolan frontier. The falls were dry, and the generators idle: the Angolans had diverted the river, rendering the entire project useless. The real excitement came when I ran into an Angolan border patrol on the other side of the chicken-wire fence delineating the international frontier, and a shootout was only averted at the last moment. When word got back to the local commander, I was escorted to a lone semi-trailer truck scheduled to travel that day and expelled from the frontier area. I cannot say I was sorry to go.

I arrived back in Windhoek a couple of days before my debut at the Shakespeare *Woche,* and the *Kulturverein* booked me into the Wienerwald Hotel, where I spent the next twenty-four hours staring at the walls. It was starting to get too confusing: staying with a marked white man in the SWAPO leadership before rolling off to entertain South African troops on the frontier and being fêted by a bunch of culture-conscious ex-Nazis the next. There were too many hats to wear, too many roles to play. Anton Lubowski, the white terrorist; the Shrinithea thing; the long-toothed whore in the whorehouse crash pad whose sisters had stolen my shell-encrusted cane; the huge disappointment in finally finding Brother Eddy; my insane ego burnt and bruised by more than a year in Africa exposing myself as a freak/genius performer of marginal cultural goods; the butcher, the baker, the candlestick maker ...

I was starting to crack up.

But onstage I was pure ice. All of culture-conscious Windhoek turned out for my series of performances and lectures, and I did not let them down. After a public calisthenics and vocal warm-up session, I launched into my first act consisting of the now familiar Launce, Shylock and Hamlet monologues interspersed with the obligatory Othello/Desdemona puppet dialogue as well as Mister and Missus Macbeth chatting about Duncan's impending doom. To lighten the load, I chipped in some *Midsummer Night* and 'Meditations on Virginity', thinking of Shrinithea.

The second act opened with King Henry's charge, followed by Richard II in prison, Lady Macbeth's 'Raven' monologue and then Mercutio's Queen Mab madness from *Romeo and Juliet*. My various introductions and social commentaries had been honed over time, and had become an integral part of the presentation, ranging in tone from the 'Caesar is Biko' and 'Prospero is Cecil Rhodes' school of political harangue to what might be generically termed 'Shakespearean lore'.

'There is the story of the Elizabethan groupie who craved the ardor of Richard Burbage, Shakespeare's leading man,' I intoned. 'The fair lady arranged a tryst with Burbage, and told him to knock at her door at the assigned hour and declare himself "Richard III". However, Shakespeare, knowing of the plan, showed himself at the lady's door first and she, being equally impressed with him, took him to bed. When Burbage arrived after the deed of darkness had been done, he sent word that "Richard III" was present – to which Shakespeare replied from within the chamber: "William the Conqueror came before Richard III" ...'

Harharhar!

At the reception that followed, an attractive German woman walked up with a cash advance, begging me to bring my show to a culturally starved German town living beyond the Namib Desert on the shores of the Atlantic, and offering me what was in effect a private plane to get there: the aforementioned empty Dakota.

And once 'there' in Swakopmund, it was starting to seem like I would never leave.

One week, two weeks, three weeks, four ...

I was at the local health-food store buying a pound of vegetarian burger for a Buddhist *Breifleis* when I saw a familiar face walk by the window and raced out of the shop in pursuit of the man I had seen on the street.

'Michael!' I called out, and the figure turned around, fear etched on his face.

It was indeed Michael, the South African drug-dealer whom I had first met at the al-Manzura in Nairobi and then recently in Jo'burg.

'Shh!' he whispered, attracting the attention of everyone within earshot. 'Quiet!'

'Where's Pam?' I asked, inquiring after his New Zealand companion.

'She's at home, waiting,' Michael hissed.

'Why all the secrecy?'

'Go get your stuff while I walk around the block,' he said. 'I'll explain later.'

I returned to the shop, paid my bill and got my sack of goods. Then I waited on the stoop until Michael performed his mysterious loop-around, and walked after him at a discrete distance once he gave the signal to follow. He led me through series of elaborate if obvious cutouts aimed, presumably, at throwing off a tail, ending up inside a building less than 100 yards from the shop where we had met.

'Quick, inside!' hissed Michael, and closed the door.

It was a dumpy little apartment, decorated in late-hippie style. A Jimi Hendrix poster graced one wall; a tie-dyed sheet with a peace symbol motif on another. There was a table, maybe, and perhaps a couple of chairs; in one corner lay a number of large, stuffed pillows, atop which sat Pam, working on some hippie-style macramé.

'Thomas!' she cried, leaping up to embrace me. 'We saw a poster advertising your show here, but we didn't dare go out to see it ...'

'Why?'

The pair was on the lam, big time.

'How did you recognized me?' asked Michael. 'I cut my hair ...'

I didn't have the heart to tell him that if he was trying to go incognito, he'd have to do better than a hair trim and sunglasses.

As Pam made some herbal tea, Michael related their tale of woe. After returning to Jo'burg, he had met up with an old school friend who turned out to be a police agent and set Michael up for a bust on dope-peddling charges. The cops had kicked in the doors, but Michael and Pam managed to escape through a back window and make their way via hedges and alleys to an uncle's house, where Michael hot-wired said uncle's car, leaving a note behind asking him not to regard the car as stolen, and certainly not to suggest anything of the sort to the police – even though the first thing Michael did after high-tailing it to Windhoek was to sell the hot vehicle to another old school friend, without bothering to tell him about particulars or pedigree. In the meantime, Michael was trying to convert the South African *rand* he had acquired into convertible currency, meaning dollars, *Deutschmarks* or British pounds.

Cashing in the ill-gotten gains was the problem. First, the couple could not show their passports in a bank without fear of arrest. Second, even if they could go to a bank, there was a conversion ceiling for foreign tourists of only $200 worth of *rand*; you were stuck with whatever was left – in Michael's case, thousands of dollars' worth of South African paper currency. The *rand* was legal tender almost nowhere else in the world, the exceptions being places like Zambia, where nervous white farmers might exchange even more worthless *kwacha* for the *rand* as a hedge against future migration to South Africa. The only other way to get rid of *rand* was to change them on the black market, which seemingly everybody else in South Africa and Namibia was trying to do. But Michael now saw a way out of this self-created pickle: me. 'You are an American – you can change the money in the bank!'

Patiently, I tried to explain that I was swamped with *rand* myself, and was actually in competition with him for changing the excess on the black market.

'I've got another idea,' Michael pronounced after a disappointed pause. 'What about buying something valuable to carry out with me?'

'You can buy gems here pretty cheap, if you know what you are buying,' I offered.

'It still does not get us out of here,' he countered. Then a light went on over his head.

'I've got it!' he crowed. 'We buy the gems and then rent an airplane to go sky-diving over the desert, but hijack it and have them drop us over Botswana, where we declare ourselves to be refugees from apartheid!'

'I am *not* jumping out of an airplane,' said Pam from the corner cushions. '*No.*'

'But Pam, it is our only chance ...'

'*No! No! No!*'

A nasty fight involving mutual recriminations followed. The highlights were that Michael was a spoiled brat who had seduced Pam with heroin in Afghanistan and led them both into the predicament in which they found themselves at present, and that she wished she had never met him. His argument focused on the central theme that she was a dumb cow whose material demands on him had forced him to do things he would never have done had she not been around, including the entire foolishness of coming to South Africa when he should have gone to London, and alone. The scene ended – predictably, perhaps – with Pam wailing and weeping and Michael moving over to comfort her with a pipe filled with dope. All I wanted to do was leave.

'What about something to carry us all out overland?' said Michael, including me in his new escape plan. 'Yes, yes ... we'll rent it here and junk it there and sell it for parts!'

'What are you talking about?'

'A Land Rover, yes!' cried Michael, already a free man in his dreams. 'Now, let me tell you what we're going to do ...'

I did not like what I heard. Michael wanted to rent a Land Rover in my name but with his money, then hide him and Pam under the back seats while I drove the rig across the border into Botswana. The idea was not very appealing for a number of completely obvious reasons, which I tried to explain. Michael did not like my response. He pulled his lips back over his teeth in a tremendously ugly, fake smile.

'You mercenary bastard!' he growled. 'It's the money you want, isn't it?'

I tried to explain that money had nothing to do with it.

'What's it worth, Thomas, *what's it worth!*' he demanded, flashing a wad of *rand*.

'Let me think about it a day or two,' I lied, just to get out of the apartment.

'*Now!* We leave *now!*'

'I'll get back to you, Michael.'

'I'm *begging* you ...'

'I said I'll get back to you tomorrow.'

I never did; I never could. The next day, Michael and Pam stole another car and headed out of Swakopmund. They did not get that far, relative to distances in Namibia and South Africa. Somewhere between Mariental and Keetmanshoop, they got in a single car accident that killed Pam and left Michael in police custody.

'INTERNATIONAL DRUG RING SMASHED', ran the headlines of the day.

'Nothing you could have done,' said a Buddhist guy named Ric, in whose home I had been camping. 'It was their *karma*, and their time had just come up.'

But the event remained with me, and reminded me that it was time to go. I ducked down to the South African exclave of Walvis Bay, and from there into the deep Namib Desert, camping along the bank of a dry creek bed. My sole companions were the dashing and dancing herds of springbok and ostriches. It was the first time in a year's wandering that I was alone because I wanted and needed it that way, and it was fine.

Towards evening, I noticed distant lightning as I made a campfire. Thinking nothing of it, I drew water from the last standing pool in my private seasonal creek to make some tea, and sat down to write. I wrote and wrote and threw more wood on the fire and wrote some more: babbling, cleansing, cathartic notes on life and death and fame and obscurity and love and loneliness. Then the teapot began to gurgle, so I took it off the fire – but the gurgling noise continued. It wasn't from the pot: fountains of water were spewing forth from the sand, and the dry creek bed was quickly taking on the proportions of a roaring river. I didn't so much strike camp as seize my tent and traveling gear, dragging them to the nearest high ground as the flash flood extinguished my fire and washed away everything I had not secured: a pair of well-worn sandals, several mismatched socks hanging on bramble branches, the teapot and other limited kitchen accoutrements – but not the several notebooks only just filled with my increasingly neurotic true confessions.

In the morning, I awoke on my high-ground perch. The torrent that had raged through the creek bed had once again been reduced to a few standing pools. Cleansed by the missing river, I shouldered my lighter load and pushed on through the desert, homeward bound. The morrow would be the day to leave White Africa for Black.

FIFTEEN

Friar Lawrence of the Kalahari

The highway linking Namibia to Zambia via Botswana is described on maps as a 1,000-mile, arrow-straight line. The problem is that the arrow flies straight across the Kalahari Desert and then the Okavango Swamps, two ecosystems justly celebrated for their pristine beauty and incredible animal life, but which are also famously difficult to get in and out of unless you fly a STOAL (Short Take Off And Landing) airplane or drive a Land Rover fitted with extra gas and water tanks. I owned neither, and was thus obliged to wait for the weekly water truck, hoping that it had not passed the day before my arrival on the frontier. I rapidly became an expert in the burning biological question about how beetles roll donkey dung off the road. There was nothing else to do. Memorise Shakespeare? You gotta be crazy ...

Then, towards evening, I heard the cough, spit and wheeze of a dirty engine blowing diesel smoke through an old muffler: there was a car in town, and it was coming my way! Again, the musical burp of exhaust as the invisible vehicle downshifted; then, two sparks of light penetrating the dusk. I breathed a sigh of keen disappointment: it was a South African Security Forces troop transport, olive-green and ugly. Even if it had room for a wandering Bard like myself, the ride would only go to the border, where I would be stuck again.

But there was something wrong with the military theory. The truck had a dozen extra gas containers strapped to the top, and was sporting outsized, all-terrain tires. As the vehicle ground to a halt, I noticed that the driver was sitting behind a steering wheel mounted on the left side of the vehicle, and not the right – clearly not regulation South African army issue. In non-verbal response to my assessment, the bearded driver rolled down his window and let out a blast of smoke: *Gitanes*.

'Good night, my friend!' chuckled the driver in a thick French accent. 'How are you?'

'Fine,' I replied, 'And how are you?'

'Very well, very well,' he returned.

'And where are you going?' I queried.

'France,' he calmly replied.

'You're a long way off!'

'Yes, of course, but you asked me where I am going, and that is my destination!'

'Well, then,' I said, 'How about a lift as far as Botswana?'

'Zambia, if you weesh!'

Great! It wasn't every day that you picked up a 1,000-mile ride! I threw my gear inside and climbed in, and my elation dimmed. There was no cover on the transmission box between driver and passenger seats, and the smell of diesel fuel permeated the cab. It was going to be a very long 1,000 miles indeed.

'My name is Marc,' shouted the Frenchman over the roar of the engine, throwing the vehicle into gear and offering me one of his cigarettes.

'*Merci*,' I begged off. 'I quit about a month ago.'

'I weesh that I could queet as well,' he replied, with exaggerated 'ee' sounds in any word that would take them. 'But my worries are manee ...'

'Sorry, I am pretty low on dough myself and –'

'What? No, no!' he laughed. 'I do not talk about *monee*, I talk about my worries being *manee*!'

'Oh,' I countered, corrected. 'But what worries could you have? Your vehicle is like a traveling hotel.'

'Yes,' he confessed with a proud smile. 'We have refrigerator, oven – everything.'

'We?'

'Yes – my girlfriend, she is in the back.'

'Sleeping?'

'No, she is hiding. Tomorrow, we shall have to steal her under zee bordair. You and me!'

'I beg your pardon?'

'She is a Zulu, and she wishes to be free.'

Marc laughed and allowed the words to sink in.

Perhaps I should have been flattered that Marc had taken me into his confidence, but a sense of unease began to infect me as we bounced towards the Botswana border. I had smuggled a little this and that all the way through Africa. But smuggling people was something else. Had I not just refused to help the unfortunate Pam and Michael?

'So, why do you need me?' I asked, or shouted over the engine roar.

'We need you to seet in 'er seat and pretend that eet ees only you and I traveling,' said Marc. 'The police, they might theenk eet strange to see one white man, traveling alone ...'

'I see ...'

I was thinking it best to tell Marc that I was so sorry, but no, I could not help him. But when we stopped to camp several miles short of the border, no sooner had he cut the engine than the door to the cab banged open and he was being dragged to the ground by a black woman with a huge round face and extra flesh in all the right places.

'My darling, my darling, I've missed you so!'

'Thomas,' said Marc between kisses, 'This is Marguerite.'

The lovebirds had been separated by the wall between cab and cabin for all of four hours. But with the surge of passion the Zulu gal threw into that first embrace, you would have thought they had not seen each other in years. I felt a pinch of envy watching them roll around on the ground: I had not been hugged like that in a long time. How could I not help this steamy pair?

My commitment to the conspiracy was cemented later that evening when Marc told me their story. A laboratory technician by profession, he had been posted by his firm to a Durban hospital a year before. Marguerite worked there as a cleaner; they had met and fallen in love, forging their union in the fiery cauldron of social defiance against apartheid. But delighting in defiance is one thing, and true love another: they could not get married, nor could Marguerite obtain a passport to leave South Africa. So Marc purchased the old military vehicle, fit it out with a smuggling chamber, picked up his beloved from work – and disappeared. Rather than chance the border crossing between South Africa and Botswana, the star-crossed couple had elected to take the long way out through Namibia and then across the Kalahari to Zambia, where Marguerite would emerge from hiding and declare herself a political refugee. Then they would marry, hawk the truck and fly away ...

No, there was no longer any question about my participation as a co-conspirator on this curious underground railway. I told them I would be honored to play a small part in this true-life story of white Romeo and black Juliet. Then they retired to their bedroom at the back of the vehicle and moaned and groaned in ecstasy all night while I pitched my sleeping bag on the ground outside, staring at the incredible heavens while jackals barked and mosquitoes swarmed, my soul filled with what can only be described as cosmic cursedness and the litany of should-have/would-have/could-haves that make up this lonely thing called life ...

In other words, I thought about Shrinithea.

After morning tea, Marc gave Marguerite a long, wet kiss goodbye before she hid herself in the dummy compartment beneath the cabin's sofa bed. Then we set off for the border.

'*Bonne chance*,' I said as we walked into the customs shed.

'*Merci*,' breathed Marc.

In retrospect, I am sure that the only reason the young guard kept us so long was because he was as lonely as I had been the night before:

we were the first vehicle to come through his post in either direction for three days, and I think the man really yearned for a few more minutes of human contact. At the time, however, every minute that he lingered over the formality of stamping our documents seemed like an hour. *He knew*, we felt, and was just playing with us before blowing the whistle.

'What's in the truck?' he asked after he had finished with our documentation.

'Kitchen, living room – eet ees a traveling apartment,' said Marc.

'Well, I'd better take a look.'

My impulse was to grab his gun, knock him on the head and make a run for it. Instead, we let him satisfy his bureaucratic curiosity, and prayed.

'Nice unit,' said the guard, poking his head around the corner and sitting down on the bed to check for bumps. 'I should get one myself.'

'It sucks gas,' said Marc.

'Don't I know you from somewhere?' said the guard, studying me again.

'Shakespeare,' I replied. This Wandering Bard stuff did come in handy at times.

'*Ja, ja!*' he exclaimed, delighted to be in the presence of celebrity. 'I did see you on the telly! Can I have your autograph?'

I guided the guard out of the cabin and back over to his little office, where I signed a sheet of paper with my John Hancock. Then I got back in the rig. Marc was already sitting behind the wheel. His hands were shaking as he put the Gitanes to his lips. Then the guard lifted the barrier and waved goodbye as we drove into no-man's-land. Still no sirens, no alarms. We were 100 yards from the barrier, then 200, then 300, and then the dirt road turned and bushes and trees obscured the customs station and we were free.

'*Mon Dieu!*' crowed Marc, 'We did it! We did it!!'

We were laughing and clapping one another on the shoulder and pounding on the window that joined the cab to the cabin, and Marguerite pounded right back.

'*Free! Free, We are free!*' she shouted through the glass. It was a swell moment.

We drove through about three miles before we reached the Botswana border station, where two ends of a 10,000-mile long barbed-wire fence came together, connected by a white aluminum beam which hung at waist-level over the dirt road. On our side was White Africa; on the far side, Black. Marc tapped on the partition glass to let Marguerite know she should hide herself again. We pulled into the station, parking the vehicle in front of a small, whitewashed guardhouse.

'Good morning!' we called out, approaching the building. There was no response.

'Good morning!' we called again, knocking on the open door. Still no answer.

'Good morning!' we called a third time, moving inside.

'*Hrmph!*' From behind a counter, something grunted. It was an official. He had clearly not had his morning tea. The guard growled something in Tswana, shoving some papers across the counter at us. No translation was needed, and we set about filling in the lines of the forms: Name, Age, Place of Birth, Nationality, Passport Number, Reason for Visit – the usual.

'You Japanese?' the guard asked me, floating his eyes from my form to my face and from there to my passport. It looked like it was going to be a repeat of my previous encounter with hung-over officialdom in Botswana, but I was determined not to fall for the bait and end up in jail again..

'Japan is just where I was born,' I replied, all smiles and courtesy.

'Then why you not look Japan?'

'I left when I was very young,' I replied. 'The climate didn't get to me.'

Same old stupid line. However ridiculous, the answer seemed to satisfy, and the customs guy reached for the entrance stamp, inked and whacked it down on my passport.

Next came Marc, and the process slowed to a crawl. The problem was that while I had a 'mere' tourist visa from the apartheid state, Marc had actually worked there, and this required explanation. How long had he been in South Africa? Where had he bought his vehicle? Was it a military vehicle? Was he a soldier? Did he have insurance? Where was the vehicle registration?

It was taking too much time. What was the hitch? Was the guy looking for a bribe?

As if on cue, Marc pulled out his wallet and began fumbling around for his driver's license, allowing a $20 bill to flutter to the top of the counter.

'It is for your collection.'

'But I don't have a collection ...'

'Then you must start collecting now, with this to be the first.'

The rusty wheels of bureaucracy had been greased, and with a loud and pleasant thump, Marc's passport came under the gavel. We all walked back to the vehicle, and while Marc fired up the engine our new friend busied himself with hoisting the barrier.

It never got beyond half-mast. Suddenly, issuing forth from another building behind the customs post, came a group of six men, all dressed in the white shirts and khaki trousers of the border patrol. One of the men waved his arms at us, while another blew on a shrill whistle.

'*Merde*,' said Marc. I couldn't have agreed more.

'Good morning!' exclaimed the first to reach us, a short and very officious man with too many bars on his shoulders and starch to his smile to bode us any relief. 'I am the District Commissioner, and here today to make an inspection! You would not mind if my new border guards received some hands-on training at your expense?'

No, the District Commissioner did not say exactly that, but that is what he meant – the novice guards were soon swarming all over Marc's vehicle, like ants on a sandwich or beetles on donkey dung. While one man went through the engine checking serial numbers, another clambered atop the roof and started dipping sticks into the spare fuel containers. Another slithered beneath the chassis to check for concealed compartments, while a fourth joined the commissioner in tearing apart the inside of the cabin.

First came the clothes. Sadly, Marc favored khakis, and in Africa such togs are associated with the military, and back then especially the Rhodesian military. All it took was the discovery of one pair of slacks before Marc's entire wardrobe was dumped on the ground and systematically turned inside out. With a deepening sense of unease, we watched as the border guards stripped the sheets off the bed and took books off the shelf, leafing through every one.

There was still the thin hope that if I could somehow distract the commissioner and his minions, we could get out of this quagmire. Accordingly, I thought it best to open my performance kit for inspection, and invited the customs men to have a peek at a couple of puppets. It had worked before at the Kisane jail, so why not again?

'What the hell are these?' asked the DC, and I was about to start explaining about the differences between Othello and Macbeth when one of the novice guards working the book shouted something in Tswana and ran over to his boss.

'Sir!' he said, handing the DC a large envelope. 'Look at these!'

I cast a wary eye at the papers now in the commissioner's hand. They were photographs of a well-endowed, naked black woman. They were nude pictures of Marguerite.

'You ... you ... *pornographer!*' shouted the DC, his hands shaking with rage. 'Guards!'

It was only a matter of time.

'*C'est fini,*' Marc said, pulling out his pack of Gitanes. I couldn't think of a better excuse to start smoking again save for impending execution, so I reached over and took one too. God, it tasted foul. So I smoked a second one and then a third, by which time they tasted like they used to. I was working on the fourth when one of the agents leapt back from Marguerite's hidden lair. The jig was up.

'Quick, get a gun!' he shouted.

'Another mercenary!' cried another.

'No!' cried Marc, throwing himself between three raised pistols and the shotgun now pointed at the hiding space. 'I confess! It is all my fault!' Real tears were rolling down his cheeks as he lifted the lid to the secret compartment.

Suddenly, the hoots and jeers subsided: even the DC seemed a little surprised and maybe disappointed that his captive was not a grimy-looking white mercenary, but a statuesque Zulu princess named Marguerite.

'I am a refugee,' she cried, hands above her head. 'I want political asylum.'

It was a masterpiece of confusion. The DC's jaw dropped open, and he was about to turn and congratulate us for aiding and abetting a freedom fighter when Marguerite committed a cardinal error: She leapt into Marc's awaiting arms.

'Oh my darling,' she sobbed. 'I love you!'

Now, the authorities in Botswana were well used to refugees. However uncomfortable it made diplomatic relations with South Africa, there were means of accommodating bona fide asylum seekers, especially those of the political variety. But love ranked even lower on the totem pole of reasons to become a refugee than such problematic categories as 'economic asylum seeker'. In fact, it was not even on the list of reasons for leaving one's own land. Then there was the little issue about the nude photographs. The face of the 'porno queen' in the pictures matched that of Marguerite exactly, a fact not lost on the DC. Marguerite was looking less like a persecuted asylum seeker than a common slut, with Marc her pornography-producing pimp. It looked bad. So did the handcuffs fastened to their wrists as they were shuffled off to jail. But no one knew what to do with me.

'You are their accomplice, admit it!' thundered the DC during my interrogation.

'Well, yes I am,' I replied.

'You knew about it all along!'

'I just told you I knew about it all along, and helped smuggle her out of South Africa.'

'Then why didn't you expose them when they crossed the border?'

'Because I was their accomplice.'

'There! You admit to being their accomplice!'

'Look,' I said, tossing in a little Shakespeare. 'They are like a white Romeo and black Juliet. You can play Friar Lawrence: take them to a cell, marry them and set them free.'

Either the DC knew his Bard better than I did, or he knew bullshit when he heard it.

'Don't give me that crap,' he thundered. 'They are breaking our laws and you are their accomplice in doing so! Admit it!'

'I just did!'

It was touch-and-go for a while. I was expelled from the country twice, but was twice allowed back into the customs house for new negotiations. The basis of my argument was that if Marc and Marguerite were to be jailed, then so should I. Why the DC never took up the offer, I cannot say. Maybe he lacked jail cells. Maybe he had seen me on South African TV. I don't know and cannot explain it, but eventually, the vicious DC caved, and I was given a one-week visa to travel through Botswana to Zambia.

'Now get out of my sight before I change my mind!' growled the DC.

But moving on was easier said than done: I was still on the trans-Kalahari highway, and the only traffic on the road consisted of the captive Marc and his impounded vehicle. Accordingly, I spent the night in a village about two miles down the dusty road, where some entrepreneurial genius had set up the only disco in the whole of the Kalahari Desert: a cinder-block room with a battery-operated boom box in one corner and a case of warm beer in another. The combination was a magnet for the hip set, which materialized out of nowhere to dance and drink the night away: Herrero girls in their strange Victorian attire, Tswana herdsmen who left their herds outside, and even a knot of domesticated Bushmen, keeping the beat with clicking tongues. It was, as they say, a rather mixed crowd. I sat in a corner drinking *pombe* (sand-brewed homemade beer) and chain-smoking Marc's foul cigarettes until I was physically sick, and fell asleep in a clump on the dirt floor.

In the morning, enjoying the delights of a splitting hangover, I began my wait by the side of the sandy road and, after an hour or two, recognized the familiar backfire of Marc's truck moving up from the border station. My first impulse was to jump for joy: they were free! My second impulse was to hide in the ditch: there were three guards in the cab with Marc, probably looking for me. My third impulse was second nature, and it was the one I followed: I walked out into the middle of the dirt road and refused to budge until the vehicle stopped to pick me up.

To all appearances, I was not the only one who had pursued this strategy; in addition to Marc and his police escort in the cab, the vehicle was packed with other hitchhikers. Besides Marguerite, there was another border patrol officer; his wife and their several children; the wife and children of one of the officers up front; and someone's crusty old granddad who looked like he was about to die from heat exhaustion and tuberculosis. It was pretty tight back there in the caboose, made more claustrophobic by the heat and dust and generally nasty behaviour of the Tswana cops towards Marguerite.

'How many cows did Frenchman pay for you,' snorted one officer, referring to the requisite 'bride price' called *lobola*. 'If I were your father, I would kill you now.'

To her credit, Marguerite countered with the only weapon she had: her not unpersuasive sexuality. What about his wife, Marguerite wanted to know, did he make her happy? Did he kiss her? Caress her? Did he care if she had pleasure? The officer turned blue with shame when Marguerite began describing her own sex life with Marc, a monologue that quickly turned into a sustained act of verbal masturbation that culminated in a long cry of yearning that silenced everyone else in the back of the truck. The rest of the eight-hour ride to the district capital of Ghanzi was of such comparative little interest that I have to admit I do not remember it at all.

Ghanzi was a dump, one of those places of which you can truly say that if it is not quite at the end of the world, you can see the end from there. It was also the place where Marc and Marguerite were to stand trial for their crimes against the laws and customs of Botswana.

'Good luck, my friend,' I said in front of the regional jail. Marc, exhausted by the drive and shattered by the experience, could scarcely talk. Still, he had the presence of mind to give me his particulars to relay to the French embassy in Gaborone. As an old hand at Botswana jails, I assured him that the SOS message would get through. Then I took a picture of the pair before they entered the jail, waving goodbye as they were led to their separate cells.

(I later received a postcard from Marc. He had been convicted on the pornography charges, fined and sentenced to six weeks in jail. Then he was deported back to Namibia, along with Marguerite – only to smuggle her back over the same border again. Either the DC was on vacation or at lunch or he, too, had finally decided to get with the spirit of Friar Lawrence and let them pass, guilty of collusion in love.) Last heard of, the couple lived in France.

The sand road from the Namibian frontier to Ghanzi was a four-lane freeway compared with the onward path to the town of Maum in Botswana, and the Zambian border beyond. In fact, at times there was no road at all, the dirt track that passed for one having been submerged in water where several rivers disappeared in the desert, creating the wonder that is the Okavango Swamp.

Yes, it looked bad. But on my second day of twiddling thumbs outside Ghanzi, I managed to catch a ride with a supply truck moving much-needed food to Maum. Our trajectory sent us over newly risen grasslands where previously there had only been the Kalahari Desert, then through the mush of the semi-flooded savannah and finally down game trails where the grassy underbrush had grown into the bushes and brambles of the swamplands.

Game was everywhere – herds of gazelle and springbok, bounding in their hundreds, stupefied by our strange presence in their midst; lumbering buffalo helpfully trampling down the tall grass and stubby trees that impeded our forward progress. About halfway through our odyssey, we ran into two extremely strange and curious creatures:

two men on bicycles. It was happy chance, because after a conference with the cyclists we adapted our course by about forty-five degrees, rediscovering the road on the far side of the washout. The muddy path seemed like a superhighway after our rumble through the jungle, and after several more hours, just as evening fell, we pulled into the mud and wattle town of Maum. Cheers and general public jubilation greeted us: aside from supplies dropped by air, we represented the first food to arrive in the town for two weeks, and the last for the next month. Maum had become the last piece of solid ground in the entire Okavango. Onward progress was impossible until the floodwaters subsided.

Waiting was not onerous. Relieved of that totally incapacitating labor, anticipation, I pitched camp and spent my days poling through the watery labyrinth in a dugout canoe, watching a wild menagerie cluster on the few standing islands left in the deluge, oblivious to former enemies and predators. I swear I saw cheetahs nuzzling warthogs, while in the muddy shallows, hippos and crocodiles splashed and played. Evenings were less bucolic. Baboons made regular assaults on my camp, and nothing was safe from their curiosity and hunger. More dangerous still were the crocodiles. Their marshy hunting grounds flooded, they had started to prowl ever closer to human settlements. It was ill-advised to walk around at night next to any body of water without a very large staff to jaw-jam the prehistoric beasts, lest they grab a leg and drag one into the green swamp for dinner.

Then, one day through the bush telegraph, I heard about a Danish doctor who had booked a private plane to Kisane – my old jail town on the Zambian frontier. The doctor, along with his voluptuous Tswana nurse-cum-housemate, was on his way to Tanzania for a little fun-in-the-sun holiday. I saw no reason why I couldn't tag along, at least as far as Kisane.

Lightning crackled and visibility was nil as we lifted off and flew straight into the next wall of water descending on the rain-stricken region. The storm battered the small plane until the Danish doctor's tan was gone and I was ready to vomit. His Tswana paramour, meanwhile, began keening a death prayer in accordance with tribal custom. Then we were through the eye of the storm, and our vantage point allowed us to peer down at the swamp and savannah below. Herds of elephants lumbered down the remains of the washed-out road, which cut like a red clay blade through the green and blue of the ubiquitous swamp, while rhino and hippopotamuses crashed through the water-world.

Kisane was like coming home. Waiting at the dirt strip called an airport was my old pal, the immigration officer, and a brace of guards from my old jail, who welcomed me back like a prodigal son returned. That night we had a special treat: my pals in the police had bagged a couple of elephant poachers the day before, and had sent the hotel staff off with axes to hack off some choice slabs of the slaughtered mammoths to roast on a giant spit. I am saddened to report that roast pachyderm ultimately tasted like third-rate beef.

SIXTEEN

Zonked in Zambia, or Camp Bitter Hunger

The border guard leafed through my passport, and stopped at the springbok stamp. 'You were in South Africa?'

'Not really,' I dodged. 'Only very briefly.'

'I see,' frowned the official. 'I shall have to consult my superior.'

The moment of truth had arrived. Due to its direct economic dependence on the apartheid republic, Botswana might have to look the other way when it came to accepting Pretoria's symbols and stamps. But the front-line state of Zambia had pretensions of political purity, and was known to often refuse entry to anyone who admitted to having visited South Africa. The only thing worse than having a South African stamp in your passport was to have one from Rhodesia. Then I felt a hand grasp my wrist from behind, and turned to see a thin, anemic-looking white man.

'Let me handle this,' he said, and began rattling away at the guard in the local lingo. The customs man looked at the interloper, and then at me, and back at the scrawny white man. He frowned, picked up his stamp and whacked it down on my passport.

'I hope your book is successful, Professor,' he said, and shook my hand.

'What did you say?' I asked the stranger once we were out of the customs shed.

'I told him you were a professor of African history, and that you were writing a book on the evils of apartheid,' my benefactor explained. 'Need a ride?'

'Yeah, it'd be great,' I replied. 'What's your name?'

'James, Bob James,' said my new friend, and threw me a pair of goggles. These were necessary, for James's car lacked a windshield. Earplugs might also have been nice, because it also lacked a muffler. But my new friend insisted on telling me his life story over the engine roar, cramming in the most salient details before we reached Livingston. I had the sense that he had not spoken to another white man for some time. On this point I was mistaken – but that is getting ahead of the story.

My companion was once a young, idealistic Communist student activist from Oxford, who had come out to Africa a decade earlier with his wife, to teach French and involve themselves in the process of decolonization. James soon decided it was silly teaching French in Zambia, and started teaching English. But what sort of contribution was that, he wondered, save for perpetuating the colonial cultural yoke? Farming, however, seemed to be an area where one could have an immediate impact upon the larger Zambian society. Accordingly, James taught himself the rudiments of agronomy and then tried to pass on his new insights to his students. Sadly, they were not enthusiastic; all most of them wanted was a government post in Lusaka or Kitwe and a new pair of platform shoes.

In despair, his marriage on the rocks, James abandoned his classes, divorced his English wife, knocked up one of his students, paid off her *lobola* (she was worth five cows to her father) and bought a broken-down farm outside Livingston. All his white farmer neighbors laughed and predicted that he would go under within a matter of months. But soon the war in Rhodesia began spilling across the Zambezi as the area around Victoria Falls became a staging ground for guerrilla attacks into Ian Smith's rogue republic, and also a favorite area for revenge raids undertaken by the Rhodesian security forces. It was not advisable to wander around at night if you were black or white, lest one stumble into a nest of guerrillas or a nest of commandos. One by one, the other white farmers in the Livingston area abandoned their homesteads, until Bob James found himself in the curious position of being the only one left, and thus one of the primary suppliers of tomatoes to the Livingston market. 'I'm working on other cash crops, too – guavas, lemons and limes,' he shouted over the non-muffler. 'And I've got so many avocado trees I can scarcely eat them any more!'

'Gee,' I shouted back. 'I'd sure like to take a look at your operation!'

'Well, come along, then!'

We stopped at the Livingston farmers' cooperative to pick up a few provisions – several five-gallon buckets of soap, a couple of 100-pound sacks of cornmeal, a few cases of beer and assorted canned goods – and then roared off towards the James estate down a half-built highway. Literally. The engineers had only managed to pave enough of the middle section of the dirt road to create one lane, meaning that we were obliged to play a harrowing game of car chicken whenever another vehicle approached. In that most oncoming traffic consisted of overloaded trucks, we found ourselves lurching off the tarmac and driving in the ditch quite often. After ten or twenty miles of this sort of white-knuckle fun, James turned off the main highway onto a gravel road, and we were instantly swallowed up by deep bush gloom.

'Well,' announced James as the car sputtered to a halt in a yard filled with rusted and broken farm machinery and general junk. 'This is it! Home, sweet home!' I had trouble identifying where the home was. At the far end of a junkyard clearing there was a house-like structure, but I had assumed it to be a tool shed or chicken coop. At exactly that moment, a hideous wailing erupted from within said structure, followed by a yelp and a howl and a scream. The door blew open, and out flew a mangy, vicious-looking dog, its tail tucked so far under its ass that it nearly touched its nose. Behind the cur came a brace of small mixed-race children, racing towards James, arms outstretched, followed by a huge black woman clutching a rooster and wailing from the bottom of her diaphragm. Then the root cause of all the commotion appeared: a rabid-looking white man with a butcher's knife in his hand and an insane gleam in his eye.

'I'll slit yer throat!' he screamed, running straight towards us.

Did I duck? Did I hide behind James? I only know that I did nothing to stop anyone's murder, and when I looked up the apparition had lunged past us and disappeared into the surrounding bush in pursuit of the sad mutt. James, meanwhile, hoisted one child onto his shoulder while his hefty wife attacked the supplies. 'That was Stan,' said Bob James nonchalantly, fetching a bag of groceries from the back seat of the car. 'He doesn't think the dog belongs in the house.'

After a repast of cornmeal, boiled chicken and a couple of beers, James took me on a walking tour of his farm. It consisted of acres and acres of tomatoes, planted, plucked and peeled by what can only be described as his population of serfs drawn from the villages in the area. Disease among the workers was high, James admitted, possibly because of an over-application of anti-bug toxins. The most recent casualty was an old hermit who used to spray DDT. Happily, the old man was single and had never been registered for anything, ever, and thus would not be missed.

'Stan buried him out in the bush without telling me where,' James casually related. 'We can't very well inform the authorities now, or they'll call it murder.'

It was curious story to tell a rank stranger: that people lived like serfs and worked like slaves and died of DDT diseases to be anonymously disposed of on the farm by an apparently mad and maybe murderous white man named Stan, and that nobody knew or apparently did not care. I found it just a tad unsettling.

'By the way,' I asked in passing. 'Who is –'

'Stan?' James helped me out. 'Oh, he is sort of a permanent fixture on the farm.'

'He seems like an interesting sort of guy,' I said, euphemistically.

'Yes, he is strange,' James remarked, using the word I had avoided.

I was starting to get a peculiar, visceral tingle that wanted to warn me of something, but discarded it. I was 50 miles from Livingston on a farm among deserted farms.

'Yes, Stan is the real item!' chuckled James. 'He's kind of like a real-life Tarzan. Spent about twenty years in the bush. Knows every bird and bug and beast. You could say that he keeps his ears pretty close to the ground.'

'How'd you meet him?'

'I came down with hepatitis a few years ago and collapsed under a tree,' James recalled. 'When I came to, there was this white jungle man standing over me. That was Stan. I was the first white man he had had contact with in years, but he saved my life, and ever since he has been coming and going as he pleases.' Our tour continued from the tomato gardens to James's most recent experiment – grafting orange rinds onto lime trees to make lemons – and then back through one of the villages, where a number of women scampered out from their huts and bowed to James. All were clutching mixed-race children, and it seemed pretty clear to me how the baron of the estate spent his leisure time. When we repaired to the house, we were greeted once more by the spectacle of the family dog flying through a window in a mad effort to escape something inside.

'Stan,' said James. 'He can't stand dogs.'

Indeed, there was the jungle man, pacing around the house with the butcher knife in his hand, keeping his eyes on the windows like he was guarding the Alamo.

'Should slit its throat,' he muttered. James introduced me as a wandering Shakespeare an actor.

'Shakespeare! *Shakespeare!*' Stan cackled. 'Do you know what Hermann Goering said? "When I hear the word 'culture' I reach for my revolver." Hahaha!'

Although I wasn't quite sure what he meant by this, I decided it best to laugh along. Stan sure brought atmosphere into a room, although I was not sure whether it was an air I particularly liked. He was not Tarzan, a white man who swung on vines through the jungle canopy, being nice to the good animals and nasty to the bad. He was just a white man who had got lost in Africa, only a lot more so than Bob James and certainly a whole lot more so than little ol' Johnny-come-lately me.

He wore tattered, cast-off clothes on his back and tennis shoes on his feet, and stalked animals with a homemade blunderbuss made from the steering column of an automobile wreck, blinding his prey with a miner's lamp before blowing them away. He was no noble savage, but a mean, predatory brute – and he scared the shit out of me.

'I first come oot here after Burma, after the war,' Stan related in a thick Scottish brogue, starring at me with unblinking eyes. 'I was one of Mosley's boys, you know, a Nazi. Didn't fit in, so I packed me bags and coome oot to the Coolonies. Worked the railway for a while. Shooveled coal. 'Oorible work. Took oop with a wooman. Black as coal. Folks couldn't see it. Droove me oot. Never coome back. Stayed in the boosh. Hadn't seen a white man for years until Bob 'ere foond me, but he's 'alf wog himself. At least his brats are. Hahaha!'

As if on cue, one of the rugrats started howling after tripping on the floor.

'Slit its throat,' Stan suggested. 'No one will ever know.'

The house shrunk as shadows lengthened. With every diminishing moment of light, I felt more confined, trapped. 'We are hungry, Stan,' said Bob James.

The real-life Tarzan went out into the yard, grabbed a chicken and slit its throat without even a split second of reflection or consideration, setting the dead bird back on its feet to lurch around the yard, spurting blood from its open neck. 'Look at the dead bird run!' roared Stan. 'Fourth one today!'

'Country has run out of meal, and the chickens will all starve to death in a few weeks anyway,' noted Bob James laconically. 'Might as well kill them while they're alive.'

When the flopping ceased, James's wife, whose name was Mercy, stripped the bird and yanked out its feathers, jamming into a pot to stew for dinner. Meanwhile, James and I played a few rounds of chess by hurricane lamp. Then Stan entered the room, took up a position near the hearth and started reading from an outdated magazine.

'Listen to this!' Stan cackled, 'Some clever Frenchman got the idea of opening up a dietary resort where fat people would go to lose weight by being locked in a barn for a week with only bread and water. He called it "Camp Bitter Hunger".'

'"Camp Bitter Hunger,"' chortled James. 'That's good!'

'I'm not finished!' shouted Stan, and continued to read aloud, or at least provide commentary. The police eventually got wind of the place, he related. When they arrived, they found half the campers already dead of starvation behind the locked barn door. But rather than thanking their saviors, the survivors tried to drive the police away. They had paid for precisely the treatment they were receiving, and wanted their money's worth.

'Their money's worth!' said Stan, erupting with insane laughter. 'They wanted their money's worth! Haha! A barn, some bread, and water – Camp Bitter Hunger! *Hahaha!*'

'People will pay for anything,' giggled James.

'Maybe we should open up a franchise, right here,' chortled Stan.

'But no starvation,' James reflected. 'We should open a work camp. Clients would pay to come and be our slaves for a month, that sort of thing.'

'Or a fear camp,' rejoined Stan. 'Guarantee clients to be frightened out of their wits.'

'The more bizarre the better,' said James. 'Camp Fear and Loathing.'

'Fear and Loathing,' Stan pronounced with finality. 'People will pay for anything.'

The only problem was getting the word out to those with enough money and sufficiently uninteresting lives to be attracted to such a camp. That's where I came in. 'It's the Americans who really go for this sort of nonsense,' said Stan.

'Advertisements in *The Village Voice*,' said James, looking at me. 'Want to be our agent? It would pay more and be more interesting than this Shakespeare business.'

'He'd need a work visa for the US, though,' said Stan. 'That might be a problem.'

'But our guest is American,' said Bob James. 'I saw his passport.'

'American?' asked Stan with mock shock. 'I thought by his accent and all that Shakespeare nonsense that he was a Brit!'

Stan let the stain sink in for a moment; he had caught me out on the lilt I had affected to my native North Dakotan tongue, twisting 'been' to 'bean' and using far too many 'ee' sounds in front of 'oo' sounds, as in 'styu-dent' as opposed to 'stoo-dent'.

'Well, what do you think?' asked Stan in a flat-out American accent, mocking me.

'About what.'

'Our idea for a camp for your compatriots, of course.'

They were serious.

'I think you are out of your minds,' I managed to utter, trying to make a joke.

'Do you mean we're *crazy*?'

The pair glanced at each other and erupted into a joint paroxysm of insane laughter, then returned their four eyes to me. A cold chill of paranoia was running up and down my spine. Was it simply the exhaustion, or were things exactly as I now perceived them to be? I had been led to the remote farmhouse by two insane, bush-bound white men, whose object from the start was to drive me mad with fear for their wicked and warped entertainment. Camp Fear and Loathing, yeah – perhaps they had had it here all along ...

'Tell me,' Stan asked all of a sudden. 'What does your father do for a living? Most travelers pretend to be something they're not, namely poor. Me, I come from a solid, decent middle-class home, and I've fucked up my life completely! I just thought it might be different with you. What does your father do? Dig ditches?'

'He's a doctor ...' I found myself admitting, almost in shame.

'A doctor, a medical doctor!' cackled Stan. 'And here is his sonny boy wandering around Africa playing Shakespeare to niggers, begging! He must be proud! Hahaha!'

'You know what I am thinking, Stan,' said James. 'I am thinking that our guest here is just kind of an early, younger version of us.'

'You mean a total fuckup who has wasted his life?' reflected

Stan. 'Maybe so. If I had it to do again, I'd have slit my own throat at thirty.'

'Slit your own throat? How?' asked Bob James.

'Well then, maybe I'd get somebody to do it for me! Hahaha!' Into the hollow silence that followed his lunatic laughter walked Mercy, bearing the kettle of boiled chicken in one hand and a new kettle of cornmeal in the other. Two children clutched at her dress from behind. Family, kids, normalcy. It had all been a bad dream; salvation was at hand. 'Jesus!' screamed Stan, lurching towards Mercy. 'Where is my knife!!'

Mercy stumbled and dropped the pot of chicken; the children wailed and cried; the dog that had followed them in from the kitchen smelling food yelped and bolted towards the door, with Stan fast behind. It was my window of opportunity to be rational, to set things straight – and I found myself almost pleading with James to ease off.

'Bob,' I said. 'I don't know how to say this, but if you could bring me back to town ...'

'Why?'

Yes, why? Because I was worried that I had been set up and brought out to a remote farm by two madmen, who intended to torture, ass-rape and kill me before sticking my stinking corpse in an unmarked shallow grave? Get a hold of yourself, now!

'It's just that ...' I began, and then Stan returned, knife in hand. 'Stan,' said James. 'Our guest says that we've been harassing him.'

'Harassing him, says he?' cackled Stan, as if I were not in the room. 'The last guy who stayed with us ran out and cut off his balls! *Hahaha!*'

'That was a vasectomy, and he went to Lusaka to get it,' James helpfully noted.

'Same thing.' Stan shrugged his shoulders.

'And he wants me to bring him back to town.'

'*What?*' cried Stan. 'At this hour of night, with no lights on your car and with half the Zambian army patrolling the area for white spies? Of all the selfish requests!'

'Well, perhaps he should walk,' suggested James, reducing me to some third-person entity privy to their deliberations.

'I wouldn't,' said Stan. 'Even if he got by the soldiers, there are the animals ...'

'Yeah. Remember that German you brought here? Fritz?'

'Poor bloke. Had to get the dogs to find him.'

'Dancing on the grave he was, howling for mercy at the moon.'

That wave of paranoia and fear washed over me again. I was trapped, and the only way out was to pull myself into a protective, psychological cocoon. But the evening dragged on and on, with my two tormentors playing chess by hurricane lamp and bantering back and forth in a coded language of familiar grunts, half-statements and keyword-groans.

'There's always the back door.'

'No, he's trapped.'

We're they referring to the board game, or to me? There was only one thing to do: get out. Easing my way out of the room with a yawn, I slid out to a dark corner of the porch. If I could make it through until morning, it would all be nothing but a paranoid dream ...

That is when the voices began talking to me.

There, said the voice of reason, *now you can sleep. Not yet,* said the other, *listen!*

And both voices fell silent as my ears tuned in on the noises emitting from the room I had just left. More cackling laughter and the click and clack of chess pieces moving on a board. And then a strange scraping sound: *drrrt ... drrrt ... drrrt.* Alarm bells were clanging through my brain again as I desperately tried to place it. *Drrrt ... drrrt ... drrrt.* Then I knew what it was: steel on stone. They were sharpening Stan's butcher knife.

No, said the voice of reason. *Yes,* said the voice of fear. A flush of nausea washed over me as the details of the day ticker-taped through my mind: The constant references to the remoteness of the place; the story of the old man's unregistered death and burial; the discussions about previous visitors who had gone mad. The psychological badgering was at an advanced stage; next would come the torture, followed a clean, cool kill before my mutilated corpse was dumped in a shallow grave. This *was* Camp Bitter Hunger, and I was its only guest.

They're insane, said the first voice. *Go.*

No, said the second. *The only insane one is you.*

Do you dare take a chance? came the other voice. *Run ...*

Out in the jungle, are you truly mad?

At least get out of the house while you still have the chance!

There is Mercy and the children. They wouldn't, couldn't.

They can, *they* will.

Drrrt ... drrrt, scraped the blade in the next room, as my tormentors chortled.

I struck a schizophrenic compromise with myself. To run for the bush was nuts, but to stay in the house was also insane. The junked machinery in the yard, however, would provide shelter for the night. Yes, the junkyard ... Silently, I slipped away from the porch towards the mechanical detritus, finding safety beneath a broken truck. Semi-safety, anyway – safety enough to sleep and rest my raging brain. Then a black shape came bounding towards me. It was the much-maligned farm dog, giving away my lair.

'Shhh ... nice puppy ... nice puppy,' I cooed, petting the dog on its mangy head despite my lifelong loathing of the creatures. In that, at least, I was in total agreement with my tormentor, Stan. Playfully, the cur began to pull at my blankets, giving out friendly little barks. It was a pity I had to do what I was about to do, but self-preservation demanded immediate action. Slowly, quietly I managed to get part of my blanket around the dog's head. Then the cur sensed my intent to kill, and with a yelp, bared its teeth and began barking to wake the dead.

And the living. Voices came from the house, and then a flicker of lamplight on the porch. They had discovered I was gone. No, someone was only going out to take a piss.

Don't be a fool, pleaded the voice of reason, making one last attempt to stop my feet from running. *They're after you!*

You're imagining it all! cried the other voice.

No! Run for your life! Go!
Stop!
GO!

The debate ended with the growl and barking of the not-yet-dead dog. I took one step away, then two, then four. I was tripping, stumbling and walk-running away from the farmhouse and then almost before I knew it I was jogging, running and then sprinting down the darkened dirt road, dropping everything behind in headlong flight, passing by the darkened shapes of the small settlement where Bob James's workers dwelled, rousing guard dogs and donkeys which barked and brayed as I thundered past, covering two or three or four miles in world-record time before my lungs gave out and I dove into the roadside brambles to collect my breath and wits. *You are crazy, but you are safe,* said both my voices at once.

But as soon as I was able to focus on anything but my panting breath and pounding heart, my terror took a new twist: behind me the night sounds became audible – baboons croaking, night birds calling; but the village dogs and donkeys were also now barking and braying at something else. It was *them*, Bob and Stan, hunting me. My system was so overloaded with adrenaline that I was sure my heart would burst, but then a new jolt ran through my veins and I raced down the road again with no illusions anymore, and very little hope. They were after me. Two bushwise, night-hunting madmen were really after me. They would hunt me down and slit my throat. My only hope, and it was thin, so thin, was to make the main road. I ran and ran for the sake of life itself, and then the canopy of trees and bush began to open and I nearly cried for joy because beneath my feet was the half-made tarmac road. I sprinted across the lifeline to civilization and threw myself into the brush on the far side, from where I could see them coming when they came.

Whumpa-whumpa-whumpa-whump went my heart/ears in combo percussion session, which surely could be heard for miles, and I pleaded with God and goodness. Then my prayers were answered by two distant lights. When they were within 50 yards I burst from the bushes, waving my arms and begging the oncoming truck to halt. *'PLEASE STOP!'* I wailed, but the truck roared right on by. Now they knew exactly where

I was. They had seen me and they had heard me and now they could probably smell my fear. They were hunters and I was just pathetic prey, hounded, badgered, cornered, caught. They could do what they wanted. I would not even resist. I was dead but for the deed.

'Here I am!' I said, maybe shouted. 'I'm here, here!'

Silence, aside from the crick-crick of the crickets. 'Hello?' I called out again into the night. 'Hello?'

Nothing but silence. I sank into a heap and wept. A year and a half of madness began to roll over me like a tidal wave of sewage: my eyes were rimmed yellow with jaundice, my skin flaky and broken from cuts and sores that refused to heal, my tongue twisted into the fakery of a quasi-Brit accent for the Shakespeare show, origins of which went back to hawking handmade pipes as curios to dumb tourists.

Then there was the emotional vacuum of sleeping with a dozen whores I could care less about, except Shrinithea, and deserting the drug smugglers Michael and Pam in their hour of need. If these seem like petty details today, at the time they seemed like moral crimes of the capital variety. I believed I deserved Stan as my judge and Bob James as my jury, and both as my executioners. But I had failed even at that. This had to stop, permanently.

Another truck was coming down the road. I walked out in front of it, inviting it to flatten me and just be done with it. But it screeched to a halt, inches from my nose. Another failure. The irate driver ordered me into the cab, and then dropped me in Livingston-on-the-Zambezi. I slept in a park, and then hitchhiked straight back out to the James estate when I woke.

The boys were surprised to see me. I explained that I had left my Shakespeare kit behind during my nocturnal stroll through the bush, and thought I might pick it up. They did not ask why I had departed so precipitously, and in the middle of the night, nor did I offer an explanation. If there was any lingering tarnish to our eternal friendship, Stan made up for it by acquiring a village lady for me, who arrived with her child.

I stayed a week. After all, I was insane.

SEVENTEEN

Temporarily Tamed *Tokolosh*

I had first heard of the tokolosh, an evil djinn-like spirit that sneaks into dwellings through open windows and doors left ajar, from some Xhosa friends in the South African Bantustan called Transkei. At the time, I just laughed. But with time and travel, I had begun to wonder why I was on such an emotional see-saw, soaring for one day (or hour) only to turn into a psychotic madman the next. I reckoned a tokolosh had entered my life, though I liked to think I had it on some kind of leash.

'Hey, Shakespeare! Hey, you!'

There was only one person on the Livingston train platform who could be so addressed, and so reluctantly, as if admitting a crime, I lifted my head and turned towards the source.

It was Colorado Ken, the very blond, very sunburnt, very blue-eyed and very racist ivory merchant, who had been my landlord at the Twiga Lodge in Kenya so many moons earlier. I did not know whether to embrace him or run, so I stood where I was.

'You can't believe how good it is to see a Yankee face!' he said, pumping my hand. 'Jesus Christ! Another American!'

'Likewise,' I replied, trying to beam enthusiasm. He seemed much friendlier now than I remembered him being then. Why was that? What did he want? Who was he, really?

We compared tickets and made arrangements to share the same compartment for the twelve-hour trip to Lusaka. Away from prying ears we began to talk, though out of general habit, much of the dialogue passed in code.

'Where are you coming from?' I asked.

'Disneyland,' said Ken.

'Well, so how are things with Walt?'

'The musketeers have given up, and Daffy and Donald are moving in,' he said, spitting out the words. 'But everybody knows that Disneyland's not big enough for two. Disneyland is next. Got the only office management on the continent but nobody wants to know.'

(Translation: Ken had been in Rhodesia; I asked how Ian Smith was doing; he reported that Robert Mugabe would brook no rivals, even among his current allies. Chaos loomed. South Africa, the only decent government in Africa, was next to be sold out.)

'Maybe it's time you got out,' I suggested. 'You've been here ...'

'Two years. You?'

'Eighteen months, but seems like eighteen years.'

'One more run and I'm through,' said Ken. 'Then I'll go home and forget about this whole goddamn continent, forever.' He sighed and leaned back, lighting a Rhodesian cigarette. They might have been tastier than the Zambian variety, but flashing a Ridgeback was asking for trouble anywhere north of the Zambezi.

Ken was casual because he had nothing but contempt for everything and everyone around him. He was getting rich smuggling ivory, but the price was cynicism and bitterness. He wasn't interested in African history or Victoria Falls or even game parks. He had become something of a gigolo, living long years with a woman he loathed, touching her only for her money, kissing her only for cash. I wanted to ask him, one American to another, whether and if so to what extent any weird shit had happened to his head during the period he had been rolling around the continent, but thought it best not to. What could he say? 'Yeah, after various and sundry life-altering experiences,

I started to go nuts, and thought perfect strangers wanted to kill me.'
Somehow it seemed that the best way to keep demons at bay was to
deny their existence.

'So, where are you off to make this last score?' I asked.

'Zaire,' said Ken. 'But not ivory. I want malachite – Green tooth.'

Green Tooth was the wild green stone out of which a room was
built in the Hermitage, they say. It was almost legal.

'The main source is Katanga Province,' Ken was saying. 'Do you
want to come?'

We arrived in Lusaka the next morning, and took a cab to a farm
about 10 miles from town, where a white Zambian was known to put
up travelers. The farmer's name was Jackson, and his spread was sort of
a bucolic al-Manzura, but with an edge: next door to the rural hippie
hotel was a training base for guerrillas loyal to the African National
Congress. The frequent visits of the guerrillas to Jackson's farm made
Colorado Ken sufficiently nervous to leave for Zaire after only two
days.

'Fuckin' *kaffirs*,' he said, 'Just let me make that last ivory run and I
am out of this fuckin' continent ...'

Ken was not the only face from the past on Jackson's farm. The
acting manager of the farm's brass foundry (Jackson fancied himself a
sculptor and had an interest in mass-producing African folk art) was
none other than California Jimmy, the long-haired American I had
met at the al-Manzura, when he was looking for a job that paid good
money and allowed him to boss natives around.

As with Colorado Ken, I had an almost visceral memory of
disliking and distrusting Jimmy, but I let it pass. He was, after all,
another American on a farm outside Lusaka, and thus almost an old
friend. It was tempting to get down to the nitty-gritty with someone
who might possibly understand, who had *lived that life*.

In addition to Jackson, Jimmy and the estate's permanently
resident African staff, the crowd there included a couple Germans, a
big-busted Dutch woman (whom Jimmy had just weaned away from
her husband, now gone), two Italian women (one of whom was having

an affair with Jackson, though neither spoke the other's language),
a Somali couple, who had been living on a trailer on the farm for a
couple of years, but whom Jimmy was trying to get removed. The
reason for Jimmy's aversion to the Somalis appeared to be that he had
been rejected by their guest – a tall, lithe, slightly bucktoothed Somali
woman who spoke no English, kept to herself and – for reasons that
were abundantly apparent but never enunciated – despised Jimmy.

'Look at that arrogant cunt,' he muttered into my ear one evening
at the nightly guacamole-and-chicken barbecue feast at the farm. (The
broilers were slaughtered as a result of the chicken-feed shortage;
avocados and lemons were basic orchard fruits; and locally brewed
beer was the only beverage around: the menu cloyed in a matter of
days.) 'If I could get Jackson's ear, I'd have all that bunch of Somalis
thrown out of here, tonight.'

Was it that night, the next? I only remember that one night among
the nights I smiled at her and she smiled back and I tried to have a
conversation but failed in English, German and even Swahili, then said
something in my pidgin Arabic – and she smiled and said something
I could not understand, while beckoning me to follow her. I did so,
and she brought me to a table where there were some remnants of
guacamole dip and a piece of bread. She scooped up the green dip on
the bread and put it in my mouth.

'My name is Sofi,' she said in almost perfect English. 'Now bring
me home.'

I followed her to the trailer. Her long, silky gown swished on the
stairs. Then we were inside and the gown was gone. I marveled at her
taut, narrow arms and delicate, tiny hands. My thumb and index finger
easily encircled one wrist, and when I put both together I was almost
able to encompass the pair. She placed her long, skinny arms around
my shoulders and gave me her version of a kiss – all lips, no tongue.

'Nice,' she said. '*Too* nice.'

I had slept with a dozen African women over the past year, all
prostitutes. Sofi was not. She was a traditional girl from a traditional
home in Mogadishu, looking forward to a traditional life with a

traditional husband, when one day her world collapsed: Her father was assassinated by the Somali strongman Mohammed Siad Barre, and Sofi and her family were obliged to flee in different directions. Her first stop was Kenya, and the welcome mat was cool: the only means of surviving for a single Somali girl in Nairobi or Mombasa was as a whore. So she next managed to smuggle herself into Tanzania, and from there to Zambia, searching for a brother who was involved in a trucking company. Three days before she got to Lusaka, he was killed in a road accident, and Sofi was again alone.

I wondered if these stories were lies, but I couldn't see the point. There was nothing to be gained through such guile or embellishment, at least not from me, a nearly broke and burnt-out Bard, ready to flip at any provocation. Maybe Sofi was waiting for the right person to come along to save her; all she got was me.

The train pulled out of the Lusaka station and Sofi leaned over and gave me a low-key, Somali-style embrace – namely, she smiled and patted my thigh.

'Nice,' she said, looking out the window at the receding sight of Lusaka. 'Nice.'

It was her favorite phrase in English.

We were moving away from Lusaka, from the farm and from California Jimmy. We were going towards Kitwe and the Copper Belt, the scene of my greatest success in the expatriate theater scene one year before. My plan was to recreate that success, and then take the accumulated *kwacha*, invest said gains in malachite and emeralds and then leave Africa forever, maybe with Sofi.

Some two hours aboard our train, ghastly little clouds of bile erupted from my stomach into my mouth – the phenomenon my brothers and sisters in Fargo referred to as 'the smelly burps'. But this was not North Dakota tummy trouble. The foul taste in my mouth was the primary symptom of what I called my 'temporary malaria'. I was used to periodic cold sweats and flush fevers, but this was different. This was bad.

By the time we arrived in Kitwe, I was vomiting and splashing diarrhea down legs that could not walk. Sofi carried me to a taxi, returned to the train for our bags and then repeated the exercise when she found a hotel, lifting me up the stairs to our room.

Then I barfed green bile on her blouse and shit fluid on the bed because I could not even crawl to the bathroom, and she washed me off and wrapped me in a blanket.

'Sleep, darling, sleep,' she cooed, placing cool towels on my face.

Then I plunged down somewhere very deep, and stayed there, churning.

'My darling, how are you today?' she asked one day, and I realized I had no idea what day she was talking about or even where I was. But the fever had broken. I even got to my feet after she left to buy some food, and took a look out the window. It was dark and raining hard. Then I heard the key in the lock, and in came a tall, lithe Somali called Sofi, soaking wet and carrying a bag of groceries.

'Now we make love!'

Faster than you can say 'recovery', she dragged both of our single mattresses to the floor and spread the sheets. She found a suitably romantic station on our shortwave radio, and tossed a towel over the reading lamp to create a little atmosphere. Then she stripped me, stripped herself and rolled up a huge joint of marijuana, taking a long toke before passing it to me.

'No,' I said.

'You must,' Sofi insisted. 'I am your doctor, your nurse, your wife.'

'No.'

'It make love *too* nice.'

Too weak to resist but still reluctant, I took the joint and pulled on it.

'You see?' she said. '*Too* nice.'

She pulled me towards her and we began to kiss and play. I brought my palm down one of her thin arms, from the shoulder to the tiny wrist, encircling it. Then I played our game by taking her other arm and placing it atop the first, and put both her wrists in the thumb and finger vise. She was so incredibly fine-boned for her height, so fragile for her size.

Then do something about it, I heard voices say.

It was the voices I had first heard at Camp Bitter Hunger, come back to haunt me, come back to drive me mad, to remind me of the Camp, but with a twist. My temporarily tamed *tokolosh* had become two.

She is so thin and small, so frail, they said. *Do it!*

Leave me alone, I begged them. *Leave me alone.*

No, they said in chorus.

Kill her.

'*No!*' I shouted, flinging Sofi's arms away. She sat up and stared at me.

'My darling,' she said, and tried to put her arms around me.

Get her by the throat, said one of the voices. *Get up and go before you do,* said the other. *Kill her, now,* rejoined the first. *No one will ever know.*

Perhaps I was growling the dialogue searing through my head; maybe I was stone silent. Sofi sat and stared, slowly sliding back on the mattress, away from me, shooting a glance towards the table that served as the kitchen in the room. There was fruit there, and a paring knife. Insanely, Macbeth's dagger speech began playing like a broken record through my head. *Stick your courage to the ...*

'*NO!!!*'

That was my voice, and I was on my feet, pedaling backwards from the bed, grabbing one of the sheets to wrap around me as I bolted from the room. I stumbled down the stairs, emerging in the lobby in a clump. The desk clerk looked up, but I was already out the door and into the pouring rain. A taxi driver honked and I stumbled in – as though picking up a raving mad white man in a toga in a rainstorm was just an ordinary event.

'*Go!*' I said, and we drove around Kitwe for some time, maybe an hour, maybe ten minutes. I had him drop me back at the hotel, and asked the clerk to pay. I collapsed in a chair, naked aside from the sheet, and just sat there – suicidal, murderous, pathetic. What was happening with my brain? Why was I set to destroy anything that smacked of joy?

An hour later, I felt a cool hand on my shoulder.

'Come,' said Sofi. 'I am *too* sorry. You are *too* sick.'

We went back upstairs. The mattresses were back on the beds and the towel had been removed from the lamp. There was fruit, but no knife in sight. I wanted to explain what had happened; whatever I said ended up as a pathetic plea: *'I'm nuts. Help me.'*

Sofi said she would, and then she rolled herself another joint and began to smoke, sitting on her haunches and watching me until I drifted off into a fitful sleep. I remember wicked dreams, demons. I lit fever fires all night and was soaking wet when I awoke.

'Good morning, my darling,' said Sofi, standing above me with a fresh, cold wet towel, while wringing out one that stank of sweat. 'Take this.'

The chicken broth she force-fed me gradually turned into pieces of chicken, and then my diet was expanded to include other local fruits and vegetables – avocados, of course, but also sweet, small mangoes, kiwis and bananas. Then one day my doctor deigned that I was well enough to accompany her to the local market, although it was not to buy vegetables. We had come to Kitwe to invest in Green Tooth, malachite, and Sofi was determined to fulfill that mission.

Perhaps if I had been alone, I would have attracted less attention – and probably paid more than I did. But I was the emaciated white man on the arm of that tall, ferocious Somali, the one who took the ancient art of haggling very seriously indeed. We would arrive at the market at noon, and spend two hours appraising hundreds of carved and polished pieces of the strange, green stone, setting aside the gems before entering into negotiations over price. Sofi was so aggressive that our favorite merchant – the man who had sold me the emeralds, I believed, but never asked – would turn to me with pleading eyes, saying: 'I rest my case under the scale of your mercy.'

Then one day, the malachite market dried up. There was trouble in southern Zaire, centering around the town of Kolwezi. Reports were patchy, but it seemed that rebels known as the Kantagese Gendarmes, who had long been the armed opposition to the Zairian dictator Mobutu Sese Seko, had infiltrated themselves into the province from bases in Angola, and then hit the mining town – and hard. The local army garrison had mutinied and joined the rebels in a popular uprising. But their methods did not seem to jibe with their rhetoric: open season was soon declared on the French, Belgians and other Europeans involved in the Kolwezi mining industry. Over one hundred foreigners had been butchered, with the number of local Africans slaughtered far exceeding that.

In the wake of the sordid and bloody events in Rwanda and Burundi in the mid-1990s, when up to half a million people were slaughtered in a great paroxysm of ethnic madness, these numbers seem paltry indeed. But at the time they generated such shock that the French Foreign Legion was parachuted in to deal with the situation as only they know how. The guerrillas once more disappeared into the bush, having to wait another two decades before re-emerging and re-raising the banner of revolt. By then, the only special forces the beleaguered president could count on were an embarrassing bunch of Serbian mercenaries, who spent more time killing and looting in the towns they were contracted to defend than defending their paymaster.

But that was twenty years later. At the time, sitting across the border in Zambia, I was stunned by my good fortune in having been laid low by disease: *There but for the grace of God go I ...* I scanned the papers for the death lists, but never found the one name I was looking for, someone who should have been smack-dab at the epicenter of the violence directed towards people with his profile: Colorado Ken.

Whether he survived the ritual killings and summary executions, I do not know. I was just very glad that I was not there with him to share the experience.

'I rest my case under the scale of your mercy.'

It was not a malachite merchant pleading with Sofi, but me, trying to explain to my lover and savior and nurse and hatchet-woman companion why I had to say goodbye.

'Africa – Green! Fresh! America – cement!' she said.

She had a point, and I had thought of that. There was nothing for me to return to in the States. Shakespeare? Theater? Why? Here I was with her. Wasn't that good enough? Was she pregnant? What if she were?

When we returned to Lusaka, Jackson implied there was room for us on his estate, maybe on a permanent basis. He had appraised my woodcarving skills, liked what he saw – and had challenged me to make a wax-relief sculpture that he would then cast in brass. If I could handle it, I would take over the artistic end of his foundry, and leave the marketing part to California Jimmy.

I threw myself into the project, fashioning a piece of art that clearly reflected the state of my soul. It was a humanoid form, or at least the head was humanlike, anyway. The eyes were deep, empty sockets and the mouth gaped open; one hand of one arm attempted to fend off what the eyes so clearly saw: two snake heads that were the extensions of the other arm and second foot (thus serving as a solid base so the monstrosity could stand), representing my hallucination-induced voices. It was a self-portrait in wax that would dissolve to become brass – and stand on its snake feet as a miniature monument to whatever was churning through my boiling brain.

'Cool,' said Jackson, when I completed the mold. 'Cool.'

The wax demon, replete with dip tubes to the elbows and knees, was placed in a vat of plaster and allowed to dry. Then it was baked, allowing the wax form to melt away and be replaced by a hollow, negative representation of the brass statue-to-be – me.

Finally, the forging night arrived. Jackson instructed his foundry workers to plant the plaster cast in a hole and collect pieces of cast-off brass and other chunks of copper alloy to heave into an iron cauldron set in the furnace. Globs of liquid brass bubbled like the waters of Hell. After checking viscosity and heat, Jackson then told his men to hoist the cauldron from the furnace with aid of extended metal poles.

They did so, and together we marched the heavy, sizzling, boiling metal mess towards the plaster cast embedded in the earth. Then they began to tip the rim, allowing the metal to pour.

Wax melts, wood burns, clay breaks – but metal is forever. I had captured that thing, the *tokolosh* demon inside me, for all time, and was taming him. The tiny waterfall of liquid red metal was my immortality, my exorcism. Sofi gripped my hand as the container slowly emptied its white heat into the living earth.

That was the moment Jimmy came running out of his tent.

'Hey! Hey! What the fuck do you think you're doing?' he screamed. *'Hey! Hey!!'*

He might have been shouting about a murder, or a Rhodesian commando raid on the ANC camp next door. He could have been shouting about anything, and the result would have been the same: the two startled assistants looked up, and in doing so, for a fraction of a second, stopped pouring the mold. They looked at Jimmy and they looked at me. They knew. I knew. Everyone knew. There had been a hiatus, a pause. Down in the plaster cast set in the bowels of the earth, the brass they had poured was cooling, hardening into a seam, which was really a break. 'Sorry,' said Jimmy, casting me the most vicious smile I have ever received from anyone, ever. Then he turned around and went back to his tent. I could have killed him. The sculpture had been ruined.

Perhaps today Jimmy is an investment banker or guidance counselor or congressman from California. I do not know and probably would not recognize him if I hit him with my truck. His long locks have probably fallen out or at least turned into a gray monk's cap, and he is now fat and flabby and uses a cart when he plays golf with his friends and no longer even reminisces about those crazy days when he was a kid in darkest Africa.

Me, I am different. I remember. And to help my memory I am still in possession of the imperfect creation that California Jimmy destroyed that day. It is precious for me, although it is cut off at the knees, a sculpture that cannot stand by itself. Yes, it is imperfect, but it is immortal metal – and a perfect monument to the most gratuitous act of mendacity I have ever encountered. I remember, Jimmy – do you?

That was also the event that made me decide to leave. There were incidents, and life on Jackson's farm became untenable. Moving to a hotel was not on, because all my money was wrapped up in the malachite. I contacted Master Carter, and we had a beer and a game of chess, but when it came to the question of floating me a loan he cooled and suggested rather openly that he did not believe he trusted me any longer. He said I had changed. I toyed, maybe desperately, with the thought of taking Sofi down to Bob James's Camp Bitter Hunger, transforming it to Camp Milk and Honey and raising an army of brown rugrats. But no.

I probably promised her that I would return after hawking the Green Tooth charms in Europe; if I did, I am sure she never believed me for an instant.

'You will forget me in a week,' she said, as she walked me out to the highway that last morning, her shadow as long and lean as she was, dwarfing mine.

'I will never –'

'Do not say.'

The bus pulled up and I got on and I left her there, waving those delicate hands goodbye. I felt like I had committed a crime. Maybe I had.

I rest my case under the scale of her mercy.

EIGHTEEN

The Foul Fiend Flibbertigibbet

Perhaps I should have checked myself into the Lusaka loony bin where I had performed the year before, and been done with it. But like a moth to the flame, I had other plans – a hopscotch return via Europe to Fargo, to complete my meltdown there. The black market in Zambia provided the opportunity to do exactly that. For a bag full of useless *kwacha* valued at around 200 real American dollars, I bought a one-way ticket to New York, with stops in Nairobi, Cairo, Berlin, Amsterdam and London.

When I walked through the doors of the al-Manzura, I was greeted like a long-lost friend. Abdullah the cook shouted a greeting from the kitchen and sent out a huge portion of the usual vapid meat-and-potatoes stew; Joseph, the front desk clerk, mimed dismay and promised to give me the best room in the house – the same one I had slept in a year before (as were the sheets, I believe). Ali, the manager, embraced me and thrust a choice handful of the speed-weed *qat* in my direction.

'You look tired, *bwana*,' he said, not knowing the half of it.

With the aid of the 'bush telegraph', I tried to get up to speed on rumors and news of the old al-Manzura crowd. Much of it was bleak; a lot was bad. Keith the schoolteacher had come down with hepatitis and had been medevacked back to England. Günther, the German wildlife photographer, was mugged by Somali bandits and had lost all his camera equipment and film along with his custom-made bicycle. Franz, the gay Dutchman from Lamu, had been caught adding a digit to the exit date on his visa to Malawi, and spent a year in an unspeakable prison for trying to gain an extra ten days in Bandaland. Another guy, who fit the profile of the wannabe 'mule' for the French Canadian gold smuggler Marco, had been killed in Rwanda, and someone who seemed a little too similar to Colorado Ken had also reportedly bought the Big One on his last ivory run in Zaire, where smuggling elephant tusks was punishable by death. The weirdest story, however, concerned Elizabeth, the Austrian nymphomaniac, who had sent me from the Sunshine Club to the Mombasa expatriate theater club so many moons before. Allegedly, she had graduated from casual sex with strangers to working the circuit of wealthy Indian businessmen in Mombasa, and had then become a common port whore.

I thought of Shrinithea, and wondered whether there were any connections.

One thing I knew with certainty was that the new motley crew of backpackers at the al-Manzura were not my people. Some came from Israel and Egypt, others from India, some flew in directly from the US. They were all contemptible greenhorns. My roommates were a Ugandan photographer named Theo who was now looking for employment while waiting for Idi Amin's tottering regime to fall; a Nigerian medical man named Johnny who was accused of malpractice back home; and Sara, a toothless German hag who seemed to have a past connected to the Baader-Meinhof gang. Sleeping in the same bed was her half-Ethiopian child of indeterminate gender, who helped the family budget by dipping his or her tiny fingers into wallets while Mom distracted the owners.

I told no one about my days as a wandering Bard. Sometimes, walking down the street near Brunner's or the Thorn Tree Bar, I would catch a glimmer of recognition in a shoeshine boy's eye, or passed a prostitute who would smile, raise her hands to shoulder level – and then twirl thumb and forefinger in simulation of my puppetry. How could I respond? I was not Edgar feigning madness in *King Lear*, but a real-life Poor Tom fleeing the Foul Fiend Flibbertigibbet, a burnt-out boy from Fargo with Shakespeare shit on his shoes.

> Who gives anything to poor Tom, whom the foul fiend hath led through fire and through flame, through ford and whirlpool, o'er bog and quagmire; that hath laid knives under his pillow and set rats-bane by his porridge, made him proud of heart, to ride on a bay-trotting horse over four-inched bridges, to course his own shadow for a traitor – Bless thy five wits! Tom's a-cold ...

'I was a gigolo for awhile,' announced my new Canadian roommate, as a knot of travelers sat chewing *qat* and smoking *bange* while talking about survival techniques on the road. 'I got tired of pushing it into dry old hags I didn't dig, so here I am.'

'I heard about some German girl working the streets down in Mombasa – now *that's* low,' chimed in a recently arrived Yankee. He was apparently referring to Elizabeth the Austrian, but there was no point in my adding to the story by correcting his error about her nationality.

'You've gotta get by,' an Australian surfer added. 'Eard 'a this bloke once, was trading stamps up and down the continent. A pocket full of stamps was his baggage, that's all!'

'Yeah, but you gotta bloody well know stamps,' somebody else said.

'You gotta bloody well know *hashish*, too,' opined another instant expert.

'Why smuggle *hashish*? Opium oil is the thing,' contributed an English smuggler named Gino. 'I filled ten condoms, tied strings to 'em, swallowed 'em – and flew to London via Moscow with Aeroflot. Stoned out'a me blinkin' mind on the fumes, I was.'

'What if it pops in your stomach?' someone asked. 'Guy died like that.'

'I thought of playing the guitar for change, you known, the

wandering minstrel business,' said a new arrival. 'Clean, no fuss, couple of bucks now and again.'

'I heard of this guy in Egypt who was doing Shakespeare in the streets.'

'Really? I heard of him too, but I think it was in Delhi.'

'He was performing Shak-es-speare in the streets?' asked my other roommate, the Nigerian doctor, who had just entered the room. 'I think I see him in Lagos.'

'Sounds like the guy got around.'

'One of those fly-in, fly-out fuckers, just doing it for publicity or to write a fake adventure book,' the Canadian Don Juan ungenerously opined.

'Yeah, people like that give travel a bad name, man,' someone else said.

Dope, *qat* and a sip of Scotch – it was a perfect flip-out environment for me. But there I sat, listening to the cant while my evil angels perched on either shoulder, waiting for a chance to interrupt the processing of information in my brain. I reached for the bundle of *qat* on the table and stuffed a few leaves in my mouth before spitting into the empty avocado skin on the floor. Then I removed a joint of dope from someone's fingers and took a long toke.

'Usually, I avoid smoke because it drives me nuts,' I said with an elaborate smile. 'But as guests in my room, I guess I will tolerate you greenhorn road toads.'

The room was suddenly quiet, wired. Dope-inspired doubt was so thick you could have cut it with a *panga*. There was something *wrong* there, and I reveled in being the source of it.

'*That's the one who was in Rhodesia, right?*' someone asked, *sotto voce*. 'He's fucking nuts and a merc, so let's get the fuck out of here!'

'Sit your ass down,' I said, blocking the door. The dope smoke was boiling my brain and the *qat* sending shivers of electric self-confidence up my spine. I could have flipped and run or I could flipped and done something else entirely, such as reach for my carving knife.

'Hey, man – *chill*!' someone cried from across the room, scared shitless. But I was deaf to it all, and sucked in a deep breath, which I then expelled at very high volume.

Is this a dagger I see before me?
The handle towards my hand? Come, let me clutch thee –
I have thee not and yet I see the still ...

I cut the soliloquy short, staring into the terrified eyes of those gathered in the room. My chuckle turned into a laugh and then a cackle, and I put the knife away.

'It's *him*,' someone blurted out. 'It's him, the fucking Shakespeare guy!'

Indeed, it was he who was I who was once me, studying how I might compare the prison where I lived to the world ...

I hit the streets hard, with a vengeance, with an obsession I had not known since the golden days of Cape Town's Green Market Square.

'*He's back,*' the shoeshine boy whispered to his client.

'Shake-a-spear ...!' a taxi driver shouted, leaning out the window for a better view.

'Othello, hello!' the proprietor of the curio store on the corner cried.

Yes, I was ready to once more go into the breach, to screw my courage to the sticking place, right back where it had all begun a year and a half earlier, in front of a crowd of cabbies, whores, backpackers and photo-safari tourists in downtown Nairobi, Kenya.

... I have looked upon this world for
our times seven years, and since I could
Distinguish betwixt a benefit and an injury, I
Never found a man that knew how to love himself ...

I mounted the show not once, not twice but at least three times a day: a matinee performance at the lip of the Thorn Tree to catch the lunchtime crowd, a late-afternoon show near the national bank to catch office workers on their way home and an evening program outside Brunner's Bar, with guerrilla assaults on the intermission audience at the National Theatre when the opportunity availed itself. I chewed *qat* to collect the necessary edge before each show and drank hard afterwards to blast my wearied mind to oblivion.

Repetition was not an issue. By my reckoning, I commanded some four hours of material drawn from twenty plays, ranging from the original puppet pieces like Romeo wooing Juliet and Othello killing Desdemona to Caliban's 'anti-colonial' soliloquy from *The Tempest* and both the Brutus and Mark Antony funeral orations from *Julius Caesar*. *Macbeth* I had aplenty: not only the dagger scene but also Lady Mac's vicious insistence that her hubby follow through on his deed of darkness and the Porter's knock-knock-knocking on Hell-Gate's Door.

Other selections I had ready on demand included not one but two Launce and Crab scenes from *The Two Gentlemen of Verona* for use as general openers; the Duke's 'death is OK' speech from *Measure for Measure*; The Night Watch duo from *Much Ado About Nothing*; Quince's rehearsal scene from *A Midsummer Night's Dream*; Shylock's tirade from *The Merchant of Venice*; Jaques's 'all the world's a stage' from *As You Like It*; Kate and Petruchio's first meeting in *The Taming of the Shrew*; the 'Meditation on Virginity' sequence from *All's Well That Ends Well*; Malvolio's love letter from *Twelfth Night*; Autolycus's 'praise of theft' from *The Winter's Tale*; Falstaff's Boar's Head babblings from the first *Henry IV*; the 'into the breach' from *Henry V*; the Horse speech from *Richard III*; the Player's lament from *Hamlet*; and Edgar's Foul Fiend Flibbertigibbet rantings from *King Lear*.

I was working on a love scene between *Antony and Cleopatra* and some more stuff from the *Henry* histories, while also trying to get my tongue around something appropriate from *The Rape of Lucrece*. The only plays from which I had not culled material were those that are seldom if ever performed, as if that made a difference: *The Merry*

Wives of Windsor, *King John*, *Coriolanus*, *Titus Andronicus*, *Timon of Athens*, *Cymbeline* and *Pericles*.

Ignatius Donnelly would have been proud. Maybe.

Nor was I content with working the streets and bars. I needed the sort of respect that only a captive audience and klieg lights could give. A meeting with the cultural attaché at the American embassy led nowhere due to the familiar logic that I was American and Bill Shakespeare was a Brit. The opposite logic applied at the British Council Library: Bill was a Brit and I was a Yank, ergo *no*. So I approached the French Cultural Mission. To my surprise, the director booked my Grand Gala Return and Farewell Performance, replete with an admission charge and even a playbill, for a date two weeks hence. My Ugandan roommate Theo shot pictures of me for a poster, which was soon plastered all over town.

'Thank you, thank you – and put money in my purse!' I theatrically intoned while passing the hat at the end of a show in front of Brunner's Bar one evening. It had been a middling performance, and the donations were not exactly generous – $20 worth of shillings. One last begging mantra, then I packed up my kit and headed over to the New Florida Club to blow the wad on a little late-night recreation.

'Thank you, thank you!' I said again. 'Put money in my purse!'

'How about dinner on me, instead?'

I was staring at natural blonde with a slightly freckled nose.

'My name is Melissa,' said the woman, extending her hand. 'I heard about you in Tanzania and I think you are just great, and tonight is my last night in Africa because I am flying home to the States tomorrow, so I want to take you out to dinner, OK?'

'Sure,' I said. 'I mean, sure.'

'Well, what are you waiting for?'

I packed away the various props into the performance bag while wondering what it meant to be picked up and treated to dinner by this American woman named Melissa. I was just a little nervous as she took me by the hand and led me down the street.

'So, where are you from?' I asked.

'Akron. You?'

'Well, kind of New York but really more like Fargo, North Dakota.'

'North Dakota! Man, you don't meet too many people from North Dakota!'

It all felt so natural, spontaneous, nice. We laughed and chatted all the way to a curry shop that Melissa had pre-selected and continued to laugh and chat and talk like old friends while we ordered the meal. I had not been around a white woman for some time, and being with a blonde made it doubly odd: people were staring at us all the time – or, rather, men were staring at her. I was no longer the centerpiece, the focal point of attention; she was. Melissa noticed my noticing their notice.

'You just have to learn how to deal with it,' she said, flicking her blonde mane. 'I thought of shaving it off.'

'Good thing you didn't,' I opined.

'I shave elsewhere,' she winked, leaving the rest up to my imagination.

'You're blushing,' she teased, calling for the bill. 'Now let's go dancing!'

'Well, the only decent club around is the New Florida, and it can be pretty raunchy ...'

'I *love* raunchiness,' hissed Melissa. 'Let's go have a drink and loosen up.'

We returned to Brunner's, walking arm in arm, but rather than going inside we stayed out on the stoop, looking at each other. Romance hung heavy in the moist and languid air, sticky with the coming rains; an African night – and Melissa's last. We were moving into an area I had not spent time in for a while.

'I'm going to miss this place,' she sighed. 'All the sights and sounds and smells. I am about to return to the States to become an upstanding citizen and pillar of the community and I will miss this place because it allowed me to get out of myself and be a little crazy. And I want to be a little crazy tonight, because it is my last night.'

I held out my hand as she extended hers in silent agreement. The distance got smaller and I noticed her lips had begun to part and I was so nervous I could feel a slight tremble in my knees as I pulled her towards me for a first embrace. At that instant, there was flash of movement behind her and my pituitary gland was shooting signals to every nerve and muscle before my brain had fully taken in what my eyes had just seen.

'*MWEZI!!*' cried a voice I realized was mine, and then I was sprinting after a retreating form before Melissa knew what had hit her. '*THIEF!!*'

'There's no money in it! No money!' I heard Melissa desperately calling behind me, referring to her snatched handbag. I ran like mad; I was sprinting in sandals, and then they were gone. My kit bag, too, was jettisoned. Then I turned a corner, shaking the street out of its slumber with my alarums: '*MWEZI!!*'

Guards in their greatcoats began to wake and lethargically join in the chase; cars swerved onto the sidewalk to flush the thief out of the lots he dashed into, pinning him like a moth on a wall in the glare of their lights. Others shouted the warning to others further up the street: *Mwezi!! Mwezi!!* Thief!! Thief!! The word seemed to evoke the most impulsive animal instincts in everyone, an excuse to legally hunt humans. Up ahead, a crowd had been drawn out of a sidewalk bar by the shouting and had almost completely blocked the road. The thief was trying to cut the angle away from the human barrier when he tripped, stumbled, faltered and then fell on the pavement, dropping Melissa's bag as he threw out his hands either to impede the impact of the fall, or to plead for mercy, or both. I was ten feet behind him. My lungs throbbed and my head was splitting but I willed myself an extra ounce of speed.

The bar crowd, coiled out in the street like a living whip, got there first. I only saw the first two blows falls: a kick to the thief's belly sent him reeling down into the gutter; the second to his head as he rose sent him down again.

'*Kill him, kill him!*' chanted women at the back of the mob, while the men in front tried to do exactly that. The weapons of choice were their shoes. 'Kill him, kill him!'

I grabbed Melissa's bag and its scattered contents, and flung myself into the melee.

'Stop! Stop!' I bellowed, fighting my way through the lynch mob. 'Call the police!'

'This is how we deal with the scum,' said a well-dressed man as he slammed his fist into the thief's battered face.

'Kill him!' shouted a woman, lunging forward with a high-heeled shoe held like an awl.

'*Mzungus* know nothing about how we must treat them,' said another man, testing out a Bruce Lee kick on the *mwezi,* who was being propped up like a punching bag. I pulled the thief towards me in a protective gesture, his blood dripping on my clothes.

'Are you crazy, *mzungu*?' shouted a man in a business suit, showering me with saliva. 'He steal your money today, mine tomorrow!'

'Kill him, now!' cried someone else. 'Maybe they are working together!'

'Stop it! Police!' I roared, no longer the man's executioner but his savior instead.

'The police!' spat the man in the sharp-looking suit, hauling off with a hard, right round-house punch to the thief's already flattened nose.

There were a few more kicks and punches, some partially deflected by my arms. The frenzy, however, had been broken, and the moment of bloodlust passed. The mob soon grew bored of the spectacle of the white man protecting the thief who deserved to die, and started to move on in ones and twos and threes until, finally, we were alone on the street.

'Please, sir ...' begged the thief, shaking from his beating, wet with blood and sweat.

'The police will deal with you,' I growled, yanking his hands behind his back and pushing him on with cuffs and shoves.

'No, please!' he whimpered. 'They will kill me. Please! I never steal again ...'

He was a pathetically scrawny and tattered little creature, stinking of garbage cans and shit. He wore shoes of two different sizes, worthless wool pants cinched at the waist with a piece of rope, his shirt effectively a grease-monkey's rag.

'Please, they will kill me!'

I pushed him forward and forced him to his feet when he stumbled, until we arrived at the taxi stand of the InterContinental Hotel. Then, as finely dressed African and European visitors climbed in and out of taxis assisted by doormen, I dragged my filthy charge up to the revolving entrance and threw him at the feet of a uniformed guard.

'Watch him while I call the police and notify the victim that her bag is safe.'

'Yes, sir,' said the guard, a malicious smile spreading across his face. Even before I entered the hotel, he was poking the thief with his club and speaking darkly to him in Swahili. Upon my return two minutes later, the thief was face down on the cement with his hands tied behind his back as if ready for execution, and three guards were vigorously kicking him in the face and ribs.

'Hey, guys, let's wait for the police,' I said. I almost felt sorry for the bum.

Then another guard decided to make his own search of the thief's pockets. The thief squirmed and wiggled, but was unable to prevent the guard extracting the contents: two foreign passports, some other documents and a wad of shillings, dollars and sterling.

'You see this, *bwana*?' asked the guard. 'This is rich thief who work with police.'

Not content with his find, the guard continued his search. Suddenly, the thief began rolling over to prevent the search of a side pocket, only bringing greater attention to it. Two other guards rolled him over and held him fast while the first removed a long narrow piece of paper, unwrapping it for all to see: it contained a cheap but deadly knife. A crowd had collected to watch the scene, and now it cooed.

'*Ooh-la-la!*' someone sang. 'It will be hanging with him!'

I looked down at the thief and thought about that sharp piece of metal stuck between my ribs, or maybe run across my throat. This time, when the guards began flailing away at the supine form, I said nothing. In fact, I was about to join in when Melissa ran up, and threw herself over the thief.

'Stop it, *you beasts*!' she screamed. 'Can't you see it's his society that makes him like this?'

'Shut up,' I pulled her rudely off the man. 'You don't understand.'

'Don't understand? Don't understand *what*! That he's a thief? What's that to me! Here, give him my money, I don't care!' She grabbed her bag back from me and started pressing money into the thief's swollen palms.

'I thought you said there was no money in it.'

'Of course there is!' snapped Melissa. 'And my passport, too!'

'Listen!' I grabbed her arm and yanked her up. 'He had 200 shillings and a bunch of someone else's foreign currency in his pocket, and a knife for my guts if I caught him alone. I saved him from a lynch mob. A little black and blue won't hurt him now.'

'God, you're as bad as they are!' she hissed. *'You ... you ... animal!'*

Then she slapped me, and the gathered crowd howled in laughter at the sight.

'Beast!' she snarled, throwing punches. 'You got the bag! Why didn't you let him go?'

The arrival of the police sent Melissa into a new paroxysm.

'I forgive him!' she implored the commanding officer, throwing herself on the thief again. 'I won't press charges! It wasn't him!'

'We will see about that,' smirked the cop, instructing his men to dump the limp form into the back of their wagon. 'Please, Madam – you must come to the station with us, and you, too, mister.' Melissa had already entered the squad car from the far side, and sat stroking the head of the thief lying in the back. I wanted to puke.

'Madam,' grinned the officer behind the wheel, looking at Melissa in the rear-view. 'We must teach them a lesson. They are everywhere.'

'A lesson? *A lesson*?!' she cried. 'Good God!'

'Madam,' the thief whimpered in the back. The policeman sitting between us reached back and slapped him. Melissa groaned as if it had been her who was struck.

We arrived at the station house in silence. When the thief was dragged in, a chorus of jeers erupted from all the night officers – and the *mwezi* was clubbed and beaten as he was hauled past the reception desk and then thrown into a nearby room. The door was scarcely shut before the first muffled cries began reverberating through the hall.

I stood in a corner and chain-smoked as Melissa wept. We didn't speak.

'Madam.' An officer beckoned to Melissa to follow him down a hallway. Ten minutes later she returned, drained and sober.

'We will need your testimony tomorrow, sir,' the officer said to me. 'Ten-thirty.'

'Fine,' I replied.

The police offered us a ride back into town, but Melissa declined for both of us. She said we wanted some air and some time alone. I only wanted the time alone, and just for me, but I thought it best to walk her where she wanted to go. Under a silver moon and star-filled African heaven, we walked in silence.

'They want you to come to court tomorrow because I can't, I'm leaving,' she finally said, breaking the quiet. 'They say you are the only witness aside from me. Otherwise, they will let him go.'

'Sounds like I'm busy.'

We walked in silence for another few minutes before she spoke again.

'Well,' she said at last, slipping her arm through mine. 'What happened?'

'I ran after him. Others caught him.'

'When the news hit Brunner's, everyone cheered,' she said. 'You were a hero. Everyone was going to buy you a drink. We should go. They probably still will ...'

'I'm tired ...'

'I had given it up for lost, everything. My ticket, passport, money, everything ...'

'Yeah.' I couldn't wait to leave her.

'I would have had to call my folks to tell them not to meet me, tell them I need emergency funds, go to the embassy to get a new passport ...'

'I go this way,' I said, nodding in the direction of the al-Manzura.

'Hey, do you want a cup of coffee or something? We could even go blow some dope.'

She was trying, trying real hard. Trying to extend the evening, tacitly offering me the hero's reward on her very last night in Africa. Do something crazy before going home.

'You've got travel tomorrow,' I replied, releasing my arm from hers. 'And I have other plans.'

'Wait!' she cried. 'Wait until I get a taxi, please!'

I assented, and waited with her until a taxi arrived. I opened the door for her. She turned and embraced me, tried to resume our interrupted kiss on Brunner's steps.

'I feel that I know you,' she said.

'You don't.'

'I want to.'

'You can't.'

There was only one person capable of that, I thought, and I had to travel back to the scene of the crime to find her. She was said to be in Mombasa, so I went there. Rather than waste time out on the highway with an extended thumb, I splurged and bought a train ticket on the Lunatic Express from Nairobi to the Indian Ocean coast. It cost something like ten bucks for a bunk in a four-person chamber for the overnight trip, and included a Continental breakfast served by a steward. I forget who my companions were, or even if I had any companions at all.

The train pulled into the station and I got out, immediately blasted by the heat and humidity of the coastal town. It was morning, and I knew she would not be up and about anywhere I could find her, so I hung around the market watching the honest folks make their honest living by carting in the fruit, vegetables and meats that would be consumed by the evening's hedonists and whores. Around noon I started making the rounds of the cheap hotels where she might keep her kit. Her description raised eyebrows and produced whispers, but no certain data. But she was around. I felt it. By mid-afternoon, during the sweaty heat of the day, I started trolling the early-bird whore bars.

'Hey, sailor – *fiki fiki*!' chortled a big-bosomed bawd as I walked into the Sunshine.

'Asante sana,' I replied. 'Thanks, but no thanks.'

'I know you ...' she said, taking a closer look. 'Shakespeare ...!'

The Sunshine Club manager, who had thrown me off the stage and then into the street, bore me no resentment – why would he? – nor did I him. I was interested in something a little different than a venue to make a laughing-stock out of myself, and he understood.

'The woman you seek is in the gutter,' he said. 'In fact, I do not know why you seek her at all. You will not find her here because we do not allow her to pass.'

'Where will I find her?'

'We are a ... respectable establishment,' said the Sunshine manager. 'She is not a respectable woman. People who require her look for her near Kilindi, the old port ...'

'I understand,' I said, cutting him off. 'Thank you.'

'By the way,' said the manager as he walked me to the door. 'I do have your Romeo puppet. The cleaning lady found it after that time when you –'

'Keep it,' I said. 'It might be worth money some day.'

I wandered over to the monumental Fort Jesus and the filthy Kilindi estuary, and sipped tea with an old *dhow* captain while waiting for the last tourists to go. We didn't talk much, just played backgammon and sipped. At the evening call to Muslim prayers he excused himself and wandered off to a mosque. I stayed at the backgammon table, waiting. There was no point in searching further. This was the place. I just did not know the time. I smoked and waited, idly reciting lines from *Richard II*:

I have been studying how I may compare
This prison where I live on to the world ...

Melissa would be back in Ohio by now. Eddy was probably in Montana, where my Mom had just moved, leaving my Dad in Dakota with the teenaged remnants of their eight-child brood. The flute player I had sublet my apartment to in New York was not only keeping the apartment, but also claiming the cats. Shrinithea was God only knew where, while here I was, facing the miasmic Kilindi under a dark fort in Mombasa, waiting for a whore who screwed taxi drivers. Two kids walked by, boys. One winked at me lewdly, and suggested an unnatural act in German. Fucking tourists. Fucking world.

I was lighting the last cigarette when I felt the hand on my shoulder.

'Hi,' I said. 'I've been waiting.'

'So was I,' said Elizabeth.

We walked the walk and talked the talk. We talked about nothing; the content was a conversation about life, about public identities that had overtaken and swallowed everything private – me a manic street performer who sold Shakespeare to sleaze, and she a white whore in a black land – or had been. Certain changes in her physical appearance and general demeanor had brought Lizzy low. Actually, she was legally dead.

'It was a stupid accident, but it changed my already rotten life entirely,' she related as we lay in the sweltering Mombasa dive she called home. 'I was dealing with some clients at a an outdoor barbecue gang-bang with me as the object of desire. Then, during a pause in the action, I got up and slipped and fell, slashing both wrists on broken glass.'

Elizabeth the Great White Whore of the Kenyan Coast bled out her life-blood to the extent that she was declared medically dead by the time her gang-bangers got her to the hospital. She showed me the death certificate to prove it. But before they did the autopsy or just plunked her in the ground, something happened.

'They took termites and had them bite the skin, and then killed them by squeezing and let the termite blood or juice or whatever it is go into and over my wounds. Anyway, they did something before they got me to the hospital and even though I was legally dead, they kept me in the morgue overnight. Somehow I came around like a voodoo whore and here I am, in that state they call being alive. Yeah ... alive, life.'

Elizabeth showed me her scars. They were deep, red and jagged. They were not your slash-your-wrists-with-a-razor-and-jump-in-the-warm-bathtub kind of attempted suicide scars we have all seen or maybe done to ourselves. Her scars were cut-by-glass-shards-you-did-not-expect scars, healed by some sort of crushed-termite-jaw juice-voodoo-bullshit miracle. She was blessed, or cursed, but whatever it was she was not natural, and knew it. But that thing the superstitious among us call Fate, the Mark, that concept we ultra-rational Western types are supposed to abhor as primitive nonsense except when it acts on us, this force kept Elizabeth alive even though she did not want to be.

I stared at her for hours that were only minutes, wondering what her mission could possibly be. Why had she been sent, why spared? Why her, why me? Why a witness? I unbuttoned her dress; she pulled off my shirt. A soft kiss on the cheek, a hard one on the lips, a hand on her breast ... But it was just too weird. I let go, and she held still.

'Es geht abwarts,' she said, marking the moment when we both knew that we were as one, more than any physical union could make us. 'It's all downhill.'

We slept and we woke. We wandered around the town. We held hands while we descended into the low-tide effluent of the *dhow* harbor, looking for something neither of us knew until driven away by stone-throwing youths who had learned the English word 'whore'. We took a bus to a beach and watched the surf roll in over frolicking, giggling, happy folks – tourists, I think, but can't exactly recall – until we were sufficiently bored by the banality of it all that we left again, returning to town almost in silence, drinking *lassi* yogurt drinks and beer and water and stronger stuff until it was evening, and then Elizabeth wanted to smoke some dope. I told her I shouldn't because I might flip and want to kill people, and I did not want to her to remember me like that, or maybe kill her. She said she didn't care, but that maybe it was a good idea for me not to flip for my own sake if not hers, because she was dead anyway.

So she smoked by herself, and we walked down a garbage-strewn side street towards the port where we had reunited the night before. Hindus were coming out of their temples and Muslims were coming out of their mosques. Someone was playing an accordion squeeze-box nearby, and in the distance you could hear a random disco beat when some invisible whore or john opened the door to get in or out. The night was hot and still and muggy-humid, and cigarettes tasted like burnt fog.

'Go,' said Elizabeth.

Maybe she was bored with me. Maybe she was frightened that somebody cared that she was really alive again and not dead. She walked me over to the train station and to the second-class ticket counter. I bought the ticket, and when I turned around she was gone. I wasn't surprised. I wasn't even sad. I just got back on the Lunatic Express, went to my compartment and let the steward make up my bed with stiff, starched white clean sheets, waited for the train to move out of the station and tried to understand this business of being dead until alive again.

I had to wait some fifteen years to really understand, but eventually did. The insight came when I found myself aboard a helicopter under fire in a rathole called Kelbajar in Azerbaijan, a situation I was not supposed to survive, and the only way to make the fear of death tolerable was to declare myself dead until proven otherwise. It took the edge off eternity, sort of. Then I survived and so did that declaration of death – and I have been unable to view the world the same since. I call it the Zombie Syndrome, but it might be better labeled the Elizabeth Fix.

I suppose I should be grateful that my farewell performance at the French Cultural Center was not an unmitigated disaster. There was a printed program with artist biography and credits, and klieg lights and an introduction and intermission and wine and cheese and all the rest of it, but it was only my ability to do the show by rote that carried me through. I won't bore the reader with excerpts. You have seen or heard them all before.

The reaction to my farewell performance was mixed. There were no official reviews or anything of that nature. A few Shakespeare purists walked out in the middle of the first act and the crowd was thinner after intermission, and at least one politicized African made it clear that he thought I should return from whence I came and not taint African culture with foreign accretions, especially via my pathetic attempt to localize and make Shakespeare relevant at Africa's expense by associating Caesar with Biko and Shylock with Kenyatta and Caliban with the mass of Black Africa as a whole.

Not all the response was negative, however: the al-Manzura crowd showed up, and enthusiastically showered me with applause no matter what I did onstage. Sara the German witch and her child presented me with a bucket of flowers they had stolen from the gardens lining Kenyatta Avenue. My other roommates, the Ugandan photographer and the Canadian gigolo, bought me a bottle of fine French wine, which I shared with a New Florida Club B-girl I encountered some hours after the closing of the show. The most curious piece of applause, however, came in the form of an invitation from a young, white Kenyan, a descendant of some very early British colonial settlers, who had a piece of property in the Rift Valley abutting the Kenyan equivalent of Yellowstone National Park. He insisted that I join him the next day on a trout-fishing expedition in the mountains.

We drove north and west in a Land Rover through the Great Rift and then shaved off to the right, first along tarmac feeder roads, then along packed gravel and then onto dirt, until finally there were no roads at all. We parked, got out and began to hike, fly-rods over our shoulders, up and down, deeper and deeper into the raw, untamed outback of Africa. We crossed bogs, lurching up to our knees in goo; we traversed thick bush and savannah, spooking greater and lesser kudu and antelopes galore. When we arrived at the river via underbrush tunnels carved by elephant and maybe rhinos, monkeys and baboons hooted and howled warnings to their brethren and showered us interlopers with whatever the upper canopy provided by way of projectiles. We were in untamed Africa – and I had to wonder what I had done with my months on the continent aside from wander from city to city, flogging Shakespeare as my calling card.

Evening found us camped along the banks of the raging river, at a bend where God had carved out a deep pool. The daybirds were going to their nests and the nocturnal ones were on the wing. The sun was setting somewhere over Lake Victoria to the west while night was rolling up its carpet over the desert to the east. A lion roared for its mate, maybe; a bull elephant trumpeted distantly; and a thousand sounds and smells and sensations that I had never heard or seen or smelled before swelled over me, leaving me numbed and stunned and utterly befuddled. The whole scene was so totally beyond my experience that I was literally in shock.

'To Africa!' said my host, raising a bottle of Tusker.

'Yeah,' I said, drunk on something I had never savored before. 'To Africa.'

Assassinating Shakespeare

I arrived in Cairo determined to never, ever perform Shakespeare again. As an alternative source of income, I packed my performance bag to the brim with malachite fetishes and strapped a prophylactic filled with opium oil to my thigh. I cleared Egyptian customs, but when I checked into a hotel and undressed to take a shower, I discovered a sticky brown leg and an empty condom. My new career as a dope smuggler was over almost before it had begun. In Munich, customs officials dragged me out of the line and went through my bags with a fine-toothed comb. Happily, I was clean, although I still needed cash.

So I resigned myself to staging the Shakespeare show – but I was just one of the many jugglers, mimes, magicians and musicians crowding every street corner. Next came a theater festival in the town of Erlangen, replete with workshops for political clowning and psycho-improvisation, and I found myself one of the last two participants from the original fifty exploring the concept of finding 'The Way to the Door'. My method was hurling myself against a padded gate with such ferocity and velocity that I cleared the stage, receiving not only great applause but also an invitation to join the troupe. I declined, reluctant to explore the lower depths of my barely contained insanity that the director was so keen to unleash onto the world of the performing arts.

In Berlin, I played the fringes of another alternative theater and arts festival and landed a crash pad in the home of a refugee Czech set designer. He lectured me late into the evenings about Eastern Europe and the Soviet Union. In retrospect, those discussions about the Prague Spring and the playwright and future Czech President Vaclav Havel might be regarded as my first real introduction to what would later become a consuming passion about the late Communist world, and the basis of whatever fame or renown or notoriety I may have today – but that was twenty years later.

Meanwhile, I tried to run down the East German puppeteer with whom I had parked my stuff almost two years before, in vain. Like Madame Dietrich, I earned the right to sing about having left a suitcase (and bicycle) in Berlin. I had also left behind something else: years later, my Czech host ran me down in Turkey to tell me that he had been obliged to fumigate his flat after I departed, because the place had become infested with lice.

The next stop was Amsterdam, where I hung around the Milky Way and tried to act like I fit right in with the other Euro-hippies trying to look like impoverished beggars. I crashed under canal bridges and tried to make a few *guilders* but the only audiences I seemed able to draw consisted of no-donation junkies. The lack of interest was a real problem, but there was a reason for it. My socio-political commentary on the plays and their relevance to the contemporary world had no resonance whatsoever in Europe. How could it? Comparing Macbeth with the local dictator was ridiculous because there was no local dictator, and suggesting that Steve Biko's killers in South Africa resembled Brutus was idiotic because no one knew who Biko was. In Europe, Shylock was a character, not a concept, and certainly not a Cape Coloured ...

There was only one place in one country in the world where I thought I might find at least someone, *anyone* who would be able to appreciate my experience – or at least throw me a dime for my efforts. The venue in question was none other than the birthplace of the Bard and site of the theater festival dedicated his works, namely, Stratford-on-Avon, smack dab in the middle of jolly old England.

Subsequently I have spent a lot of time in England, and I actually kind of like the place. I have spent weeks in West London as the guest of the BBC in White City, stitching together television documentaries on post-Soviet nastiness in Chechnya and Abkhazia; I have crashed in slummy joints in Islington and hung out at Blakes and have had house seats at new Tom Stoppard plays at the National and hung with buddies at the Groucho Club. I have done London by motorcycle, car, hansom cab, train, Tube and just plain shoe leather. Chip in several trips to Oxford, Land's End, Cornwall, Bath, Brighton, Dover, Bristol and even Glasgow, and I think it safe to say that I know England fairly well, with a bit of Scotland thrown into the mix.

But all that came much, much later. At the time of my pilgrimage I was a dirty, hollow-cheeked psycho with jaundiced eyes, carrying a lice-infested sleeping sack on his shoulder and murder in his heart towards the long-dead white man who allegedly created all those characters and many more. Yes, I hated Shakespeare. And I hated all the smiling, shutterbugging, tombstone-touching tourists who spilled in and out of Anne Hathaway's house by the dozen, when not tripping over each other to register for Shakespeare seminars like 'The Meaning Of *Macbeth*', 'The Problem of Ophelia' and 'Death, Delusion and Desdemona'. I hated the eminent scholars pontificating on these themes and I hated the bored, snot-nosed children of the culture-vultures, putting together Shakespeare jigsaw puzzles or flying Bill the Bard kites ...

Yes, it was stuffy, neat and clean, and it was all too much for me. From the moment I woke up, cold and aching from the cardboard box in which I bedded down by the Avon River, I knew I was the wrong person in the wrong place at the wrong time. But unlike the others who flogged donkey to get to the Birthplace of the Bard as an obligatory stop between Westminster Abbey and Madam Tussaud's Wax Museum, I was not a regular tourist. I was a man with a mission, a pilgrim with a purpose, to foul the fount of my psychic sorrow. Had he not already achieved the status of having been a Dead White European Male for four hundred years, I might have made him one, had I seen him walking down one of the manicured lanes of New Place.

Assassinating Shakespeare, yeah – killing Bill the Bard.

I had not worked out all the details, but the plan required my getting inside the main stage of the Stratford Summer Shakespeare Show and then gloriously sabotaging it. Perhaps I would swing down from the balcony like John Wilkes Booth after he bumped off Lincoln, screaming obscenities about how Ignatius Donnelly had been so maligned all these years. The alternative to the Tarzan swing (a nice Africa-touch) would be to wait until intermission and, while the audience was chatting and laughing and smoking and drinking tea and eating clotted cream crumpets, to sneak backstage and wait for the curtain to rise again on the second act – only the second act would be me, lecturing on the true nature of William Shakespeare and how it was really Francis Bacon who wrote all the Greene, Marlowe and Shakespeare plays ...Yes, I had options.

The problem was getting through the door. Lacking the funds to buy a ticket to *The Tempest,* which just happened to be the only show of the week, I was reduced to trying to convince the guy manning the ticket office that he should let me in for free.

'Sorry, mate,' said the ticket man. 'We've been sold out for months.'

'*But do you know who I am?*' I queried, the ire of the insane in my eyes.

'Yeah,' he sneered. 'You're an unshaven, foul-smelling lout o' a Yank who thinks he can sneak into a twenty-quid Shakespeare show for free.'

I thought about his assessment for a moment, and realized a profound truth: the attendant was perfectly correct. I had not bathed in a week, and the sun-parched skin of my sunken cheeks and receding forehead had begun to peel. My clothes were the one set of trousers and shirt that I had been wearing for months, maybe a year – and both needed a good crease as well as a patch or five. I will not even mention the color of my teeth.

'You clearly do not understand,' I said. 'I *have* to see the show. Caliban is *the symbol* of the *oppressed* colonial peoples of this world. *The Tempest* is about Africa – *and me.*'

'Look, Yank,' said doorman between his teeth. 'If you want me to call the guards ...'

'No,' I replied. 'Just listen. *Please*! ...'

And I proceeded to tell him a story. It was a bit convoluted but I tried to make it succinct. I told him about Ignatius Donnelly and his obsessions with Francis Bacon's secret codes. I told him about success and madness and delusion. I told him about Africa, about how after two years on the road, I was calling it a day – and that he had to break every rule he had sworn to uphold as a ticket-taker and let me in before the curtain rose.

'Jeez,' he said, after a pause. Then, for reasons he could probably not explain to himself and certainly not to his manager, but which were perfectly obvious to me, he handed me the keys to the director's box – Peter Brook's seat, I believe.

'He's out of town,' whispered my new friend at the box office. 'Have a good time.'

The delicious irony of it all – *yes!*

I had finally arrived, was sitting in a silk-upholstered chair and in the perfect position to carry out my scheme. I quivered with delight as the curtain rose on a play I knew so well, a play that was about *me*:

Master: Boatswain!
Boats: Here, master – what cheer?
Master: Good, speak to the mariners. Fall to it, or we run ourselves aground! Bestir!

It sounded like the cue for me to bestir myself and launch my assault – and it would be to the tune of Caliban! If the metaphoric and symbolic connection between Prospero's island and Stratford seems a little thin to me today, they did not then. It was *perfect!*

Too perfect, in fact. As I edged my way out of my director's seat and inched towards the railing, allowing all the suffering and abuse ever inflicted on any actor, ever, in the history of any kind of stage anywhere to infuse my being and give me the courage needed to sabotage the cultural pretensions and pleasures of the sneering, selfish and servile bunch of Shakespearean savants down in the pit below, I made the mistake of looking at the stage.

There were actors on it. They were, maybe, people like myself who as youths had dreamed of running away to join the circus, to revel in the smell of the greasepaint and the applause. Now they were faced with the fact that their wishes had come true: here they were, strutting their meager egos, desperately trying to believe they were someone else, anyone else but themselves for the period of time allowed by literary disguise. But could I blame them for my predicament, or ruin their show for the sake of my own revenge?

I sat there in the director's booth for the duration of the three-hour show, not even leaving during the intermission, waiting until I finally heard the words I knew meant the show was over.

Now does my project gather to a head
My charms crack not, my spirits obey, and time
Goes upright in his carriage ...

What would Bill have thought about it all, if he was indeed Bill at all? According to Ignatius, Prospero's final soliloquy was the most direct evidence available that it was Francis Bacon, true author of the plays, announcing the closing of his own, secret curtain. It was a monologue that I, too, had memorized with great pain but had never been able to make sense of, until that moment. Sitting high above the crowd of Shakespeare sophists, it suddenly made perfect sense – and I whispered the words along with the false prophet Prospero who, like me, was bowing out forever.

But this rough magic
I now abjure; and when I have required

Some heavenly music (which even now I do)
To work mine end upon their senses,
I'll break my staff
Bury it certain fathoms in the earth
And deeper than did ever plummet sound
I'll drown my book ...

Standing on the banks of the muddy Avon, I tried to do exactly that. My lousy sack was the first thing to go into the drink. Next came the carving kit and dyes, plunk, plunk, plunk. The wooden puppets would float, so I kept them. *The Collected Works*? It seemed, on reflection, almost criminal to destroy it. It remains on my bookshelf today, in the section I reserve for author-signed or family-authored books. Whether the real author was Shakespeare or Bacon is immaterial to me. They both owe me. So does Iggy.

Lastly, there were my notebooks, the diaries. It was tempting to flush them down the Avon forever, but I resisted. You have just read the result of my having retained them.

Then I hitchhiked back to London, to Heathrow airport, and managed to board the first aircraft back to New York with my shoddy, black-market ticket from Zambia. I bounced through New York, Chicago, the Twin Cities and finally Fargo, where I gave my final performance to a massive and amazed crowd ...

No.

Trying to hitch my wagon to that of the Community Theater, which happened to be performing *A Midsummer Night's Dream*, I launched a street performance on North Broadway that drew a crowd of five, most of which consisted of deeply confused friends of my parents, and whose one- and five-buck donations into my extended hat reflected their silent concern about what the hell had happened to Debbie and Neill's second son. Drummed out of Dakota, in effect, I set off for Montana, where I found Brother Eddy driving a school bus and living in my mother's new house with the only African American woman in the state, a girl from Chicago who went by the name of Aroma Flowers.

Yes.

I then sought and found a venue to perform my Shakespeare show, not only to make some cash from the box office but also to make some new friends in a strange environment through the tried and true method of public exhibitionism.

Yes, yes!

The show was to run for three nights, and the hundred-seat theater-in-a-barn was full on the first, and the applause almost deafening ...

No.

Thanks mainly to the presence of my mother and a bunch of her friends, the opening night audience was respectable, and people listened courteously and attentively.

Close enough.

The Grand Finale was totally sold out, with standing room only, and so packed that the fire marshal arrived to close the show for safety's sake.

No, no, no.

I was tempted to cancel the last performance because there were only four or five people in the audience, one being my mother and another a younger brother.

Yes!

I was shattered, relieved – it was over at last.

'What are you going to do now?' asked Mom as we drove back to her log cabin.

'Dunno,' I replied. 'Go back to school and get a degree in something. They have this program where you collect credits for life experience, so maybe I could pick up credits for all this Shakespeare stuff. That or study Arabic. I am pretty good at memorizing weird stuff.'

That is what I did. Before I knew it, I was back abroad – first to Syria, then Egypt, then Turkey and finally to the newly independent states of the Caucasus region of the former Soviet Union, embracing the real-life theater where characters such as Iago, Macbeth and Richard III were all too real and where assassinations were permanent. As for Shakespeare, my interest did not wane; it died altogether.

One day, during an interview for a government job, I was confronted with a two-year hole in my resume. 'Please explain,' demanded the interviewer. From his expression, it was clear that he thought I had something to hide – like a twenty-four-month indoctrination period in Lebanon. Two hours later, I was ejected from the interview.

'You expect us to believe *that*?!'

By then, I had a new project to complete. It was time to go back to the diaries and delve through the tattered, dog-eared and ink-marked pages of *The Collected Works*, stitching it all together in the form of this book. There were different versions. The first was dry, if bizarre, but true. The second was a much better read, but described things the way they should have been, and not the way they really were. The third removed the little fictions, better known as lies, and formed the basis for the work at hand. And there it languished for some twenty years, unsold, unpublished and unread.

Then feckless Fate offered up two seemingly unrelated events: my literary agent, who had inherited the original manuscript from her boss, was obliged to move a mountain of books-in-boxes that had accumulated over the years in order to let repair men paint and re-carpet her office. Almost on the same day, the Divine Miss Kidder told me about her new movie, based on that much-maligned Donnelly work, *The Great Cryptogram*.

The result is the work in your hands, my secret history. I would end it with Prospero's plea:

As you from crimes would pardoned be
Let your indulgence set me free.

(And by the way, I never found the emeralds.)